The Kazakhstan Way

The Kazakhstan Way

Nursultan Nazarbayev

Translated by Jan Butler

Foreword by Margaret Thatcher

STACEY
INTERNATIONAL

The Kazakhstan Way

STACEY INTERNATIONAL
128 Kensington Church Street
London W8 4BH
Tel: +44 (0)20 7221 7166; Fax: +44 (0)20 7792 9288
Email: info@stacey-international.co.uk
www.stacey-international.co.uk

ISBN: 978-190529-965-2

CIP Data: A catalogue record for this book is available from the British Library

© Nursultan Nazarbayev 2008

1 3 5 7 9 0 8 6 4 2

Edited by Anthony Gardner & Charles Powell
Picture research by Kitty Carruthers
Mapping by Cartograph
Printed and bound in Turkey by Mega Print

CONTENTS

The Photographic section is located between pages 162 and 163

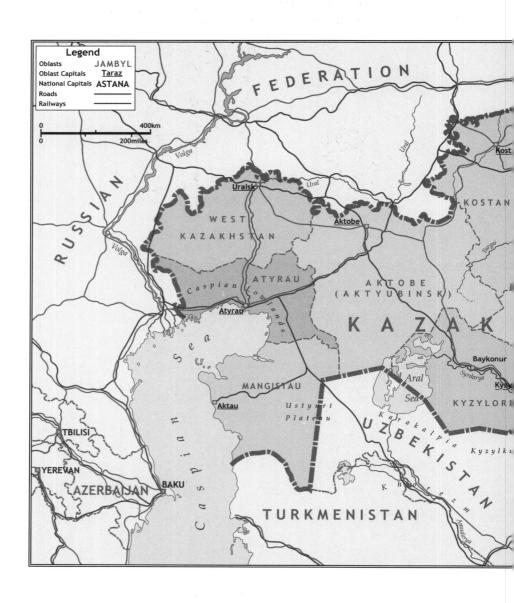

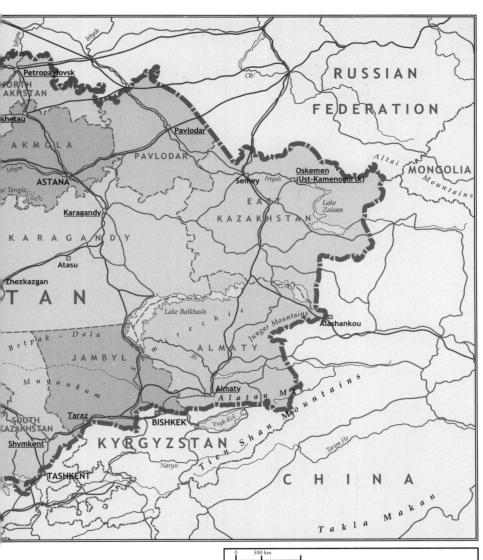

FOREWORD

The founding fathers of nations almost always tend to be larger than life figures and Nursultan Nazarbayev fits comfortably into this category. Such leaders can attract both glowing admiration and noisy criticism in varying measures. Much of this is due to the fact that they stand astride a crucial moment in their nation's history and therefore become more iconic figures than those who have gone before or those who come after.

How far does the character of the leader determine events? How far do events shape the character of the leader? These are questions which historians spend volumes trying to explain. But what is clear is that such leaders do leave a greater imprint.

This imprint is even more important when the contrast between the old and the new is marked. From the establishment of the Kazakh khanate in the fifteenth century, through Russian domination and conquest, to Soviet oppression, the history of the Kazakh people had not embraced many of the freedoms which were developing in the West during those centuries.

The transition from totalitarianism to freedom is never an easy one. Though in some ways obvious, that is still worth saying because sometimes we in the West are in danger of expecting too much too quickly. This does not mean that we should refrain from pressing for more – that is the prerogative of friends. But it does mean that we should be realistic.

In this book, President Nazarbayev tells the story of those years of transition and of his central part in the decisions which have shaped a new direction for Kazakhstan. And there is much to praise. Unlike many of the former Soviet satellite states, Kazakhstan has not been troubled by much of the uncertainty, violence and turmoil which have marked other transitions. Potential inter-ethnic rivalry has been minimised. Widespread political unrest has been avoided. Today, Kazakhstan is fast becoming an economic powerhouse. State industries have been privatised. Small businesses have been encouraged. And people have been given the opportunity to own both their land and their homes. A new middle class is beginning to emerge.

Of course, there is more still to be done. Greater political opportunities, greater electoral transparency and more open access to the media have been cited as areas where further progress is needed. But the announcement that Kazakhstan will become the first former Soviet republic to chair the Organisation for Security and Co-operation in Europe, demonstrates the confidence of her friends that the Kazakh Government can meet these future challenges.

President Nazarbayev has combined both boldness and caution in bringing Kazakhstan to where it stands today. A nation has emerged form under the yolk of communism, with a distinct Kazakh character. He has sought to open up the economy and society in a way in which some of his neighbours have fiercely resisted and he has given Kazakhstan a strong voice in world councils. This book sets out in detail how President Nazarbayev approached the problems of transition and shows us what progress has been made so far. It also tempts us to hope about the direction in which he, and Kazakhstan, may yet head in the coming years.

Margaret Thatcher
- January 2008

PREFACE

Every family dreams of building a house of their own. It all starts with a simple idea and the father of the family imagining what the house will look like. Ideas and details slowly begin taking shape in his head. A location is found, and then work begins on the design and the draft. The house is built in stages, from its foundations to its walls and roof. Many families devote years to its construction, doing a high-quality and thorough job. The head of the family builds it for his children, grandchildren and great-grandchildren. Nothing can beat a house you have built with your own hands. You see, a house is much more than just windows, walls and rooms. It's a shelter, a haven – it's your living space, your home.

As the writer Antoine de Saint-Exupéry said, 'Someone wanting to understand the essence of a house may pull it apart and have a look at the bricks and roof tiles but never will he find the silence, comfort or coolness created by the brick walls and tiled roof. Bricks, tiles – what can they teach you if the intention of the architect who put them all together has been lost? Stone needs a human heart and soul.'

Many people, especially the older generation, know how hard it is to build a good house. Building our shared home, the young state of Kazakhstan, was even harder. State-building required a clear overall plan providing precise guidelines on the type of state we would be living in.

A concise official history of independence is scarcely capable of shedding light on all the intricate details of history and human destinies when every event was fraught with passion and tragedy, vitriolic conflicts of interests between various groupings and even between generations. What's more, such is human nature that it quickly forgets the past, particularly unpleasant times.

The peace and tranquillity, the economic boom we have been experiencing, and our citizens' lively optimism, their confidence in their own potential and the foreseeable future, are becoming the given features of daily life. We scarcely notice them, just as we hardly remark the warm rays of sunlight slowly ascending Astana's tall buildings every morning. And yet a decade ago nobody believed it would turn out like this. Who could have believed that Astana would become the spiritual, economic and political focal point of the entire Eurasian continent? Who would have supposed that Kazakhstan would become a leader of economic and political reforms, the continent's epicentre of peace?

This is precisely why I set about writing this book. I want to tell of how much effort it has taken us to build the independent Kazakhstan of today.

The urge to write such a book came to me a while ago. Over the years I have accumulated a great many speeches or mere notes on ideas I have spoken about at meetings and lectures with talented young people, university students, scholars on the Bolashak Programme (which funds the higher education abroad of some of Kazakhstan's most talented students) and graduates at the higher level of education. Whenever I have looked into their eyes, so full of youthful enthusiasm and curiosity, I have been aware that very often our young people have not had enough hard facts or objective accounts of the events that have shaped our recent past – about how it all began, and all the changes that have taken place – nor a grasp of the fundamental logic behind the various decisions taken during such a critical period for the country. This is why I want to lay forth how painful and difficult every step was on the way to this success.

Though describing events in the past, my book is very much focused on the future. I trust it will serve as a touchstone for Kazakhstan's future leaders.

Our country's future leaders, the students and schoolchildren of today, must have the chance to know every brick in Kazakhstan's foundations. I would like them to appreciate how immense and grave the responsibility has been in making decisions at every stage of our state's formation when it took coercion, a staunch display of will and tremendous vital energy to get the most unpopular tasks done.

As I shall always keep repeating – you young people of today – are a special generation. You have been born and are growing up in independent Kazakhstan. Your young days coincide with a time of growth and prosperity for our country. And you have absorbed this spirit of achievement and determination to succeed. Our country's destiny will be determined by what you make of your own.

Nowadays not only specialists in international affairs but the leaders of the world's most advanced states acknowledge the success of Kazakhstan's modes of reform. Kazakhstan's leading position is grounded in a political and economic model carefully altered for a transitional period: strong presidential power plus rapid, energetic economic reform. Our model has consisted of a synthesis of radical, rather than abrupt, reforms intended to lay the foundations of a market economy and of democratisation without diminishing the authority of the state.

An author invariably has something else to add to his writing. So much formidable work has been completed during the years of independence that it can hardly be condensed in a single work. And then there's the title to live up to.

Kazakhstan's chosen way cannot, of course, be cast merely as a particular economic model. It is also a political model comprising not only general constitutional provisions but also a political system of government, infrastructure, and indeed religious adherence. It maintains a singularly diverse assemblage of faiths, and in these relations it has performed like a model state in the modern world. Achievements in this area have won praise both at home and abroad.

Maintaining an ethnic and religious consensus in such a fragile region of the planet for the past one and a half decades has, to a large extent, determined the Kazakhstan way. It is a delicate balancing act: any serious violation would lead to rapid destabilisation. A lot, moreover, is tied up with personalities.

The next key component of the Kazakhstan way is security. From nuclear disarmament, the maintaining of frontiers with regional and global powers, the fight against terrorism and military-political blocs to an individual's personal security - these are all part of this far-reaching way. But a separate analysis is needed here. To my mind, it is still impossible to reach conclusions on such matters: work is still in progress.

It is very important not to get complacent now, as the vital requirement is to keep striving onwards. Figuratively speaking, any champion's aim must be not only to win gold but also keep his lead. And this can only be achieved if he sets himself increasingly more difficult and ambitious new challenges.

This is what my book is about: how we freed ourselves from the Past and arrived at our Present, and how difficult it has been, this way of independent Kazakhstan.

Nursultan Nazarbayev

1

THE STRATEGY FOR INDEPENDENCE

The period of history directly before the emergence of sovereign Kazakhstan displayed the distinctive symptoms of clinical death throes that the world's largest state, the Union of Soviet Socialist Republics, was experiencing. Paralysed by economic and political crises, the state organism sank into a coma while its brain, society, conducted a brief critical reassessment of history. Social awareness then underwent a very strong reaction to this painful process.

Starting with the April Plenum of the Central Committee of the Soviet Union's Communist Party in 1985, which marked the start of 'perestroika', and until the Soviet Union's final disintegration, the country kept trying to make sense of its complex, labyrinthine history. Millions of cases of people persecuted in one way or another, of members of the intelligentsia eliminated by the totalitarian regime, came to light, and peoples, both large and small, began rediscovering their true histories. In various regions of the former USSR these processes were frequently accompanied by sporadic national conflicts, stormy political battles and armed clashes. So advanced was the 'disease' that certain regions of the former USSR have yet to recover and still make alarming news headlines as the planet's trouble spots.

This also reminds me of the joint press conference I held with Georgia's President Mikhail Saakashvili, during his first official visit to Kazakhstan in March 2005. Responding to a journalist's question, he compared his country in the fifteenth year of its independence to a patient 'in a post-comatose state'. The economies of a number of other countries of the Commonwealth of Independent States (CIS) are still in a relatively similar condition. There is evidence that we are eleven to twelve years ahead in development terms.

Despite suffering the symptoms of the social problems accompanying the transitional period such as collective hopelessness, apathy, and psychological tension, Kazakhstan emerged from the crisis much earlier than the other former republics. Moreover, this phase rid us of our illusions of the Soviet period, leaving us free to build an entirely new country – independent and successful Kazakhstan.

We understood that this peculiar comatose state was so unstable and dangerous that any delay or wrong decision could have fatal consequences. There was a serious danger of our railing futilely against past iniquities and attempting to put right the past when it was already part of history instead of focusing our energies on the present and future. A sinking ship's crew has to work flat out and not just look for someone to blame for their problems.

A sound managerial approach and considerable effort were required of each and every one of us to get out of this difficult and complex situation. Exactly how tough the going is depends on society's perception of it. There's no point making a drama out of a crisis, as the main purpose of a crisis is always to usher in change. I was convinced then, and still am, that any crisis has to do, first and foremost, with development. The end of the old always marks the start of something new.

No country in the process of finding its feet has ever avoided crises affecting, in particular, its economic foundations. Other states including America, France, England, Turkey, Germany, and India have lived through great depressions and slumps. Only the scale of the upheavals has differed. Certain countries, such as the so-called tigers of South-East Asia, had to pass through phases of internal political instability, land reforms and financial crises on their way to forming a market economy. Other countries went through coups and civil wars, as was the case in Latin America.

Once through all these ordeals, some states succeeded in strengthening their economy and became shining examples to others. Less fortunate ones are still struggling to cast off the shackles of civil war, instability, economic depression, and extremely burdensome foreign debts.

One could, of course, retort that every state has a different starting position. The specifics of geography, economic development, past experience and people's mind-sets all influence the outcome of reforms and end results. However, in my opinion, it is not always the objective reasons that play the most crucial role here: much depends on the subjective qualities of the leaders of these countries. That is precisely why, when our state-building got under way, I set about studying the biographies of the founding fathers of numerous countries by way to pinpoint the reasons for the successes and failures they had experienced. Among those to have played outstanding roles in the history of their countries are Turkey's first President, Kemal Ataturk; the 31st President of the United States, Franklin Delano Roosevelt; the 'father of Chinese reforms', Deng Xiaoping; and the ex-Malaysian Prime Minister, Mahathir Mohamad.

I singled out two eminent founding statesmen in particular who set me personal examples in certain ways. They were the late French President, Charles de Gaulle, and the founding father of Singapore, Lee Kwan Yew, who is still alive and well.

After the Second World War, the French Republic continued to be torn apart by one parliamentary crisis after another. Embroiled in political rows during the 1930s, France had failed to put up an effective defence against German aggression and ended up losing a major part of its overseas territories. Before the French had time to recover from the humiliating war, a protracted bloody civil conflict flared up in Algeria. Stuck in Indo-China, the French army suffered a humiliating loss of face in their war against Vietnamese peasants. By the end of the 1950s it looked as though France had lost its world power status for good.

The political crisis also left its mark on the economy. France had to turn over a new leaf as fast as possible, and needed a strong person capable of uniting its citizens. Such a person was General de Gaulle.

Immensely popular and an incontestable authority among his compatriots, de Gaulle succeeded in creating a strong, stable presidential republic. Within a short time he had raised France off its knees, restored its reputation after the Nazi occupation and returned it to the ranks of world powers. The constitution that de Gaulle had bequeathed to his compatriots regenerated France and put it at the heart of the European Union. Quite a few critics of the day accused de Gaulle of virtually burying French democracy. His response once was, 'I'm astounded by voters' boundless forgetfulness and French people's old tendency to take sides under the influence of contradictory trends and become involved in political games. Under the influence of these trends, and by stirring up hostility towards a strong regime, parties would regain their supremacy and lead the country yet again into decline. It was political party policy that led France to shameful defeat in the early 1940s.'

The next example is Lee Kwan Yew who in a matter of thirty or so years managed to transform Singapore into a developed city-state with a high standard of living. Today, Singapore's education and health-care systems rank among the very best in the world. The average annual income there is now over US$25,000, compared with an average of under $1,000 when it first acquired independence. With its population of two million the megapolis is now a most attractive Asiatic workplace for major transnational companies.

In May 1991, Lee Kwan Yew paid an official visit to Almaty, marking the start of our friendship, which continues to this day. During his five-day visit to Kazakhstan he familiarised himself with the situation in our country and, at my request, gave a talk to a group of young economists working at the Council of Ministers of the Kazakh Soviet of Socialist Republics.

During his informal talk Lee Kwan Yew spoke about the city-state's formation and development, explaining the problems Singapore encountered when it gained independence in 1965. These problems had to do with the formation of state institutions and a domestic army, maintaining inter-national concord and the non-interference of neighbouring states in Singapore's affairs. Singapore's economic policy evolved as a result of Singaporeans' initiative and industry, and by reaping the benefits of the port's advantageous geographic position and highly skilled work force.

The Prime Minister of Singapore captivated listeners with his extraordinary personality, forceful delivery and great charisma. With quintessentially Oriental subtlety and expressiveness, Lee Kwan Yew compared a large state to a liner that required a lot of space and a deep channel to turn round in so as not to capsize. The USSR and China, for example, needed a lot of time and profound groundwork to carry through radical economic and then political reforms. But in the case of Singapore and Kazakhstan, history had simply not given them much time for deliberation or hesitation, requiring of them immediate radical changes and harsh methods.

The Strategy for Independence

During his talk, Lee Kwan Yew sought to convince his audience that Communism had no future, citing by way of examples the development of East and West Germany and North and South Korea. Despite comparable cultures, climates and natural resources, the countries with Communist systems found it impossible to compete with their capitalist relatives.

An experienced politician and state leader, Lee Kwan Yew was convinced of the inevitable collapse of the USSR, but with genuine confidence he forecast a great future for Kazakhstan. And, although at the time many considered his comments about our country to be merely the diplomatic compliments of an Oriental guest, subsequent developments have shown them to be prophetic.

It was 1991, and an uncertain future stretched ahead. Only weeks were left before the disintegration of the USSR, one of the most powerful empires of all times. A new age was dawning, bringing with it unpredictable changes. During the 1980s and 1990s the world swiftly moved from an industrial to a post-industrial society. Scientific and technological progress inexorably changed the structure of state economies, and this had a knock-on effect on their social structure. Globalisation gathered momentum, threatening to leave ill-prepared countries out of the historical picture.

Let's leave it to the political scientists and economists to argue over exactly how the fall of the Communist system and accelerated rise of globalisation are interconnected. The fact remains that the Soviet Union with its unwieldy economy and military-industrial complex failed to adapt to post-industrial society. It failed to change along with the changing world, and no longer had a place in it. The USSR had made attempts to carry out reforms, but this had been a transformation focused on the political system in the first instance. Economic reforms had been put on the back burner. As a result, it was an economic crisis that brought about the vast state's collapse.

When the planned administrative economy began to disintegrate and the Union's productive and economic links to fall apart, Kazakhstan, along with the other Union republics, reached an impasse. It was obvious the transition had to be made to a market economy.

However, modern economic theory had no ready-made model for a transition to a market economy that would meet present-day trends. There was no single method or integral formula for a transition of this kind. One way or another, we had to look for a way of our own: the Kazakhstan way.

In the course of our search we travelled extensively and met with figures of global importance. The formation of our state was watched with lively interest by such eminent world figures as Margaret Thatcher, Francois Mitterand, Helmut Kohl, George Bush Snr., Lee Kwan Yew and Pope John Paul II. We formed our global vision through our contact with such people. Discussions and meetings with them enabled me personally to understand what stage the world had reached in its development and Kazakhstan's place in the international arena. We were always open to dialogue, eager to listen to new and unfamiliar ideas and respond positively to any criticism levelled at us. If we found other countries' methods interesting, we boldly adopted them and made them our own.

So, for instance, we spent a long time analysing why the years of economic crisis in post-Soviet space were highly prosperous times for the Asiatic tigers who managed to adapt most fully to the conditions of international competition.

We asked ourselves how it was that in just 30 years the poorest countries of South-East Asia had succeeded in dragging themselves out of poverty and turning themselves into booming industrial states. First came Korea, Taiwan and Singapore, followed by Malaysia, Indonesia and Thailand. When Soviet astronauts were being launched into space from Baikonur Cosmodrome, these countries were only just completing their land reforms, and illiterate peasants were flooding into future major cities.

What's more, many of these newly developing countries had to contend with a system where the state was responsible for setting the economic benchmarks and intervened daily in the country's economic life. At a certain point in the development process these countries' governments must have decided to step back from total planning and give private initiative a freer rein. Far from limiting the market, the state used its own methods to stimulate it and encourage development. Subsequently, the Asiatic method of state control followed in these countries acquired worldwide acclaim as the 'regulated market method'.

The Strategy for Independence

What concerned us when designing a market-economy model for Kazakhstan was not merely coming up with a portfolio of judicious economic measures, but also then having the political will to carry them through and consolidating the country's sovereignty. It was crucial to gain a full understanding of the radical changes taking place, predict likely development trends, and then select the most effective strategy for the reforms that would meet the needs of tens of millions of people. What's more, time was of the essence. History was not setting time aside for lengthy research and deliberation. The world was changing at an exponential speed. And we had to adapt not only our economic system but also our entire state structure, from its very foundations upwards, including the mind-set of each and every one of our citizens. We were well and truly playing catch-up with the rest of the world.

Many of our personnel from the previous regime failed to understand that these changes were irreversible. Cut off from the rest of the world for so many years, we did not fully appreciate the threat of globalisation or, incidentally, the opportunities it afforded us. The Singapore premier's talk in 1991 served as a pointer as we worked out our long-term strategies. To find the right course of development, we first had to identify exactly what we wanted to achieve.

A Strategy for Kazakhstan as a Sovereign Country

The *Strategy for Kazakhstan's Formation and Development as a Sovereign State*, the policy document developed in early 1992, was our first attempt at medium-term planning and defining the course of our development in those chaotic times, and can be referred to as the first three-year state plan.

Independence brought with it a plethora of challenges. First and foremost, we had to qualify as a state. And this meant having to form state institutes of power, gaining recognition in the international arena, and joining different international organisations. It was to a large extent a survival plan, and with hindsight we can say it achieved what it set out to. It primarily identified who we were and what we would turn out like in the short and long term.

7

'Individuals, power structures, society – none of these can exist without a clear goal. People living without a set ideal, a worthwhile dream, are inevitably consumed by a host of petty, shallow interests, and a longing for instant material gratification. And this triggers social degradation. That is why a precise, clear idea of the way in which Kazakhstan society is to develop is so crucial today, as it enables everyone to see the azimuths of our course, become more assured of the predictability of events and achievement of the final result.'

Strategy for Kazakhstan's Formation and Development as a Sovereign State, 1992

The Strategy was one of the republic's first official documents, underpinning its ideological foundation: the principle of the Kazakhstani nation's self-determination. The Strategy explained by way of a brief survey of history how different ethnic tribes once lived throughout the territory of what is now known as Kazakhstan. These later joined together to make up the Kazakh nation and controlled the entire territory of present-day Kazakhstan. We officially declared that the independent state in its present form had not been gifted to the Kazakhs but was our historical homeland, Kazakh land from time immemorial. We gave the people precise points of reference as well as a clear indication that the authorities intended using all the constitutional means available to guarantee the state's unitary integrity, and the unity and inviolability of its territories. It was an important declaration for such an unstable time.

Developing a sovereign state with strong presidential power was set as our strategic goal. The young republic had to define the precise contours of statehood. Fully aware of the danger of losing time and further aggravating the crisis, presidential power enabled us to focus on resolving pressing problems and conducting the most urgent reforms as swiftly as possible instead of being sidetracked by protracted discussions and quests for compromises and half-measures. This period saw the setting up of new ministries focused on resolving fundamental challenges. Also established for the first time in the history of independent Kazakhstan were other state institutions such as the armed forces, diplomatic corps and customs service. Measures were taken to regulate and strengthen state borders. All these required considerable financial resources and decisive action.

With this document we made our first and, arguably, most difficult steps in changing attitudes towards property, overcoming conservative and outmoded economic methods and the inert mind-sets of managers and officials and the population as a whole.

The Strategy advanced two fundamental economic principles: the formation of a social market economy based on competition, and the establishment of a legal framework and other conditions to realize the principle of individual economic self-determination. The state officially announced a projected reduction in the percentage of state property to 30-40 per cent. These economic goals were to be achieved by using indirect methods of regulating the economy as the appropriate budgetary, fiscal, monetary, credit and social policies were implemented.

> 'A process characteristic of a post-totalitarian period will begin in the republic to delimit political and economic power and surmount the state's absolute monopoly of property. The latter will be seen in more active privatisation and the introduction of sufficiently effective and substantial non-state forms of property, in the formation of a solid middle stratum of private owners, bringing stability to economic development and society as a whole. This stratum will facilitate the removal from society of such negative phenomena as parasitic tendencies – the habit of calling upon the authorities for social aid and assistance in times of economic hardship.'
>
> *ibid*

Work on the document itself encountered a fair amount of difficulties. I drew up a list of the Strategy's basic tasks and aims for a group of young economists who then used it in drawing up a draft document. Numerous discussions were held on the subject in my presence. I enlisted the help of various experts and my foreign advisers. Naturally, a fair degree of conservatism – or should I say backward thinking – made itself felt among our specialists. However, the right wording for the document was produced in the end.

The Kazakhstan Way

The Strategy stated that Kazakhstan was transferring from a planned to a market economy, from totalitarianism to liberal politics. Many did not understand us. The Supreme Soviet and its leadership requested a review of the individual principal positions, arguing that the people were not yet ready to take on such ideas.

I am grateful to the then Vice President Erik Asanbayev, responsible for heading the group of young economists who included S. Akhanov, U. Shukeyev, O. Zhandosov and G. Marchenko. They defended the document before the deputies of the Supreme Soviet (as the Soviet parliament was called) and stood up against the numerous critics who had yet to understand the real significance of the changes taking place or were simply afraid of anything new. The debates raged on in the Supreme Soviet.

'Prosperity for one and all' was arguably the Strategy's key concept. The author of this idea, the renowned German economist, Minister for the Economy and later Chancellor of the Federal Republic of Germany Ludwig Ehrhardt, was once hailed as the architect of Germany's astonishingly effective market reforms. For ten years the German economy's average annual growth rate was consistently around 8 per cent, the highest in the world at the time. The expression 'German economic miracle' was coined directly in response to the results of Ehrhardt's reforms. Following the principle of 'prosperity for one and all', our state announced that it would be achieving this by guaranteeing an individual's business freedom and right to enter any sphere of enterprise he or she chose. Given conditions such as these, the most competent, hard-working and entrepreneurial people would gain a higher status in society. We also promised an increase in earned income, pensions and benefits in line with the economy's growth rate, increasing stability and integration into the world community. As history has shown, we have kept our promise.

In the Strategy we also outlined our intention to introduce a national currency, inserting the proviso that we would only be considering this issue when the crisis was over and the economy had stabilised. The Soviet rouble was adopted as the common currency of the transitional period because we were not yet ready then to change to a new currency. Moreover, all the settlements in commodity circulation were in roubles, and the Russian leadership promised to keep the same rouble zone going for the time being.

The Strategy for Independence

However, there were then people in Russia who wanted us to agree to remain in the rouble zone and informed us that they would ruin our economy if we refused to. Events during the next eighteen months confirmed our misgivings – but more of this in other chapters.

At the end of 1992, hardly anyone believed me when I announced that the Strategy only marked the start of our long journey. At the very height of the crisis, the Strategy set the guidelines for forming a normal democratic society with a multi-structure market economy guaranteeing everyone equal opportunities for pursuing their economic, social and political interests. We sought to create a society in which the law, the will of the people and common sense would prevail: a society in which the enterprising and intelligent people would prosper and achieve their goals.

Despite the obstacles we encountered in the political sphere and others during the first three years (1992-94), the Government tried to liberalise the economy, setting up the legislative and institutional bases for market relations, and filling the market with consumer goods. Liberalising the economy uncovered a great many problems that had an impact on the country's economy by reducing its production and economic potential. The prime causes were backward technology, numerous noncompetitive goods and services, an inadequate market and legislative base and insufficient institutions in the state system, as well as a lack of financial and human resources.

During this period a great many incisive criticisms and at times quite preposterous opinions and commentaries were aired by foreign media with regard to Kazakhstan and its leadership. Some fiercely contested the expediency of conducting reforms in Kazakhstan, and argued in favour of border reviews and so on.

American political analysts headed by Zbigniew Brzezinski predicted terrible internal, inter-ethnic conflicts resulting from the republic's multi-national population, or that we would be swallowed up by Russia, or China or the Muslim states. The following excerpt from Z. Brzezinski's book *The Grand Chessboard* is a good example:

'It's becoming inevitable that not only representatives of the elite but even more so ordinary people in these republics are

11

going to get increasingly nationalistically inclined and will, most likely, all to a great extent adhere to the Muslim religion. In Kazakhstan, a vast country with vast reserves of natural resources but with a population of nearly 20 million made up more or less equally of Kazakhs and Slavs, linguistic and national frictions must surely exhibit a tendency to get stronger.'

Z. Brzezinski, *The Grand Chessboard: American Primacy and its Geostrategic Imperatives*, 1998

It was Russia's independent press, it has to be said, who set the critical tone. Particularly vociferous was Vladimir Zhirinovsky who, like Solzhenitsyn, argued that Kazakhstan was a temporary phenomenon and would be incapable of existing as an independent state, and that Russian people's rights were supposedly being violated there. Neo-liberal politicians and economists in Russia argued that once it lost its ties with the Russian Federation, Kazakhstan would go bankrupt and 'crawl back to Russia on its knees'.

'...if economic policy continues as it is today, experts in Russia also predict, in the near future Kazakhstan can expect hyperinflation or, more precisely, the collapse of its national currency and a total financial and economic catastrophe...the disastrous endgame will be played out no later than March next year'.

Nezavisimaya Gazeta, 27 May 1994

History has proven all these predictions wrong. Indeed, ten years after declaring its independence, Kazakhstan occupied a leading position in many areas of activity in post-Soviet space. Kazakhstan's main achievements in the initial stage of its economic reforms were maintaining social and political stability in the country, successfully introducing a national currency, joining international financial institutions, totally renouncing the principles of an administrative-command economy and, as a result, gaining the recognition of the international community.

As Kazakhstan's independence and economy continued to expand and develop, the shortage of highly skilled personel became increasingly acute. We ended up searching all over the former Soviet Union for Kazakhstani specialists – economists, lawyers, military personnel, financial advisers, and so on. Many did not need persuading to return to their homeland. They were all professionals in their particular area and patriots. Many of those highly qualified people who came back to Kazakhstan went on to become senior state officials.

It was also important during our quest for the most effective economic model that we marked our course with ideological pointers. I summarised my thoughts in a short work entitled *The Ideological Consolidation of Society as a Condition of Kazakhstan's Progress*, published in 1993. In those days public opinion was in a state of total confusion. However, three principal ways forward emerged through the mists of uncertainty. Firstly, there was the socialist idea, which was still very strong; then traditionalism; and thirdly, liberal ideas. We had to choose between these different options. However, an analysis of the situation convinced me that not all the ready options for developing society, tried and tested by many other countries, were actually right for us.

The situation was more or less clear as far as the socialist idea was concerned. The total chaos in the economy, politics and international relations were there for all to see. And as someone who had personally experienced the statistical 'marvels' of a socialist economy, it was clear to me that there was no going back to the past.

Things were more complex with traditionalism. Important though it may be for preserving a nation in cultural terms, it is not a valid option in politics. I was often obliged in those days to explain that a political ideology of a traditional type based on reviving archaic forms of social organisation and on 'tribalistic' psychology was definitely not right for us. I was already well aware of all the dangers of various 'tribalistic' attitudes and issues. All my practical political work over one and a half decades had been firmly focused on suppressing all kind of tribal sentiments.

Just then, traditionalism as a political ideology was inevitably causing an acute rise in tribal disputes. I remember how in 1993, a group of young political scientists brought me a paper on the mechanisms of tribalism in Kazakh society and its influences on the

13

state's future. It was a serious critique with a detailed analysis of possible outcomes. However, I put it to one side and told them that while the issue definitely needed studying and constant monitoring, there was no need to stir up public opinion, or, indeed, organise public discussions on this subject. Time has proved me right.

It was an equally complex situation with liberal ideas. In the early 1990s, many members of the elite regarded these as the panacea for all ills. In my position as state leader, I could not afford to be so credulous. Yes, liberal ideas are one of the West's most visible, striking contributions to world political theory and practice and, yes, they did become the dominant political ideology in many regions of the planet. And yet it was already clear then that the people attempting to transfer Western liberal ideas directly to Kazakhstan would run up against cultural difficulties in the broadest sense, including political culture as well. It would be impossible to instantly change its character and ideals. Political culture had to be transformed gradually and in a civilised manner by carrying out real reforms.

Let me remind you, all this was said in the now far-off year of 1993. Exactly the same, word for word, can be said of it today. And the system of our pointers was set just as clearly. It was a compact programme with four directions in the political and economic sphere, and four in the realm of consolidating ideas. I have not changed the pointers since they were first announced. So, now it's up to you to judge.

First, we decided to turn our formal, legal independence into genuine independence. Secondly, we made it a strategic priority at this stage to strengthen our statehood. You see, we only had incipient attributes of statehood at the time. Thirdly, we agreed to carry out full-scale economic reforms to the system. Fourthly, we decided to go for pragmatism not only in our choice of foreign economic partners, but also in our foreign policies overall.

The ideas section consisted of issues under the following four headings. First, there had to be inter-national harmony. We were to achieve this objective brilliantly over the following years. Secondly, there had to be internal national unity. We saw to it that the Kazakhs did not split up into *zhuz* and clans, regions and other territorial units. As we can see today, for many countries this is not just a problem still under discussion but even one with serious political resonance. Thirdly, we announced the framework of ideas within which Kazakhstani society was to be modernised. This involved the creation of the institutes of a civil society, a multi-party system, free and independent mass media, and non-governmental organisations. Finally, we correctly assessed the potential of religious movements and clearly stipulated the need for religious tolerance and religious freedom.

All these propositions have withstood the test of time.

The President's Memorandum, 1994

Even with the initial successes, there were still plenty of other problems left to resolve. One causing me particular concern was that people were still refusing to embrace the changes under way. Faced with an extreme crisis and economic collapse, I made a speech that subsequently became known as 'The President's Memorandum', at a sitting of the Supreme Soviet of the Republic of Kazakhstan. Its principal aim was to get the highest echelons of state power, political parties and alliances to take stock of the current state of affairs in Kazakhstan and at last start working in a co-ordinated and constructive manner. It was the third year of independence, and the population had to be told categorically that there was no going back to the past.

The year 1994 marked a turning point in many respects. The Memorandum proposed radical reforms in the currency, credit and banking systems. The country had had a currency of its own for half a year by then. The next decisive step was aimed at stabilising the course of the tenge and curbing hyperinflation.

We told our citizens outright that the state would be cutting back on its spending, including the various direct and covert subsidies, grants, and spending to maintain state bodies. It was the government's task to keep strict control of all budgetary revenues and spending. Any sort of pressure and lobbying in favour of individual departments and branches was clamped down on. The government officially announced that the state budget was an instrument of state policy, and that it would not be pilfered to benefit corporate, regional and other interests. Another really important task was attracting as much major foreign investment

15

as possible in key areas such as transport, energy and mineral resources. One other landmark event of this period was the National Bank being given independence from the Supreme Soviet and Government.

It was at this time, too, that unprecedented measures were implemented to reduce the state apparatus. During Soviet times it had been fashionable to divert money from the centre to increase the number of provinces and regions. This also resulted in an increase in the numbers of state officials. A republic's leader was only entitled to become a Politburo member if there was a minimum of 20 provinces, as in Ukraine. There were by then 19 of them in Kazakhstan, with the twentieth about to be created.

But they were provinces in name only, as, in fact, they failed to meet the stipulated requirements in terms of economic potential or population. Even so, each had a complete power structure of its own: a provincial committee, executive committee, judiciary, and departments of internal affairs, education, health and so on. And the same was true at regional level. Such a bureaucratic hydra did not take kindly to innovations or changes. It was precisely for this reason that administrative reform was one of the first measures we took in the course of our announced reforms.

To make the most of our resources, in 1994, we formed 14 provinces from the existing 19, and 169 regions from the 230. 25,000 officials lost their jobs, thus saving millions of tenge previously used to pay wages and pensions. Only a decade later was Russia to first attempt similar administrative reform.

We were guided by the simple logic that it was pointless for a working person to have so many bosses if he had to pay for their salaries out of his taxes. It would have been different if a province had been able to pay for them out of its income. But what happened was that the funds had to be raised against solvent provinces. The officials who lost their cushy jobs of course objected to my course of action, and certain politicians have opportunistically seized upon this to call for the reinstatement of the provinces and regions. We must not lose our resolve over this, however, just because we are now enjoying higher levels of prosperity. It is most tempting at times of great affluence to increase the state apparatus and spending on its maintenance, but it is essential, in my opinion, for the state to keep this spending under control in the future as well.

16

The Strategy for Independence

We have not completed the administrative reforms. They still lie ahead of us.

It was impossible to overcome the non-payment crisis without adopting mechanisms for classifying enterprises as 'thriving' or 'failing'. The plan was to eradicate weak enterprises by means of regeneration or bankruptcy.

The process of reducing state ownership and that of privatisation envisaged the creation of a stratum of potential proprietors and the establishment of a securities market and its infrastructure. Another massive challenge facing us was that of conducting legal reform. It was to be used as a 'strut' to underpin the economic block of reforms as well as a sort of engine for dynamically implementing them.

However, what arguably mattered the most at this crucial time for the country was maintaining a balanced psychological climate in society. While some populists attempted to promise a rosy future just around the corner, others predicted certain doom. But only a forthright position could be an honest one, as I tried to explain to the deputies.

> 'If we are true patriots of our country, if we really want to get out of the crisis and give people a better life, we must face the difficulties and get through them. Fifty years ago during the war against Nazi Germany, the British Prime Minister Winston Churchill told his people: "It will be a difficult and hard war that will demand sacrifices of all of us, but we have no choice." He did not try to conceal from people the fact that pain and suffering would have to be endured for victory to be won in that war. Kazakhstan has gained political independence, but we are now struggling for our economic self-sufficiency. That is why I am going to be frank with you and say that considerable effort will be required of literally each and every citizen of Kazakhstan and, first and foremost, of you and me.'
>
> From the speech to the Supreme Council, 9 June 1994

During those years of crisis, attention had to be given daily not only to the economic reforms but also to the public mood and maintaining social equilibrium, inter-national calm, and stability throughout the country. At a time when an increasing number of trouble spots for inter-national conflicts were cropping up in post-Soviet space, Kazakhstan continued to be the shared home of many nationalities.

We were, however, particularly concerned by the numbers of Russian-speaking people leaving the country. We realised the loss of this most valuable human resource was seriously affecting the republic. That was why I came up with the initiative called 'ten simple steps towards meeting ordinary citizens' needs' which we adopted to try and stem the flow of emigrants and simplify the procedure for acquiring citizenship. That same year I brought in the idea of a Eurasian Union as the ideological basis for future economic integration.

By the start of 1996 the reform process was already well under way. At this stage, the main thrust of the reforms was to provide macroeconomic stabilisation and improve the legislative base, financial system, public service and production sector: this included demonopolisation, privatisation, and the bankruptcy and reorganisation of enterprises. We also reviewed the reforms that had already taken place.

'It should first be pointed out that Kazakhstan is now well and truly an independent sovereign state and, figuratively speaking, has acquired its place on the political world map.

Secondly, the passing in August 1995 of the New Constitution has paved the way for establishing the country as a state. Thus the first phase of state building has been accomplished.

Thirdly, while consolidating and strengthening the state system, we have attached, and continue to attach, the greatest significance to deepening inter-national accord, political stability, the development of democratic processes, and the formation of new political institutions. From the very outset, priority has been given in the country to civil rights and individual liberties.

Fourthly, this period characterised by the turbulent, chaotic and, in many respects, critical process of carrying out reforms and achieving economic self-sufficiency is drawing to an end. It is increasingly entering a comprehensible, controllable phase, enabling action to be taken on precisely formulated programmes and plans – that is, making it possible to predict the course of events instead of lagging behind them.

And, fifthly and finally, we have succeeded in tackling social problems head on. We have begun increasing pension sizes and calculated our outstanding debts to pensioners, and a start has been made on increasing salaries in the budget. Real support is now being given to the countryside.'

From the speech *The reforms' success depends on the regions' active participation in them*, 1996

The transition we were making involved providing key conditions for a functioning market economy, such as putting enterprises on a commercial footing and giving them the freedom to take charge of their own affairs; free price formation and the end of state interference in enterprises' economic management; consistent integration into the world economic relations system, and expansion of market relations into spheres where they are the most effective.

It is no secret that many considered these tasks unrealizable. There were numerous diametrically opposed views, but we had to follow our chosen course and carry the reforms through. I am deeply convinced of the importance of identifying the lines along which the transition to a functioning market is to go, the various interconnected measures that are to be implemented, and the sequence they are to follow.

'I am far from thinking that in the course of the reforms we have carried through everything we set out to. There have been mistakes and miscalculations. There are difficulties today and there's probably no way of avoiding them in the future either. But the most important things have been done. Statehood has been established. The foundations of a political system, democracy and civil liberties have been laid. An inherently market economy is functioning on a new legislative base. Meanwhile time is going by. Reform undoubtedly needs to be extended and developed on a new, larger scale.'

ibid

Deep social orientation and high-quality restructuring were needed for Kazakhstan to achieve optimum economic development, bound up with this transition to a new market model of social and economic development for the republic as a sovereign state. It was also important at this juncture to analyse the causes of the economic crisis, and chart the right ways of getting out of it.

We again returned to Singapore's example. Without any land resources, natural riches or even its own food products and water, it was still transformed into the leading country of South-East Asia within a relatively short time. A thorough study of Singapore's experience showed that one of the major factors in the country's success was having a long-term strategy, clear goals and a high-skilled policy for implementing them. In many respects, this served as a starting point for developing a long-term strategy of our own.

Strategy for Development to 2030
I took the decision to develop the long-term strategy at the end of 1995, just as Kazakhstan embarked on its fifth year of independence. By that time the economy was showing promising signs of stabilising, thanks to the reforms already carried through. For the first time in independent Kazakhstan's history, at the start of 1996 the economy recorded a growth: not very substantial (0.5 per cent) but at least positive. Sizable oil reserves allowing production for the next 30-40 years, and the increasing presence of foreign investors in the Kazakhstan basin of the Caspian Sea, indicated that oil extraction revenues were going to increase substantially over the coming years. The period of 'putting out the fires' was over, and it was now time for us to stop and imagine what our country was going to be like in 10, 20 and 30 years' time.

The Supreme Economic Council (SEC) was established under my chairmanship in April 1996. Its main aims were to draw up strategic proposals for tackling social and economic problems, analyse the progress of the reforms, and develop new initiatives for carrying them through. The setting up of the Council was an important advance in forming the institutional foundations of a market economy. The SEC comprised eminent scientists, senior state officials and specialists in various fields.

The Strategy for Independence

The SEC's core personnel were young people who had none of the baggage of outmoded dogmatic opinions. They had been selected for employment primarily on the basis of their fluency in foreign languages, academic achievements and managerial experience. Each of them was put in charge of a different branch of the economy. Their employment created a pool of fresh, new ideas on the country's future development. These energetic young people stood out in sharp contrast to the conservative apparatchiks. Today they are all working in different departments and putting the strategy into practice.

This group had two principal challenges to meet throughout 1996. The first was to conduct thorough research into other countries' experiences of strategic planning and structural reform and then visit as many of them as possible. The second was to set up a group of national and foreign specialists in every branch of the economy to develop and systematise all the feedback. So complex were these challenges that it took each of the young managers an entire year to assimilate all the necessary information.

Once this was done, a methodological base had to be set up to work out a long-term strategy. And here we turned to other countries' track records. Thanks to the active support of the UN Development Programme in Kazakhstan, we were able to establish contacts with Harvard University and hold a strategic-planning seminar.

In April 1997, a group of Kazakhstani experts travelled to Boston to attend the ten-day seminar for senior managers, which Harvard hosted. The Kazakhstani group learned about the strategic-planning experiences of countries such as Korea, Singapore and Malaysia and long-term business strategies of world giants like Boeing, General Electric and British Petroleum. The lectures threw light on how Kazakhstan compared with other countries and transnational corporations in terms of territory, population, GDP and hydrocarbon reserves. The seminars' materials and subsequent contacts with individual world experts provided the methodological base we needed.

A 30-year term was set for the planning for two main reasons. First, because it represented a generation's active life span. Secondly, in terms of oil reserves and the possible introduction of alternative energy sources, Kazakhstan was also looking at a 30 to

40-year span: for instance, its contract with Chevron – which was to be a benchmark for other oil companies – was set at 30 years.

The 'Kazakhstan to 2030 Strategy' was divided into four phases: the preparatory phase (1997-2000); the first phase (2000-2010); the second phase (2010-2020); and the third phase (2020-2030), at the end of which Kazakhstan was expected to rank among the developed industrial countries. The Strategy set out three development scenarios for the country based on optimistic, average, and pessimistic forecasts of energy reserves and prices. It should be said that in subsequent years oil-price levels exceeded even the Strategy's optimistic scenario based on US$18 a barrel. By way of a comparison, it was already US$28.2 in the year 2000, and US$60 in 2006.

The main focal point of discussions on the document's structure was drawing up priorities and the order to put them in. During many hours of heated discussion, each expert argued for his department to be given priority. For instance, it was argued that healthcare and education should be separate priorities. No less heated were the debates on the sequence the priorities should be in. The working group finally settled on five of them. However, during the course of the work it became clear that infrastructure and energy issues would be playing such major roles in Kazakhstan's economic future that they should also be treated as separate priorities. In the end, the Strategy listed seven priorities.

I can certainly say that serious, intensive work involving state management and psychology went into setting the number of priorities. The main conclusions drawn from other countries' experiences and Kazakhstani and foreign experts' feedback were used as a framework for formulating the Strategy and, in particular, identifying the importance of the priorities and the order they should be put in. During this process it gradually emerged that we needed to shift our attention away from global priorities to ones relevant to our country, and think not in terms of phases but of potential resources. So, we identified our main priorities as being national security, social stability, the economy and public welfare. In other words, the Strategy's priorities were identified by the 'gradual shrink ring principle' of selecting only the most important points from a total number that became progressively smaller at each phase of the process.

The Strategy for Independence

The Strategy was reworked and examined time and time again, from fundamentals through to individual aspects. Experts, for instance, repeatedly reworked the wording of the priorities so that people could understand them more easily, making sure the text was succinct and pithy. We also decided to limit the number of priorities for the same reason (to five and, later, seven) because a large number of priorities might have been less engaging or easy to comprehend. What's more, for Kazakhs seven is a magic number.

During the summer of 1997, the document was drawn up in detail. Once every two weeks the Strategic Planning Agency sent me revised and updated versions. In the meantime experts honed each paragraph, reworking all the ideas to incorporate my amendments.

Work on the Strategy was a complex challenge on many levels, involving a thorough analysis of the theory and practice of world economics; thematic, branch and indicative plans; mathematical and economic estimates and the feedback from numerous foreign visits and discussions with eminent experts; and, finally, the intuition of all those involved.

It has to be said that we were given considerable help in developing the Strategy by international organisations and donors – first and foremost, the UN Development Program. Suffice it to say that over 40 acclaimed international experts worked with us as consultants, including H. Berstock, K. Grey, V. Hudzhong, G. Allison and R. Blackwell.

It is worth noting that we did not get any Government members working on this project. It was brought to my attention that the then Prime Minister did not want to get involved in it and was actually slowing down the process of gathering material. How could such a Government be trusted with carrying this Strategy through? That is why, in the autumn of 1997, I released Kazhegildin from his duties and dismissed the Government.

In August 1997, we put the finishing touches to the full text of the Strategy. The final list of basic priorities read as follows:

1. **National Security**
   To ensure Kazakhstan's development as an independent State with the retention of total territorial integrity.
2. **Internal Political Stability and Social Consolidation**

To preserve and enhance internal political stability and national unity, enabling Kazakhstan to implement the national strategy in the current and following decades.

3. **Economic Growth based on an Open Market Economy with High-Level Foreign Investments and Domestic Savings**
To achieve real, steady and accelerating rates of economic growth.

4. **Health, Education and the Prosperity of the Citizens of Kazakhstan**
To constantly improve the living conditions, health, education and opportunities of all Kazakhstanis, and improve the environment.

5. **Energy Resources**
To make effective use of Kazakhstan's energy resources by rapidly increasing oil and gas production and export so as to achieve revenues promoting steady economic growth and the improvement of the population's standard of living.

6. **Infrastructure, in particular Transport and Communications**
To develop these key sectors with a view to strengthening national security, political stability and economic growth.

7. **A Professional State**
To create an effective and modern workforce of Kazakhstani state officials, dedicated to their duties and competent to act as the people's representatives in the achievement of our stated goals.

From *Kazakhstan's Development Strategy to 2030*, 1997

The issue now was about launching the Strategy as policy, and about the mechanisms for subsequently implementing it in practice.

The first of these concerned me deeply for two reasons. First, because the Strategy's subsequent success in practice depended on how people took to it, and, indeed, whether they took to it at all. A strategy nobody believed in could not fulfill its purpose. And, secondly, after all the hard work, efforts and ideas that had gone into it, every member of the working group, including myself, took everything concerning this document very much to heart. This may have helped us find a superb solution to the issue of the Strategy's launch.

Kazakhstan's Development Strategy to 2030 and the immediate measures for implementing it were officially announced on 10 October 1997, when I delivered my first address to the people of Kazakhstan in Parliament. I liked the very idea of a presidential address to the people, and I am pleased that it has been adopted as an annual tradition. And at the time it was just what was needed, and by addressing the people as a whole – all the citizens of the Republic – we underscored the Strategy's special role and status.

The Strategy identified the national goal, and the system of priorities for achieving it. Our country's declared mission was to build an independent, flourishing and politically stable Kazakhstan with intrinsic national unity, social justice, and economic prosperity enjoyed by the entire population. To cite my words from the address, security and increasing prosperity for all Kazakhstanis defined the Kazakhstan we all wanted to build.

As for putting the Strategy into practice, measures were developed for each of the long-term priorities which could be implemented consecutively in the annual, three- and five-year plans that all the state bodies were to be accountable for. These priorities were to become points for the state and all citizens to focus their efforts on. They defined the methods of approach and criteria in working out the budget and human resources policy in the years that followed.

To implement the Strategy as quickly as possible, we identified a series of challenges that had to be completed no later than 1998, and the Government was given eight specific tasks for that year.

1. To guarantee punctual, full payment of pensions, benefits and wages in budgetary organisations.
2. To issue in the course of the year microcredits worth the equivalent of US$400 to a total of 30,000 disadvantaged citizens for a three-year term to create jobs, first and foremost, in the rural sector.
3. To guarantee, with effect from 1998, the issue of credits to develop small- and medium-scale businesses, agricultural enterprises, and create jobs worth a total of US$100m.

25

4. To start implementing a broad-based programme to computerise schools, first and foremost in rural areas, having allocated in 1998 a total of US$22m for these purposes.
5. To ensure the reduction of credit rates for peasants and farming enterprises to a total of 2.5b tenge.
6. To start a public campaign to promote a healthy lifestyle.
7. To start implementing a programme of housing construction, having allocated a total of US$40m for this purpose. To issue a public report in April 1998 on the principles and anticipated results of this programme's implementation.
8. To guarantee a 100 per cent attendance rate at schools.

ibid

The postulates in *Kazakhstan's Development Strategy to 2030* are constant pointers in developing any of our plans, and are still just as relevant as ever. There is no role here for political and economic radicalism: these are sufficiently energetic economic reforms – predominantly political in the first phase – democratising the administrative system without diminishing the vertical line of power, and developing a market while retaining the state's quite distinct regulatory functions. As far as I know, this method is quite unique.

It should be noted that Kazakhstan was one of the first states to apply 'synergic principles' in the development of its state from the moment of gaining independence in 1991. To implement this strategy, various structures have to be in place to develop state policy, forming an open network of state regulation in which healthy emulation is encouraged.

'Political stability is what matters most. In Asian society discipline and order are more important than democracy, which has to develop over time'. This was the political credo of Lee Kwan Yew. I never concealed the fact that this approach appealed to me. 'Economics before politics' was what I always used to say. I was criticised for saying so. But I had seen the disintegration of the USSR with my very own eyes, when politics had taken precedent over people's prosperity and peace of mind.

The Strategy for Independence

From a Planned Economy to Competitiveness

When we Kazakhs were citizens of the USSR, we used to think we were building an ideal state. With its population of totally diverse peoples, the 'Sixth of the World's Land Mass' was united by a single idea. It was possibly this that caused politics to dominate all the other constituent parts of the Soviet state.

Industrial and commercial links that failed to comply with any economic laws were set up with the particular aim of connecting the 'threads' of the Soviet republics to a single centre and spinning the idea of an 'integral great Motherland'. However, the laws of economics, like those of nature, are objective and cannot be dismissed or rewritten at someone's whim. The political course set to achieve a 'shining future' foundered. There were numerous reasons why, of course, but, principally, it was because there was no proper economic base. When the idea was debunked and the state was left to live out its final years, these artificial economic 'threads' were stretched to breaking point by a tumultuous crisis, and then snapped.

In search of a solution, the Soviet leadership tried to make the transition to a new system – but in keeping with their old methods, they started with politics. The transition ended in an impasse. The economy is the key to political independence, and whereas our first steps to reform the country's economy were actually urgent measures to survive at that particular point in time – in post-Soviet chaos – the reforms currently under way are targeted at a specific result in the future: namely, building a sufficiently strong, diversified economic system to allow our country to compete successfully at global level and find its 'place in the sun'.

The President's traditional annual address to the people of Kazakhstan began with the *Kazakhstan to 2030 Development Strategy*. Every address is a part of our general Strategy and part of our way ahead. And the Message 'To a competitive nation' became a landmark in the years that followed.

In my opinion, a country's competitiveness is determined by establishing favourable conditions for raising the competitiveness of each and every one of its citizens. On the subject of people, I would like to cite the Austrian economist Joseph Schumpeter, whose definition of an entrepreneur impressed me greatly. According to Schumpeter, being an entrepreneur is not just about running a business, but also about taking new, original managerial decisions. An entrepreneur introduces innovations and takes responsibility for economic risk. I would very much like to see Kazakhstanis becoming entrepreneurs of this kind – thirsting for knowledge of new things, experimenting and being creative, prepared to take risks and accept responsibility.

Following the axiom 'if you want to change the world, change yourself first', each of us must learn to compete and be winners. And, ultimately, our general competitiveness must bring prosperity to our people. Here I want to underscore the deeper meaning of this idea I have just expressed. Kazakhstan's competitiveness must bring spiritual as well as material prosperity to our nation. A flourishing economy should bring with it a flowering of culture and art, the Kazakh language, and our people's traditions and philosophy of life.

A nation's competitiveness is the sum total of the competitiveness of every one of its representatives, the level of his training, education and personal development. And a country's competitiveness derives from its people's prosperity and degree of social and economic development. The principle of dynamic programming is bound to apply here: in order to achieve one's goal, one first has to define one's means.

Designing a new economy is a difficult and risk-laden task. In doing so, we are basing our course on *The Strategy for Kazakhstan's industrial and innovation development 2003-2015*. Implementing its first phase will enable us to change radically the structure of our economy and the dynamics of its growth. Achieving the Strategy's goals will solve the problem of our economy's dependence on the state of world prices for natural resources, and one of these goals – diversification – will assist the economy to move away from primary commodities. The foundations will also be laid for the transition to a service and technology economy. According to our experts, the industrial innovation policy being conducted will result in guaranteed economic growth rates of no less than 8.8-9.2 per cent per year.

But the Strategy for industrial and innovation development only covers the preliminary period. The formation of post-industrial society in the world is still far from complete. Kazakhstan still has a chance to make a breakthrough to join the ranks of the industrially developed countries. And carrying through the Strategy should radically change the course of events and prepare the country for this breakthrough. The main question is in which direction we should be making this leap forward.

It is essential, on the one hand, to make full use of what we already have, since survival instincts tell us that for the breakthrough Kazakhstan should rely on fairly traditional branches of the economy such as mining, heavy industry and agriculture, as well as nuclear energy and the development of space technologies; and, on the other, to use innovations and high technologies as a means of increasing economic productivity.

Take the example of Finland. Having concentrated on the development of high technologies, this small northern country with a population of five million that until recently had no firm scientific base or advanced industry, is now hailed as the world's most competitive economy. The Finnish national production model or 'innovation wonder' is now hailed as one of the most effective in the world. Its hallmarks are a high standard of education, the competitive principal in the allocation of science funding, and a developed innovation infrastructure linking the state, science and business together.

For several years now, Finland's indices have topped the Davos Competitiveness Index, followed by the USA, Sweden, Taiwan, Norway, Iceland, Singapore, Australia, Canada, Switzerland, Japan, Britain, Germany and Israel. According to the 2005-2006 results, Kazakhstan came 56th out of 117 countries. I shall mention that according to this index we did better than all the other CIS members.

The current division of labour around the world enables countries to concentrate their resources on the areas of science and technology where they have the most potential. For instance, the USA is the largest producer of computer and office technology, while Japan occupies a dominant position in the electronics industry and Switzerland is the absolute leader in pharmaceuticals. The USA, Britain and France are the leading exporters of aerospace technology.

However, all this does not mean that the scheme cannot be altered. The situation is certainly not disastrous for any economy, even the global one, and the emergence of new players, new producers and markets marks a step towards a new phase of development. A fine example of this is India that has rapidly caught up with the world leaders in Information Technology (IT). I specially visited Bangalore and 'Asia's Silicon Valley' to have a look at this phenomenon myself. In 2004, India's IT exports were worth over US$17b. Nowadays Indian specialists are much in demand in the best IT companies, making up 34 per cent of Microsoft's human resources, 28 per cent of IBM's and 17 per cent of Intel's.

After successfully implementing our strategic documents, we can see to it that the revenues from enterprises of the non-commodities sector become the main source of replenishing the state budget, constituting about 85 per cent of its total. At the same time, the economy's monetarisation level will not exceed 30 per cent, and inflation, 4-5 per cent.

Then, from 2008 onwards, we shall start work on the Strategy for the second decade – *Kazakhstan to 2020*. Two objectives were set in the first strategic plan ending in 2010: firstly, to double the GNP of 2005, and, secondly, build the foundations of a competitive economy. While the first phase – *Kazakhstan to 2010* – began in the post-crisis years and consisted of 'sliding' three-year state programmes, the second phase will coincide with a more predictable economic situation, affording us the opportunity to adopt five-year development plans, like Japan and the South-East Asian countries. Our economy also has to raise its index levels and choose new key pointers. For instance, by 2015, our GNP should be three and a half times higher than it was in 2000. Also, the per-capita GNP should by then reach between US$8-10,000, putting it on a par with that of Saudi Arabia and a number of European countries, such as Portugal and Spain.

In line with the *Kazakhstan to 2030* Strategy, Kazakhstan has now set itself the ambitious goal of joining the ranks of the 50 most competitive states within the next decade. Taking advantage of the positive results of strategic planning over recent years, we have devised a development Strategy for Kazakhstan to achieve this goal. It lists seven crucial lines of development that will make it easier to achieve.

'We must be prepared for stiff competition and use it to our advantage. Kazakhstan can and must play an active part in multilateral international economic projects that will facilitate our integration into the global economy, based, among other things, on our advantageous economic and geographic position and available resources. The state, for its part, has to remove the legislative, administrative and bureaucratic barriers in the way of business initiatives and provide direct support to promising private-capital business undertakings.'

From the Address to the people, *Strategy for Kazakhstan to join the ranks of the world's 50 most competitive countries*, Astana, 1 March 2006.

The key development areas in the field of new technology over the next decade are going to be bio- and nanotechnology, artificial intelligence systems, global information networks, high-speed transport systems, and energy-saving technologies. Automated production, space technologies, the production of construction materials with preset features and nuclear energy are also going to continue developing. Production will become increasingly 'intellectualised' and the transition will be made to a constant process of innovation. The move towards a knowledge-based society of a new type will gradually be completed.

We must keep these areas in our line of vision as we implement the Kazakhstan Strategy for increasing competitiveness.

We have a chance of achieving significant results in science and technology areas such as biotechnology, nanotechnology, space exploration and information and communication technologies. These specific areas will require thousands of highly qualified specialists and scientists.

The first successful steps have already been taken in implementing our plans.

Kazakhstan's first satellite, 'KazSat', was successfully launched in June 2006. Over a thousand Kazakhstani scientists are currently working on scientific projects within the framework of the state space exploration development programme. Kazakhstan's first Information Technology Park (ITP), Alatau City, was opened on 15 September, 2006. The idea of creating one came to me in 2002, during my visit to India and, in particular, Bangalore, a major centre of machine manufacturing, the food and textile industries, arts and crafts, and space research. A decree was issued in August 2003, 'On creating a special economic zone, an "Information

Technology Park"', and the construction of this complex began in 2004. Eleven of the 25 companies tendering for work in the Alatau City ITP have already been selected. I invite all the world's leading IT companies to come and work here and guarantee that we shall provide all the essential conditions for your work and do everything to make your business profitable for you, and Kazakhstan.

'Alatau City' is our first high-tech industry project, and destined to become a new intellectual centre in Central Asia. We have enlisted the services of world IT and communications leaders in the ITP. Co-operation agreements have been signed with Microsoft, Hewlett-Packard, Siemens, SISCO Systems, Talis, LG, Macrosystem and Samsung.

We are in the initial stages of setting up a National Nanolaboratory that all Kazakhstani scientists will have access to. A new complex housing the National Centre for world-standard biotechnology is to be built in Astana in 2008. Kazakhstani scientists currently working abroad have already expressed interest in working at this centre and are currently taking part in joint scientific ventures.

The Samruk state holding company linking the country's top national companies together has been set up with the principal task of advancing our economic interests in world markets. The Kazyn Fund for steady growth has been founded to coordinate the development institutes' work, promote economic diversification and finance industrial projects. Five hundred and twenty investment projects have been completed since 2005. Ninety projects worth a total of US$2.2b are currently being financed under the development institutes' aegis.

Encouraging as this may be, the fact remains that the state cannot be solely in charge of the development process. There needs to be an active business environment to launch scientific projects and put them on a commercial footing. And while the State may regulate the sphere of scientific development by means of, say, whole and subsidy-based financing, an initiative revolving around science and production integration does best in private hands. It is up to our citizens to take up the challenge.

When considering various scientific matters in the past, I came to realise more and more that the role of business had to change. During its years in crisis there was a period of 'intermediary' business in the country. At present, the service sector is undergoing rapid development. But it is now time for us to set our sights further. What we need now is business based on the production of high-tech goods and services. Science-based production must become a dominant part of our economic development in the years to come.

Kazakhstan tomorrow: breakthroughs and priorities

It is fifteen years since the Republic of Kazakhstan gained its independence and embarked on a course of independent political and economic development. Of course, in historical terms fifteen years is virtually no time at all. During this period Kazakhstan – like, indeed, all the other post-Soviet republics – faced grave economic and social challenges.

Speaking about positive results is always pleasant. However, at that moment in time, at the very start of our journey, there was no theory to hand, let alone a complete strategy for the transition from a planned to a market economy. Nor were there examples of effective ways and means of transforming post-totalitarian societies, especially of the imperial Communism type several generations of Soviet people had lived in. We had neither the know-how nor trained personnel. We relied on invited foreign consultants and our managers' vast experience. Even then, however, it was clear that in our human resources policy we should set store by our young professionals – economists, financiers and legal experts who were unfettered by outmoded ways and, most importantly, outmoded mind-sets. All that time I personally spent searching for, educating and nurturing several generations of new managers, among whom there were examples of both successes and failures.

Kazakhstan was the first in post-Soviet space to take up strategic planning, acclaimed worldwide as an instrument of state management and regulation, and also for establishing the institutions for a market economy. Not only did the strategic documents define the main priorities and phases of development in that time of crisis and turmoil, they also charted our way and prevented us from getting sidetracked into solving issues of a serious but transitory nature.

When I get free time, I often re-read each of the three strategic documents we have discussed in this chapter. Each of them is a reflection of past events in our society. They contain the spirit of their time in a compact form: you can refer to any of them and see at once what was going on in Kazakhstan at the time and what problems there were. *The Strategy for forming and developing Kazakhstan as a sovereign State* and *The President's Memorandum* reflect all the severity and specific features of the crisis in the country at the time. *The Strategy for Kazakhstan's development to 2030*, on the other hand, already epitomises the optimism and confidence in Kazakhstan's success. It has helped people gain self-belief and take responsibility for their future instead of waiting for state handouts.

At the time, the word 'strategy' struck the wrong chord with a lot of people. I started discussing *Kazakhstan to 2030* in 1997 when the country was only just starting to emerge from its systemic crisis, and a financial crisis had begun to affect South-East Asia and Russia. We were also suffering a setback just then on account of oil prices, which had reached an all-time low in world economic history. Even this, however, did not make us totally lose heart.

Each of the strategies mentioned in this chapter played an immense role in building an independent Kazakhstan and marked qualitatively new, consecutive phases of development. Initially, we started from zero, effecting the transition from a planned economy to its total antithesis, a market system. In the second phase of strategic planning we are now faced with entirely different tasks: ensuring macroeconomic stability, improving the country's legislative base, financial system, social sphere and production sector. The third phase envisages the transition from an agro-industrial to an industrial and post-industrial state, and the transformation of a developing country into a developed one.

'Kazakhstan has been an independent state for only 15 years – since the disintegration of the Soviet Union and collapse of Communism. Prior to this, it had never been independent in modern history. It had to build democracy, political awareness and a free market economy from scratch. All things considered, the growth Kazakhstan has succeeded in achieving in the said fields is outstanding and promising.'
Martin Stiff, United Press International, 6 December 2005

The Strategy for Independence

Of course, during the most difficult initial years the market reforms were bound to encounter obstacles and did not always go as planned. Many of the programmes aimed at stabilising the economy were of a temporary and localised nature. The solution of one task usually gave rise to other problems that were just as difficult to resolve. However, these years helped us not only to achieve successes in later years but also consolidate our position as an independent State.

Kazakhstan headed towards its targets step by step, developing its state economic policies not by tying them in with electoral terms but by following the objective logic of economic development, as defined by so-called investment cycles with estimated time spans of 10 -15 years.

We are living at a very important, complex and also remarkable time. Very often I catch myself thinking about how the contribution each of us makes in the present and short term will determine the kind of country all coming generations of Kazakhstanis will be living in. That's why the government's task must consist of providing its citizens with equal opportunities for growth and fulfilment, regardless of their sex, age, national or ethnic origin, region they live in or any other differences.

There is also a need to understand clearly that development and the parasitic attitudes generated by high social spending are incompatible. The opinion still persists today that the funding of all social programmes should be considerably increased in line with oil revenues. But remember that the availability of significant revenues from oil sales is not always a good thing for a state. You only have to recall the sorry experiences of countries such as Venezuela, Nigeria and Saudi Arabia.

We must not repeat these mistakes. We must not sink our citizens' and economy's competitiveness in oil dollars. The *Kazakhstan to 2030 Strategy* argues that we must live and work as though we do not have any oil. This idea has a deep significance.

Rational consumption of our available means – this is the principle our strategy should be based on. Like any family, our state should be keeping something back for a rainy day. Only a fraction of the revenues from oil sales will be used to set up a modern socially engineered infrastructure inside the country in areas such as health care, education, drinking-water production and road construction. These are areas with so-called 'market gaps' that definitely require state intervention. For instance, the nation's health and its standard of education are areas that cannot be neglected under any circumstances.

No other country in the world has set itself such ambitious tasks in such a short time scale. But I believe that one day this will be referred to as 'the Kazakhstan way'.

In the first years of independence Kazakhstan was like a traveller crossing a mountain pass, battling against the elements, fatigue and fear, and trudging on, come what may.

The first steps were the most difficult. As we set about building our new state, we realised what we needed, first and foremost, was a reliable base, the very foundations of our home: a new Constitution.

We did not arrive at our present 1995 Constitution straightaway. It was preceded by the first Constitution of 1993, and over 140 Presidential decrees with the force of law, and several years of constant battles with people who could not understand the urgent need for the changes and refused to accept them. I shall describe exactly what happened in the next chapter.

2

THE 1995 CONSTITUTION

Charles de Montesquieu, the eighteenth-century lawyer and author of tracts on the division of authority, has said, 'The principle of democracy is corrupted not only when the spirit of equality is extinct, but likewise when the spirit of equality is taken to an extreme and every person wants to become an equal of those he has chosen as his leaders.'

During the final years of the USSR, deputies of all levels in the republics became self-appointed critics of the administrative command system. The media ran live broadcasts of debates in the Supreme Soviet and at Congresses of the People's Deputies, making them out to be clashes between different branches of power. Paradoxically, the Soviets, the very cornerstone of the USSR's might, subsequently became the arena for its public deposition.

Instead of carrying out its basic function of providing people with objective information, discussing burgeoning new issues and preserving universal human values, the media actually heightened tensions.

After decades of censorship and bans, society sought an extreme alternative where the principles of freedom of speech and glasnost were changed beyond recognition. Glasnost is fine as long as the information being broadcast has been verified. False information is not freedom but an infringement of freedom of speech. This was understood long ago in developed societies where jurisdictions allow legal actions to be brought against slander. In these most complex conditions politicians of all stripes, speculating on people's emotions, rushed to gain power, shattering the foundations of the state system and creating a threat to the state's integrity.

What did we actually gain as a result? A protracted multilateral political conflict between various embroiled political groupings both of the Centre and of union republics. The political opposition of the early 1990s coincided with the most horrendous economic crisis throughout the country, during which enterprises stopped working, unemployment increased, and a chronic shortage of all essential goods developed while the union budget just crumbled away.

Such was the reality we were facing when we announced the country's independence on 16 December 1991.

Kazakhstan was the last of the already former Soviet republics to officially declare its independence. Many well-wishers said at the time that Kazakhstan had received its independence unexpectedly, rather like a gift of destiny. Certain of them even considered independent Kazakhstan's days numbered.

Paradoxically, however, it was after gaining independence in 1991 that the most difficult and serious phase in our struggle for self-determination began. It is much harder being genuinely independent in the political and economic sense than simply gaining someone's recognition for being independent. The battle is still raging, only nowadays it is more like a systematic process of building a sovereign state. The foundation of this building is the Constitution, which is to be discussed in this chapter.

After gaining independence we needed a Basic Law that would keep pace with the new realities and prospects, and encapsulate both the experience of previous generations and our confidence in a better future. Independent Kazakhstan's Constitution was to consolidate the basic principles by which we intended building an open and democratic society.

The challenges facing us during the first phase of designing the Constitution were exceptionally complex, diverse and demanding. Firstly, there was a need to strengthen the newly created statehood and the entire state authority and management system in every possible way. Secondly, we had to solve the pressing problems of radically reforming the economy and lifting it out of dire crisis. Thirdly, we had to make foreign policy. Fourthly, we had to guarantee internal political stability. And, finally, there was a need to complete a whole series of tasks linked with the affirmation of citizens' rights and liberties, universally accepted in the civilised world, and with the development of democratic institutions.

Nowadays our country lives by the 1995 Constitution. With its adoption, Kazakhstan definitively established the choice of direction its future development was to take. This Basic Law, adopted in a nationwide referendum, essentially became a social contract in accordance with which the authorities committed themselves to consolidating Kazakhstan as a democratic, civic, rule-of-law, social state, and its citizens accepted responsibility for observing the country's Constitution and laws. Such mutual commitments create a firm basis for the continuing successful development of society and the state and enable us to look to the future with confidence.

The adoption of the Constitution was preceded by a lengthy period of intensive work. Numerous Constitutions were analysed, particularly those adopted in the second half of the 20th century. What mattered most for us was understanding how in countries at different levels of development with diverse socio-cultural, national and other features and different legislative systems, Constitutions resolved the principal objective of helping to strengthen stability, increase national prosperity and develop democracy.

Our search was also extensive in geographical terms, taking in Europe, Asia, North and Latin America. I personally made summaries and analysed 20 Constitutions from all over the world.

As a result, when the decision was taken regarding the need for a new Constitution, we already had five years of our own experience learning to define priorities and goals and how to achieve them.

The adoption of the Constitution was preceded by several years of persistent work overcoming the stereotypes that had formed in people's minds over the decades, solving the great many objective and subjective problems that had arisen in the course of radically reforming the state and society. Yes, our solutions sometimes were makeshift compromises; errors were committed of a kind inevitable in any new situation. All this was reflected in the work of the state institutions and legislation of the time which bore all the hallmarks of a transitional character.

However, looking back at those trying years from today's perspective, I am confident that I did everything to enable us to avoid serious social cataclysms, preserve the country and build a modern state that would become a fully-fledged member of the world community.

The 1995 Constitution did not appear out of the blue. It was the embodiment of all the previous experience of constitution building in sovereign Kazakhstan, as well as the most progressive experience abroad that best reflected our conditions at the time. That is why anyone wishing to fully understand the spirit and significance of our country's Basic Law needs to know how it came into being.

The Declaration of State Sovereignty of the Kazakh SSR

The formation of constitutional legislation began in Kazakhstan just as the Soviet Union was in the process of disintegrating. The adoption of the Declaration of State Sovereignty of the Kazakh Soviet Socialist Republic by the Supreme Soviet of the Kazakh SSR on 25 October 1990, marked the first step towards sovereign statehood.

It reflected certain of the fundamental principles that were later to be developed in the two successive constitutions of sovereign Kazakhstan: the intention to build a humane, democratic and rule-of-law state; the definition of the people as the only source of state power and the declaration of the indivisibility and inviolability of the territory of our country and so on.

Of course, the Declaration of State Sovereignty was more of a political document than a legal one. Its principles, strictly speaking, were not legal norms: that is, they had no legal force. The enactment of an appropriate constitutional act was required for sovereignty to be legally consolidated.

Such an act was the Constitutional Law on 'The state independence of the Republic of Kazakhstan' that came into force on 16 December 1991. This is now Kazakhstan's Independence Day.

Here I shall allow myself a short digression. Independence Day should not, I consider, be regarded solely as an official public holiday. This day has much greater significance. It became a milestone and also a new beginning in our struggle for independence. Today every Kazakhstani can celebrate this day as the day of his or her own independence and success.

The Law *On the sovereign independence of the Republic of Kazakhstan* declared and legally consolidated the state independence of the Republic of Kazakhstan as a sovereign state possessing integral, indivisible and inviolable territory, and forming its relations with all states on the principles of international law. The right to act on behalf of the people of the Republic was bestowed not only on the Supreme Soviet but also on the President of Kazakhstan, as Head of State.

The law also made provision for an independent economic system in Kazakhstan. This system was to be based on the diversity and equality of all forms of property, the envisaged establishment of Kazakhstan's own financial, credit and monetary systems, and the formation of its own gold reserve, diamond and currency funds. The formation of Kazakhstan's own armed forces was also announced.

The law declared that, together with the Declaration of State Sovereignty, it served as the basis for designing the Republic's new Constitution. It was also established that the provisions of the Constitution and other laws of the Republic of Kazakhstan were valid, since they did not contradict the law. Thus, this first legislative act of sovereign Kazakhstan acquired legal precedence over the 1978 Constitution of the Kazakh SSR in effect at the time. This was an essential step since the Constitution of the Soviet Socialist Republic and constituent members of the union State, no matter how patched up, was totally incapable of meeting the needs of the rapidly changing country, making the transition to a new socio-economic formation and embarking on totally new social relations at home and abroad. The new sovereign, democratic and rule-of-law state was being built on entirely different principles and needed other constitutional foundations. Such foundations were laid in the Constitutional Law *On the state independence of the Republic of Kazakhstan*. However, the adoption of a new Constitution was required for the independent state to be definitively formed.

The 'Red' Supreme Soviet

Work on the draft first Constitution of sovereign Kazakhstan began almost immediately after the adoption of the Declaration of State Sovereignty. The Constitutional Commission of the Kazakh SSR formed by a resolution of the Supreme Soviet of the Kazakh SSR on 15 December 1990 was initially headed by Erik Asanbayev who was then working as the Chairman of the Republic's Supreme Soviet.

The membership of the Constitutional Commission was made up of the entire leadership of the Supreme Soviet: the Prime Minister, Minister of Justice, Prosecutor General, Chairman of the Supreme Court, eminent legal academics, renowned legal practitioners, one of the secretaries of the Central Committee of the Kazakhstan Communist Party, the first secretary of the Central Committee of the Lenin Communist Youth League, and other specialists – 35 people in all. The Commission was very representative, as was the custom in the days of the Soviet Union. Unfortunately, however, it was unable to work effectively for a number of reasons. For instance, there were a great many members and, correspondingly, opinions and most of the Commission's working time went on gaining a consensus. Then, there was the constantly changing political situation in the country.

For instance, in the year following the formation of the Constitutional Commission, amendments and addenda were made to the Constitution of the Kazakh SSR then in force no less than seven times (on 20 November 1990 and 15 February, 20 June, 25 June, 25 August, 10 December and 24 December 1991), not to mention the rest of the legislation. Thus, the members of the Constitutional Commission did not even have a stable foundation to start with. Nor were the directions the country was to develop in clear either.

After the turbulent events of 1991, culminating in the disintegration of the Soviet Union, the renaming of the Kazakh SSR as the Republic of Kazakhstan and enactment of the Constitutional Law *On the state independence of the Republic of Kazakhstan*, some kind of certainty emerged at last. It became clear that there had been a final break with the totalitarian past and the pressing issue was now to build a sovereign, democratic state. Kazakhstan's entire future was now in our own hands. The time had come to take a serious stand on designing the country's new Constitution. This for me, as President of Kazakhstan, became one of the most urgent tasks.

My appointment as Chairman of the Constitutional Commission was confirmed by a Supreme Soviet resolution of 15 December 1991, and the new Chairman of the Supreme Soviet, S. Abdildin (appointed in place of E. Asanbayev, who had by then been elected as the Republic's Vice President) became my vice chairman on the

Commission. Using the powers given to the Constitutional Commission, I set up a working group consisting of a small number of people under the renowned legal academic, Gairat Sapargaliyev. Also in the group were Y. Kim, A. Kazhenov and the still young but already promising lawyers B. Mukhamedzhanov, K. Kolpakov, Y. Maltsev and T. Donakov. Slightly later, the group was joined by N. Shaikenov, who by then was my legal adviser. The working group's general management was placed in the hands of Zinaida Fedotova, then vice chair of the Supreme Soviet.

The working group was given the specific task of preparing the groundwork for the draft Constitution of the Republic of Kazakhstan, which could then be brought for discussion to the Constitutional Commission.

The Constitution's first draft was soon ready and discussions began at the meetings of the Constitutional Commission in a fairly tense atmosphere. The Constitutional Commission was made up of the entire Presidium of the Supreme Soviet and all the chairs of its committees. Most of them considered their main objective was to preserve the soviets' vertical of power with the Supreme Soviet at the apex. They were not ready for an open dialogue and discussion of alternative propositions. It became clear that moving forward was going to get increasingly harder.

The Constitution of the Kazakh SSR in effect at the time provided for the enactment of the new Constitution exclusively by parliament. The Supreme Soviet therefore retained a significant portion of its decisive authoritative powers while presidential power was still being developed. In these conditions compromises had to be sought to avoid a schism in society and the state, and maintain peace and stability in the still emerging state and multi-ethnic society. In the final analysis, the need to maintain internal political stability took precedence over the task of fundamentally and irrevocably resolving problems of paramount importance for the country.

It should be said that an external political factor also played its part in achieving a compromise: everyone in those days was witnessing how the disagreements in issues of constitutional design and delays in adopting new constitutions in the different CIS countries were eventually erupting into conflicts. The uncertainty surrounding Kazakhstan's new constitutional model was hampering the start of systemic socio-economic, political and legal reforms, and causing unnecessary tension between the different branches of power, as their jurisdiction was not clearly defined on a constitutional level. All those involved in the Constitution's design acknowledged the need to reach a compromise.

Despite all the disagreements, it was essential for the Constitution to be adopted as swiftly as possible. After all, the country was already in its second year as an independent country and still living by the totally obsolete Constitution of the Soviet period.

Well aware of all these circumstances, and having to deal with a conservative-minded majority in the Supreme Soviet who had been elected in Soviet times, I decided to settle on a compromise that would guarantee the new document being adopted. The result of having to make concessions on numerous issues was that the first Constitution was unable to meet the vital needs of social and state development.

Attempts to uphold the idea of a bicameral Parliament, the development, on an equal rights basis, of all forms of property, (first and foremost, private property) and to embed in the Basic Law elementary rules of a democratic rule-of-law state – the right to dissolve Parliament and impeach the President – ended in failure. The majority of the Presidium and leadership of the Supreme Soviet vetoed these proposals.

Certain pre-eminent figures in Kazakhstan's legal system were also maintaining a conservative position. For instance, at one of the Constitutional Commission's meetings, corresponding member of the Academy of Sciences S. Sartayev asserted that the establishment of a bicameral parliament would put an end to the national statehood of the Kazakh people and insisted on the Supreme Soviet reserving the right 'to withdraw any issue from executive power at any time and resolve it directly at a session'. Evidently, such a proposal contradicted the principle of the apportionment of authority declared in the Declaration of State sovereignty. At another meeting of the Constitutional Commission, the no less authoritative lawyer S. Zimanov actually proposed rejecting the new Constitution and introducing amendments to the old one instead. I have great respect for these people, renowned lawyers in our country; they were, moreover, of constant assistance to me. But during that turbulent and troubled time, many made mistakes.

Highly vociferous discussions also developed on the subject of the so-called 'national' issue. Certain members of the Constitutional Commission, presenting themselves as advocates only of the Kazakh people's interests, proposed announcing a development programme to build a Kazakh State without regard for the interests and rights of other citizens of different nationalities. Let me remind you that at the time Kazakhs made up less than 50 per cent of the country's population. Correspondingly, a motion was proposed to establish that the President and Chairman of the Supreme Council had to be Kazakhs – that is, concerning itself solely with national origin. Motions of such a kind created a serious threat to Kazakhstani unity. I had to decisively repulse such pseudo-patriots. Time and again, I reminded all those present that the Constitution we were devising had to unite the people, not divide them on the basis of their nationality. So as not to allow a dangerous shift in direction affecting the interests of the republic's nations and peoples, we were obliged at times to uphold virtually every article of Kazakhstan's draft Constitution.

Another critical issue was that of the status of languages in the Republic of Kazakhstan. On the one hand, it was essential to take measures to regenerate and develop the state language – the Kazakh language, which had by then been in a critical state for quite some time. On the other hand, on no account could the Kazakh language be allowed to develop to the disadvantage of Russian and the languages of the other peoples of Kazakhstan.

Recognising the Kazakh language as the state language was not in itself an infringement upon anyone. It was a logical and natural decision. What might have had a negative effect was a rash decision to introduce Kazakh as the language of business, giving free rein to the arbitrary rule of inveterate bureaucrats, especially in the provinces. This even gave rise to conversations here and there about the need to revoke the law on languages already in force.

This then very topical issue was discussed in detail not only at meetings of the Constitutional Commission, but also at many other conferences. In my address to the heads of the administrations and chairs of the local soviets at a Republican conference that took place on 11-12 November1992, I drew the attention of all the participants in the conference to the following:

> 'On no account should the language problem be an object for cheap populism and demagogic speculation. Does anyone really think that having revoked the Law, we can hope for calm in Kazakhstan? Is it really not clear to any unbiased person that the Kazakh language is in an almost critical state and it's now a question of saving this language? The language of many generations of our forebears must not die. Does anyone really want to lose their voice through their own choice? Both in law and real life our language policy must promote conditions for the development of the Kazakh and Russian languages and those of the national minorities.'
>
> From the address to the heads of administrations and chairs of local soviets at the Republican Conference,
> 11-12 November 1992

A majority of the deputies eventually supported the following edition of the Constitutional norm: 'The state language in the Republic of Kazakhstan shall be the Kazakh language. The Russian language shall be the language of international intercourse. The state shall guarantee to preserve areas for the use of the language of international communication and other languages, and concern itself with their free development. The limitation of citizens' rights and liberties on the basis of their non-command of the state language or the language of international intercourse shall not be permitted.'

On the whole, such formulations met the urgent needs of Kazakhstan's multinational people, although the status of the Russian language as the language of international intercourse, remained, from a legal point of view, insufficiently defined. Subsequently, in the 1995 Constitution, this issue was resolved somewhat differently.

The right to dissolve Parliament caused deputies particular concern. Understandably, having taken advantage of the troubled time and absolute power, they had assigned themselves a great many privileges, were able to put pressure on any minister, and possessed unprecedented guarantees of immunity not only during their term of office as deputies but for two years after the expiration

46

of their term. Generally speaking, they had created for themselves an ideal climate for individual ingenuity in the 'personal business' sphere. Only a small number thought about their electorate.

As the legislative body, as represented by the Supreme Soviet, did not function all the time, deputies carried out their official duties as well as holding top-level posts in the provinces. The Supreme Soviet's sessions were only held a few times a year, and forming an independent state meant adopting hundreds of new laws which, in turn, called for serious legislative work. Instead, the deputies representing the regional party nomenclature would report on problems in their regions, of which there were indeed not a few. These representatives of the people were unable to raise their awareness to consider the state's general needs, or understand that the time for parochial interests was over. As a result, the sessions turned into a kind of tug of war, with each deputy trying to grab a little more money from the state budget for his region. So there could be no question of serving the state and the entire people as a whole.

Most of the deputies simply failed to understand that Parliament already had to fulfil another role now that statehood was being established and the transition to a new economic model was under way. Many deputies went on believing they had an 'imperative mandate', an erstwhile Soviet tradition whereby a deputy would use the regions as a means of extracting additional finance for local needs.

There was a general tendency during the course of the reforms to try and take on the function of apportioning and shifting responsibility onto the shoulders of the executive branch of power. Unfortunately, this tendency continued in other independent states as well. The majority of deputies of the first post-Soviet parliaments still failed to understand that their main task was not to assign responsibility, but create the legislative conditions for developing a civilised legislative base and new economic relations.

What specifically characterised this situation was that these parliaments were functioning in the absence of a developed market economy and a civil society, before a modern system of representation had been worked out, and before the protection of economic and political interests had been instituted. Indeed, these very interests and the people who would hold them had not fully materialised yet.

In these conditions parliaments turned into clubs of consumers battling for the redistribution of incomes to their advantage. They passed populist motions on wage increases and financially precarious social programmes, while the bodies of the executive branch bore the responsibility for carrying them through at a time of an acute budget deficit and profound crisis.

As a result, the executive branch of power came under fire from all directions, criticised by the press, the deputies and society. Deputies representing regions genuinely in the most terrible crises inadvertently caused more damage to them through their actions. The economic decisions taken on a populist wave began fracturing the entire management system – the state's regulation of the economy, in the final count, causing the economic situation to deteriorate even further.

Despite all their importance, the laws of the first-wave transitional period (1990-94) had many populist norms that were impossible to carry through because of the state's insufficient financial resources. The Supreme Soviet worked on the following principle: 'We publish the laws and allocate the money, and it's up to the Government to carry them through if it wants to.'

It was then laws were passed on the pensioning of dairy workers and tractor drivers at the age of 45, as well as financially unsustainable laws on compensation payments to people living in ecologically damaged areas. Such laws ratified at a time when the economy was not functioning and the coffers were empty resulted in long-term arrears in social payments.

Later on, the relevant articles of the laws were suspended. This only caused indignation and disillusionment, because people felt they had been cheated. What's more, it was the measures to carry through such laws that led to the hyperinflation in the first years of independence which almost entirely wrecked our economy, already in a critical state.

Many laws of that period also failed to contain the mechanisms for regulating the legal relations arising in the course of building a market economy and a democratic society. Sometimes I used to wryly joke that I spent my entire working day in the Supreme Soviet, only to come home to work at night and deal with even more pressing issues.

Still inertly sticking to their erstwhile ideological viewpoints and stereotypes, the parliamentarians kept blocking all our actions to reform the state and society. The economy's obsolete structure was thus preserved, and all initiatives to form new social relations were halted. Many of us realised that it was now well and truly time to set up a new system of representative bodies to meet the needs of a democratic rule-of-law state.

Getting ahead of myself, I shall say that eventually the deputies came to realise this themselves and, on their initiative, at the end of 1993, the soviets at all levels started dissolving themselves. It should be acknowledged that before its self-dissolution the Supreme Soviet of the Republic of Kazakhstan fulfilled its historic mission by adopting the first Constitution of sovereign Kazakhstan.

The draft Constitution prepared by the Constitutional Commission was adopted by the Supreme Soviet at the first reading on 2 June 1992 after many days of public debate with Supreme Soviet deputies (including a nationwide television broadcast). A week later the draft was published in the republican and provincial press for a nationwide debate which continued until December 1992. Finally, on 28 January 1993, by roll-call vote, the Supreme Soviet of the Republic of the Kazakhstan almost unanimously (1 abstention, 2 opposed) adopted the first Constitution of the Republic of Kazakhstan. When the results of the vote flashed up on the electronic panel inside the Supreme Soviet, the chamber erupted in an ovation and ecstatic roars of 'Long Live Kazakhstan!' I noticed tears of joy in some deputies' eyes.

It was a truly historic event in the life of the people of Kazakhstan, who had embarked on a course of independent development. Adopted in the conditions of 1993, the Constitution was a compromise between one section of society who opposed the introduction of socio-economic and political reforms, and the rest who recognised the inevitable, urgent need to transform the Kazakh SSR into a democratic, civilised state. It enabled the first steps, so essential at the time, to be taken on the way to reform.

However, not long after coming into force, the shortcomings of Kazakhstan's first Constitution became obvious. First and foremost, there was its patent detachment from real socio-economic and political processes.

The absence of mechanisms in the Basic Law to overcome the differences of opinion that emerged between different state institutions was one of the causes of the real increase in conflicts between the executive and legislative bodies. In other words, the Constitution of the 1993 model was a legal barrier in the way of improving the state organisation and the future development of socio-economic and political reforms. The issue of supremacy was constantly being contested.

As a 'historical compromise', the Basic Law failed to live up to all society's expectations. Primarily, this was because it did not contain a definition of our aims and priorities in social development.

Indeed, the method by which the country's Basic Law was adopted also came in for criticism. The way things turned out, it was not the people who had adopted the Constitution but the Supreme Soviet, formed in accordance with Soviet laws, and these officials had gifted it to themselves, and the people while they were about it. Suffice it to say that regardless of the Constitution's articles on the President being the Republic's representative inside the country and in international relations, the Supreme Soviet that had adopted the Basic Law (and, accordingly, consolidated the presidential form of government) reserved for itself alone the right to act on behalf of all the people of Kazakhstan. This revealed its still intrinsically 'Soviet' aspiration to retain supremacy. Even so, as the English visionary Thomas Paine once said, 'A constitution is a thing antecedent to a government, and a government is only the creature of a constitution.'

Encountering numerous similar gaps in the legislation on a daily basis, we realised that the 1993 Constitution model was not suitable as a legal foundation for the building of a sovereign Kazakhstan.

Time was passing, however, and there was no longer any way of maintaining the status quo. The issue of the Soviets' absolute power, which was hindering the President and Government's introduction of reforms, particularly of an economic character, had to be resolved without further delay. I was even prepared to put this issue to a referendum, as I said openly, repeating time and again that the Supreme Soviet was putting a halt to reforms. This is essentially what caused the strain in my relations with the Chairman of the Supreme Soviet, S. Abdildin (now leader of the Communist Party) who then took steps aimed at establishing his supremacy in all decision-making. I am not going to speak about his views, which are now common knowledge.

We found ourselves in a kind of impasse, with neither the Government nor the Supreme Soviet able to find a way out of our confrontation. On more than one occasion I had to speak candidly to the people about the perniciousness of individual deputies' actions.

It was then, on 16 November 1993, that the Alatau Regional Soviet of People's Deputies of the city of Almaty passed a motion, unprecedented in the state's social and political life, on self-dissolution that was to make it possible to elect deputies in accordance with the new laws. This was when the address to the people's deputies of the republic and local soviets was published:

> 'The Soviets have in many ways remained synonymous with the previous regime and old ideology. The narrow frameworks of the irredeemably antiquated laws regulating the work of the Representative System, the dwindling interest of the deputy body itself in its work has increased the Soviets' detachment from real life. Their inability to carry through the will of electors is becoming increasingly apparent. And this is not the deputy body's fault. The cause lies elsewhere: in the Soviets' fundamentally flawed absolute power model and its total failure to meet the realities of the present day.'
>
> From the address of the people's deputies of the Alatau Regional Committee of the city of Almaty to the people's deputies of the republic and local soviets, 16 November 1993

On 17 November, the deputies of the capital's Lenin and Oktyabr regional soviets also decided to relinquish their plenary powers before the expiration of their term of office. The Auezov and Frunze soviets followed suit, and so, finally, did all the others right across the republic.

A group of Supreme Soviet deputies then presented me with a notice requesting me to accept their resignation and release them from their plenary powers as deputies. As the Constitution did not authorise me to do so, I suggested they raised this issue at the forthcoming session of the Supreme Soviet. Frankly, I have to say that I am grateful to the deputies who displayed responsibility during that most crucial period for the country.

The Kazakhstan Way

Common sense prevailed and rank-and-file deputies became the initiators of the termination of the Supreme Soviet's plenary powers ahead of schedule. Of the 360 deputies, over 200 tendered their resignations. It was as a result of this total collapse of the soviet system that the Supreme Soviet passed a motion on self-dissolution.

The Supreme Soviet's self-dissolution was one of the most dramatic events in independent Kazakhstan's history. Historians will continue assessing for some time to come what made the deputies pass a motion of such paramount importance for the country's future. In my opinion, the Supreme Soviet's dissolution was inevitable. The far-reaching economic reforms could not be implemented unless the contradiction posed by the soviets' system had first been resolved. This contradiction consisted of the fact that many of the deputies were representatives of both the legislative and executive branches of power. In such a situation the deputies could block the work across the vertical of executive power in the provinces, as well as using the Supreme Soviet as a means for keeping the reforms in check in the centre.

As the 16th-century French philosopher Montaigne said, 'The best state organisation for any people is one that preserves its integrity.' Kazakhstan succeeded in resolving the antagonism between the executive and legislative branches of power by peaceful means and maintaining order without the use of force. We were able to transfer smoothly, step by step, over to an effective, democratic system of government providing increased stability and rapid economic growth.

Some of the other CIS countries have been less fortunate in this respect.

In 1992, the seeds of such a confrontation were sown in the fertile soil of Tajikistan's regional antagonisms. The confrontation that started with many days of meetings in two squares of the capital, Dushanbe, ended up as a fratricidal war lasting over five years and claiming around 100,000 lives.

No less bloody were the conflicts in Georgia and Azerbaijan, where the demagogue dissidents Gamsahurdia and Elchibei gained power on a wave of populism and not without the help of the Supreme Soviets. Their term in office may have been short-lived, but the results of their dilettante internal and foreign policy, which had some pernicious repercussions for both their countries, is still resonating. Even a decade on, Georgia and Azerbaijan are only just emerging from the most crippling economic crisis and still unable to restore their territorial integrity.

The most dramatic events of global significance took place in Russia in 1993. All over the world, television channels broadcast live coverage of the tanks of the Kantemirov division loyal to President Yeltsin firing at the smoke-blackened building of the Supreme Soviet of the Russian Federation. The unpredictability of the situation in Russia at the start of the 1990s left a serious imprint on Kazakhstan's political landscape. Attentively following events in Moscow, and analysing the confrontation between the executive and political powers that had caused complete chaos and lawlessness in Russia, I became convinced once and for all that strong, centralised presidential power was an essential prerequisite for Kazakhstan to actively liberalise its economy.

Along with the intensive work on the legislation, there were also a host of different problems all over the country to attend to. I remember how many towns and villages were not ready for the cold at the start of the winter of 1993-94. The room temperature in thousands of apartments in north and central Kazakhstan did not get above 10-15 degrees Celsius.

In December 1993, we ended up in an even more critical situation. Even though the urgent introduction of the national currency, the tenge, had gone exceedingly well, the situation throughout the country was exacerbated by the rapid pace of inflation. Rapid, decisive actions were called for. A single day's delay in passing legislative acts in the economic sphere could cause damage that would take years to put right. However, the Cabinet of Ministers' operative efficiency was being hampered by the Supreme Soviet. Economic destablisation became a real threat yet again.

The Supreme Soviet proved incapable of passing laws now that the country's financial and economic policy-making was entirely independent. Extended and unproductive discussions took place at its sessions, with lengthy intervals between them. We were forever waiting for Parliament's rulings and gained the impression that it was simply blocking the formation of a legislative base for economic reform. This, in fact, was one of the reasons for the sharp fall in the course of the tenge at the start of 1994. The leadership of the Cabinet of Ministers of that period gave in under pressure from the deputy body and local authorities' strong lobby, and introduced an ill-considered system of mutual payments between enterprises.

The new Constitution: a democratic start

The elections of a new body of deputies to the Supreme Soviet were held in March 1994, and I placed great hopes in it. It has to be said that after a fairly lengthy period of highs and lows, this Parliament gradually embarked on a constructive course of cooperation, and this I found truly heart-warming. Undoubtedly more professional than its predecessor, it still, however, failed to live up to our expectations. The deputies very quickly forgot what they had been elected for. During its term this Soviet passed no more than seven laws, whereas over one billion tenge from budgetary funds were spent on the 177 deputies' upkeep.

I had been counting very much on these new parliamentarians' professionalism and felt disappointed. Stormy and unproductive debates of many urgently needed laws continued in Parliament. One only has to remember the enactment of the law on the 1994 budget: introducing the draft budget to Parliament, the Government discussed it with the deputies for over three months. It was only after the threat of the Government resigning that it was finally adopted.

Despite the fact that in December 1994 the Supreme Soviet declined a rating ballot on the status of languages, the character of state organisation and private ownership of land, I continued working with the deputy body. There was an obvious need to create a better defined and more consistent power structure and, on a constitutional level, resolve issues of a fundamental economic nature and considerable social and political significance.

At the end of December 1994, I invited over Minister of Justice Nagashbai Shaikenov, whom I knew well and trusted as a consistent supporter of the reforms and highly professional lawyer. We spoke for over two hours. I outlined the basic methods of approaching the constitutional reform and gave him a rough draft of the new Constitution to work on. Naturally, the draft was drawn up in strict secrecy.

The 1995 Constitution

The original plan was to submit the draft of the new Constitution for the consideration of the re-elected Supreme Soviet of the 13th convocation, which by then was ready to conduct constitutional reform. Evidence of this had been provided by the Parliament's positive steps during the discussion of economic problems, and contacts with a number of influential deputies' factions. I remember that period well. I was confident a compromise would be found and constitutional reform successfully introduced.

But something unforeseen happened.

Time and again, a small incident in history has set off a series of events that have gathered speed like an avalanche and led to in unforeseen consequences. Just such an incident for the whole of Kazakhstan was the ruling passed by the Constitutional Court of the Republic of Kazakhstan on 6 March 1995.

Tatiana Kvyatkovskaya, now a household name but then a rank-and-file journalist, took the Central Election Commission to task in the *Kazakhstanskaya Pravda* newspaper, alleging a violation of the election code in the Abylaikhanov electoral district.

The investigation went on a very long time. Eventually, the Constitutional Court of the Republic of Kazakhstan passed a ruling that the method of counting votes introduced by the Central Election Commission not only entailed a large-scale violation of the constitutional principle of 'one man, one vote', but might also distort election results and essentially change the electoral system established by the election code. In so doing, the Central Election Commission had violated Article 60 of the Constitution by exceeding its jurisdiction.

Consequently, doubt was cast on the results of the previous election and legitimacy of the authority of all the Supreme Soviet deputies. In view of the complexity of the situation and in an attempt to avert the impending crisis, I made the following public statement on 8 March:

'The Court's ruling has come as a total surprise to us all. Nothing like this has ever happened before in the history of the state. I was, and still am, an advocate of stable state authority.

After all, the fate of our intended reforms in many ways depends on this. The role reserved here for the Parliament

55

the country elected a year ago is not a minor one. I have great hopes for the Supreme Soviet. Of course, sometimes there are arguments and emotions run high. However, from the very start we have succeeded in establishing a constructive dialogue.

The signed agreement on maintaining co-ordinated action between the legislative and executive branches of power is testimony to this. And then, like a bolt from the blue, came the Constitutional Court's ruling. Only common sense, tenacity, and a strict adherence to the laws can lead us to the one and only correct solution and avert a parliamentary crisis.

At the same time, a respectful attitude should be adopted to the Constitutional Court's rulings, regardless of whose interests they affect. Only then is it possible to speak of Kazakhstan's genuine move towards a rule-of-law state and of the triumph of the law.'

Source: Archive of the President of the Republic of Kazakhstan

That same day I exercised my legal right and raised an objection to the Constitutional Court's ruling. The following day, 9 March, an objection to it was also raised by Chairman of the Supreme Soviet Abish Kekilbayev.

However, in keeping with Article 131 of the Constitution, which states that 'if the Constitutional Court by a majority of no less than two thirds of the votes of the total number of judges shall approve a previously adopted ruling, it will pass into effect from the moment of its adoption,' the Constitutional Court overrode the objections we had raised. This found expression in the ruling of 10 March 1995: 'Guided by Article 131 of the Constitution of the Republic of Kazakhstan, Articles 14, 25, 26 of the Law "On constitutional judicial procedure in the Republic of Kazakhstan", the Constitutional Court has decided: to decline the objections of the President and Chairman of the Supreme Soviet of the Republic of Kazakhstan and reaffirm the ruling of the Constitutional Court of 6 March 1995. The decision is not subject to appeal'.

Despite this decision, on 11 March, the Supreme Soviet passed the Constitutional Law *On the implementation of amendments and addenda to the Constitution* and resolution *On suspending the activity of the Constitutional Court*. However, from a legal viewpoint and pure common sense, these documents no longer had any bearing on the Constitutional Court's ruling. In view of the ruling, I made an inquiry to the court on the legal implications of this resolution. My inquiry read as follows:

'In view of the passing into force of the resolution of the Constitutional Court of the Republic of Kazakhstan of the 6 March 1995, adopted in accordance with the action brought by T.G. Kvyatkovskaya, I request an explanation of the following issues: does this ruling of the Constitutional Court signify the unconstitutionality of the election to the Supreme Soviet of the Republic of Kazakhstan that took place on 7 March 1994, and also the unconstitutionality of the authority of the deputies of the Supreme Soviet; if the authority of the deputies of the Supreme Soviet of the Republic of Kazakhstan is unconstitutional, who is entitled to make decisions of a legislative character; does the ruling of the Constitutional Court signify that the Law of the Republic of Kazakhstan "On the temporary delegation of additional powers to the President of the Republic of Kazakhstan and heads of the local administrations" adopted on 10 December 1993 continues in force?'

ibid

On 11 March, the Constitutional Court in its additional definition gave explanations of the issues I had raised. The fact of the unconstitutionality of the country's Parliament – or, in other words, the illegitimacy of its activity – was recognised.

What's more, the Law of 10 December 1993 *On the temporary delegation of additional powers to the President of the Republic of Kazakhstan and heads of the local administrations*, granting the President the right to make decisions of a legislative character, came into force again. This law continued in force until the moment when the new Constitution was adopted. During this period a total of approximately 140 Presidential decrees, having the force of law, were issued with respect of all the main directions of the state's vital functions which helped the country to speed up the reforms (first and foremost, in the economy) and accurately chart the course of development.

To this period belong the Presidential Decrees *On land*, *On mineral resources and mineral exploitation*, *On oil*, *On foreign investments*, to name but a few. This block of essentially market laws made it possible significantly to speed up economic reform. In particular, it was directed towards liberalising the economy, demonopolising the state, and giving freedom and support to enterprise. Thanks to these successful, timely reforms, work started on a two-tiered banking system that was to develop into the best in the CIS, and enjoy considerable public confidence.

The extensive system of commercial banks that have opened across the country have, in turn, played a decisive role in the development of private enterprise. The right conditions have been created by means of legislatively secured guarantees to attract substantial foreign capital into the country. The country has become an attractive location for the development of major international projects to exploit mineral resources. And this has provided employment for thousands of our people and raised revenues for the state budget.

Guided by the Constitutional Court's ruling, that same day I signed the Decree *On measures issuing from the ruling of the Constitutional Court of the Republic of Kazakhstan of 6 March 1995*. A state commission was set up in accordance with this decree to offer deputies assistance with finding employment, providing security for Supreme Soviet property, and resolving other issues relating to the cessation of the Supreme Soviet's term of office.

If the Parliament's plenary powers were unconstitutional, so, too, were those of the government, as the illegitimate Supreme Soviet had participated in its formation. On 11 March, the government also offered its resignation, which I accepted. The resignation of the Central Electoral Commission was accepted at the same time. In accordance with the Constitution and the Law *On the temporary delegation of additional plenary powers to the President of the Republic of Kazakhstan and heads of the local authorities*, I appointed Akejan Kazhegeldin to the post of Prime Minister of the Republic of Kazakhstan and instructed him to implement the proposals on the new membership of the Government as a matter of urgency.

The 1995 Constitution

The events of those days yet again showed our aspiration for stability and rigorous adherence to the legal principles of resolving conflicts. This was highlighted more than once by representatives of the international community.

'It's a triumph for democracy. There has been no crisis because all the branches of power have carried out their functions. The Constitutional Court has worked in a quite cautious and considered manner to reach the conclusion that the election was not legitimate...

We respect the ruling of your Constitutional Court. The whole world understands today that democracy has been significantly strengthened in Kazakhstan. You have gone through all this calmly and very swiftly, and that's why there has been no crisis... This is a good model not just for the CIS states but also other countries who consider themselves democracies, including the US. Kazakhstan is no longer a student of democracy but a teacher. All Kazakhstanis may take pride in this, and the US has reason to be proud of Kazakhstan... The latest events... have consolidated the political rating of your leadership which has shown respect for the Constitution.'

From an interview with W. Courtney, US Ambassador to the Republic of Kazakhstan. Archive of the President

It should be mentioned here that some deputies attempted to oppose the Constitutional Court's ruling. There was an obvious intention to repeat the Russian events of October 1993. The deputies also took over offices, stayed in the building all night and organised pickets. However, none of them won popular support, and the crisis was successfully overcome.

Despite all the criticism, I consider that both convocations of the Supreme Soviet in the post-Soviet period were a great schooling for us all in the incipient democratisation of society, and in political compromise.

Work on the Draft Constitution

Once the Supreme Soviet had been recognised as illegitimate, it became clear that there could be no further delays in designing the new Constitution. Now that the country had neither a Parliament nor a Government, it was important for me to get support for my plans directly from the Kazakhstani people. The Assembly of the Peoples of Kazakhstan proposed holding an all-nation referendum on extending the President's plenary powers. A positive outcome to this issue would also act as a seal of the people's approval for stepping up political and economic reforms. Subsequent events showed this to be the correct decision.

The Decree *On the holding of a republican referendum on 29 April 1995*, No. 2152, was published on 25 March 1995, which, in part, read as follows:

> 'Given that the highest expression of the will of the people as the sole source of state power in the Republic of Kazakhstan is all-nation voting, with due regard for the appeal of the Assembly of the Peoples of Kazakhstan, and guided by Article 78 of the Constitution of the Republic of Kazakhstan, Article 3 of the Law of the Republic of Kazakhstan "On the temporary delegation of additional plenary powers to the President of the Republic of Kazakhstan and heads of the local authorities", I resolve:
>
> 1. To hold a republican referendum on 29 April 1995.
> 2. To put to the republican referendum the following question:
>
> "Do you agree to extend until 1 December, 2000, the term of office of the President of the Republic of Kazakhstan, N.A. Nazarbayev, elected by an all-nation election on 1 December 1991?"'
>
> From the Archive of the President of the Republic of Kazakhstan

The referendum's results convincingly demonstrated Kazakhstanis' support for the course of the country's further reform. The Central Commission of the Referendum on the issue of extending the President's plenary powers summed up the results of the voting on 29 April 1995. They were as follows: votes were cast by 8,309,637, or 91.21 per cent of the republic's 9,110,156 citizens registered to take part in the referendum. 7,932,834, or 95.46 per cent of the total number of voters, were in favour of extending the plenary powers.

Having gained all-nation support, it was possible to focus on the design of the draft of the new Constitution. The March events once again highlighted the need for its urgent adoption. The legal foundations for a solution to the situation were then found. However, it was impossible to keep responding like this every time. Well-defined safeguards were needed to prevent similar events happening again.

In the spring of 1995, I invited B. Mukhamedzhanov and K. Kolpakov to work on the project I had placed under the supervision of Minister of Justice N. Shaikenov. They had both worked actively on the 1993 draft Constitution, and so were familiar with all of that Constitution's flaws and all the compromises we had been forced to make under pressure from the Supreme Soviet. We now had to design a more effective Constitution on the basis of which a modern and genuinely democratic state could be built.

Later, when the draft was ready, an Advisory Council of Experts was set up by a presidential resolution of 22 May 1995, to analyse it thoroughly. This Council consisted of twelve members. For the working group Shaikenov enlisted leading figures of the law Yuri Basin, Gairat Sapargaliev and Maidan Suleimenov.

The working group also consisted of the following:

Membership of the Advisory Council of Experts under the President of the Republic of Kazakhstan

Basin, Y.G.   professor of the Kazakh State Institute of Law, Ministry of Justice, doctor of law;

Kim, V.A.   head of the department of state law, Kazakh State People's University, doctor of law;

Kolpakov, K.A.   personal representative of the President
                       of the Republic of Kazakhstan in the
                       Supreme Soviet of the Republic of
                       Kazakhstan, candidate of law;

Kotov, A.K.   vice director of the Scientific Research
                       Centre of Private Law, Kazakh State
                       Institute of Law, the Ministry of Justice,
                       doctor of law;

Mukhamedzhanov, B.A.
                       head of the Department of Legislative
                       Initiatives and Legal Expertise of the
                       Apparatus of the President of the
                       Republic of Kazakhstan;

Nurpeisov, E.K.   director of the Kazakh State Institute of
                       Law, the Ministry of Justice, candidate
                       of law;

Sapargaliev, G.S.   director of the Institute of the State and
                       Law, Correspondent Member of the
                       People's Academy of Sciences of the
                       Republic of Kazakhstan (supervisor of
                       studies);

Suleimenov, M.K.   director of the Scientific Research Centre
                       of Private Law of the Kazakh State
                       Institute of Law of the Ministry of
                       Justice, Correspondent Member of the
                       People's Academy of Sciences of the
                       Republic of Kazakhstan (supervisor of
                       studies);

Saikenov, N.A.   Minister of Justice, doctor of law;

Foreign experts appointed by agreement:

The 1995 Constitution

Alexeyev, S.S.   chairman of the Scientific Council of the
                 Research Centre of the Russian
                 Federation;

Jacques Attali   adviser to the State Council of France;

Roland Dumas   chairman of the Constitutional Council
                 of France.

From the Resolution *On the Advisory Council of Experts under the President of the Republic of Kazakhstan in respect of the draft new Constitution of the Republic of Kazakhstan of 22 May 1995*, No. 2292

I briefed the working group on drawing up, as quickly as possible, an agreed draft to serve as the basis for a definitive version of the Constitution.

The members of the working group, temporarily released by me from carrying out their regular duties, installed themselves in the Alatau Sanatorium and set to work.

To protect them from lobbyist pressure, I forbade them to discuss the draft with anyone else. It had not been possible to avoid such pressure during the design of the 1993 Constitution. At the time, everyone taking part in its design had tried to ensure the future Basic Law fitted in with their interests, depending on the position they held: deputies sought to gain more plenary powers for the legislature, government officials for the executive, and so on. Only a few had considered the need to produce a document for the country's future instead of just for themselves.

Prior to preparing the draft, the working party studied dozens of other states' constitutions, both from the CIS and further afield. The experience of Asiatic countries, and not just Western democracies, served as a crucial pointer. This had a positive effect on the quality of the new Constitution, which took account of the errors committed during the design of its predecessor.

I then had a two-week holiday which I spent reading and, as I have already mentioned, personally summarising some of the provisions in 20 countries' constitutions. Later on we bound the two drafts together.

An analysis of the Constitution now in force will reveal apparent similarities to that of the French Republic. However, this is only at first glance. My brief to the members of the working group was not to copy another country's Constitution but analyse their experience and then, on this basis, prepare a draft of the Basic Law that would meet our country's needs as fully as possible. That is why our Kazakhstani imprint – our own identity, according with Kazakhstani mind-sets, the past traditions of the Kazakh people and the future we are setting our sights on – is apparent in all the provisions of our Constitution.

Time was running out, and there was not enough left to wait for the working group to design the draft themselves and for the next discussion to take place. I visited the sanatorium nearly every day, analysed the work completed by the members of the working group, and immediately introduced amendments.

Each norm of the future Basic Law was elaborated in a great many versions and thoroughly discussed. Since the document being drawn up was of major significance and defined our country's future, it was essential to consider all the factors, all points of view, and select only the right one. I encouraged the working group members to express their opinions openly and engage in frank debates but, naturally, only until they had come to a decision. Then they had to quickly formulate it all and move on.

The discussions began at once – from the draft's very first articles. I listened to all the opinions and then a final decision was reached on each article. Very often when we failed to reach a consensus during our evening discussions, I would leave the decision-making until the following morning, and then come back with a complete, edited version of the controversial article. What's more, I always tried to explain in a well-argued manner why the article was worded in exactly this manner, citing various foreign countries' constitutions.

One of my proposals was that there should be a definition of the fundamental principals of the Republic's activity in the first article of the future Constitution. This proposal resulted from my deliberations over many years regarding the importance of defining the main priorities of state policy in the Basic Law. At first, the lawyers working with me raised objections, arguing that principles were not legal norms and so should not be in the Constitution which, unlike a Declaration, was a legal document of direct effect.

The 1995 Constitution

After a stormy discussion, I still insisted on the following principles being included in the draft: social concord and political stability; economic development for the benefit of all the people; Kazakhstani patriotism; and the resolution of the most important issues of the affairs of state by democratic methods, including voting in an all-nation referendum or in the Parliament. Such principles were not established at all in the 1993 Constitution, making state policy unpredictable in many respects. Fundamental principles are pointers designed to help us on our way and not to stray from the course we initially set ourselves, regardless of the reforms we failed to carry through. They reflect the spirit of the Basic Law, in accordance with which all its remaining proposals are to be understood and interpreted. Subsequent practice confirmed the correctness of the decision to enshrine them in the Constitution.

The outlines of the country's new Constitution gradually began to take shape, revealing it to be different from its predecessor in many respects. The 1993 Constitution stated that Kazakhstan was a democratic state. However, it was obvious this was merely an intention, as genuine democracy was then still a long way off. Then there was the statement that Kazakhstan was to be not only a democratic but also a rule-of-law and socially orientated state. This, too, still had to be achieved.

That is why the decision was taken to write in the new Constitution: 'The Republic of Kazakhstan proclaims itself a democratic, secular, rule-of-law and social state'. It means that Kazakhstan is in the process of building such a state.

It was exceedingly important in the new Constitution to resolve once and for all the issue of the form of government. There had been no clear resolution to this issue in the 1993 Constitution, which had proclaimed Kazakhstan a republic without specifying exactly of what type. At the time, there were elements of both a presidential and parliamentary republic in Kazakhstan. The President was the Head of State and yet the structure of the Constitution, in which the article on the Supreme Soviet preceded the one on the President, envisaged the highest representative body's definite supremacy in the state hierarchy. This was evident in certain other provisions of the Constitution: for instance, the fourth provision on the fundamentals of the constitutional structure

65

stated that the right to act on behalf of the people of Kazakhstan was to belong only to the Supreme Soviet and the President (that is, the Supreme Soviet was indicated in first place). The Supreme Soviet also accepted the resignation of the President and Vice President with two-thirds of the votes from the overall number of deputies, although they were elected by the people as a whole.

Thus, in Kazakhstan there was no clear constitutional apportionment of rights and responsibility for the resolution of state issues.

A parliamentary republic, by definition, is a form of executing state power where the principal role belongs to political parties, each of which has its own agenda. Given that there were no major political formations with their own social base, and given their immature condition, there could be no question of a parliamentary republic. The experience of countries with developed democracies also showed that this model was unsuitable for Kazakhstan. Frequent political crises, re-elections of the legislative bodies and changes of government were all features of parliamentary republics. For a young state in the process of consolidating its independence, this would have inevitably resulted in chaos and stagnation – and the main prerequisite for a state to carry out reforms is stability.

The new Constitution proclaimed Kazakhstan a Presidential Republic. The choice of a presidential form of government was, as I have already said, not fortuitous. This form of government is best for Kazakhstan, creating the most favourable conditions for the successful reform of society's political and economic systems.

However, the plenary powers of the President of Kazakhstan are not unlimited. The system of restraints and balances preventing the committal of an abuse of power also applies to him.

The principle formulated in Article 3 of the Constitution in respect of the unity of state power and its division into branches became the subject of lengthy discussions. In the previous Constitution, in line with certain Western countries, the issue had concerned the apportionment of power itself. In Kazakhstan's case, as practice had shown, this had been the wrong decision, increasing the tendency for conflicts between the different state institutions as each considered itself independent of the others.

The new Constitution envisions a mechanism for the division of integral state power into three branches, based on the one hand on the potential for their close cooperation, and on the other for their mutual restraint and protection from interference in each other's competence established by the Constitution and other laws.

What's more, Article 4 of the Constitution introduces the concept of 'functioning law' that had not been in the previous Constitution. It also stipulates that only ratified international treaties shall have priority over the Republic's laws (but not over the Constitution). The inclusion of this norm was not to the liking of certain supporters of the priority of international law. However, it was this that was passed in the final count. And it subsequently proved very helpful in establishing the uniform practical application of the law based on the supremacy of the Constitution's norms.

For the first time, ideological and political diversity – a most important indicator of democracy – were proclaimed in Article 5 of the Constitution. This envisages, apart from everything else, the freedom of activity of political parties and other social organisations. Questions then arose regarding whether our country at its present stage required so much freedom in issues of ideology, whether our society was ready for this, and whether it would harm its stability. Nevertheless, we decided in favour of democracy.

I did, however, stress that the existence of political diversity was not to turn into a free-for-all situation. With this in mind, a ban was introduced on the creation and functioning of social associations whose actions were directed towards a violent change of the constitutional system, violation of the integrity of the Republic, undermining of the security of the state, or inciting social, racial, national, religious, class and tribal enmity. This decision proved to be justified, especially in view of the increasing threat of international terrorism and setting up of extremist groups within the territory of Central Asia.

The principle of equally protecting state and private property enshrined in Article 6 of the Constitution had great practical significance. It could have been left at that, but despite some experts' objections, the following was inserted in the Constitution: 'Property shall impose obligations, and its use must simultaneously benefit the society.'

One of the achievements of our Basic Law is that the land issue is resolved in it. The Constitutional formula states that land may be in private ownership on terms, conditions and within the limits established by legislation. The 1993 Constitution excluded such a possibility.

However, underground resources, water, flora and fauna remained exclusively in state ownership. Not everyone who took part in the drawing up of the draft Constitution supported this point of view. The ardent supporters of private property wanted to provide for the potential private ownership of everything. At the same time, the majority of the working group's membership considered it unfounded for resources to be in private ownership that had not been created by human hands. Our land's natural resources have been bestowed upon us by the Almighty and preserved by our forebears; it is what has existed before us and will exist after us, and therefore belongs not only to us but to our future generations. A great many comments to this effect were received during the all-nation discussion of the draft.

The correct solution of the language issue, satisfying the full diversity of the spectrum of national interests, is an undoubted achievement of the Constitution. The Basic Law states: 'The state language of the Republic of Kazakhstan shall be the Kazakh language. In state institutions and local self-administrative bodies the Russian language shall be officially used on equal grounds along with the Kazakh language. The state shall promote conditions for the study and development of the languages of the people of Kazakhstan.' All these norms of the Basic Law alleviated the misgivings of a section of the country's population regarding their own future and that of their children. It is, however, essential to stress that the Russian language, as objectively the more widely used, ceased to be legally referred to by the meaningless term of 'language of international intercourse' and gained the constitutional guarantee of being used on equal grounds along with the state language.

When the principles of state foreign policy were being formulated in Article 8 of the Constitution, various proposals were considered, including the proclamation of neutrality. It was finally determined to be expedient to carry out an active policy of integrity with other states to overcome jointly the difficulties of the transitional period.

The status of the individual established by the Constitution meets generally accepted world standards, in so far as it included the most important principles of international documents on human rights and freedoms. The core features of constitutionally regulated space as a whole and the statehood in particular are stipulated in the Basic Law, from the position of the innate and inalienable rights of a person as society's most valuable asset.

An extremely important achievement of the new Constitution is, undoubtedly, the fact that it contains a clearly formulated rejection of the vacuous, unsubstantiated declaration of rights and freedoms. It is well known that an unparalleled number of rights were enshrined in Soviet constitutions. However, these were mere political slogans. They were detached from reality and never fully carried through. Nobody used the Constitution's norms in practice. Everything was basically regulated by acts of the Communist Party's Central Committee and Soviet of Ministers.

It was my view, and I expressed it to the working group members, that reality should not be glossed over as this would devalue the Basic Law's significance, turning it once again into merely a fine-sounding declaration. It was essential to act in such a manner that all the constitutional rights were practicable and the norms of the Constitution directly applicable. In modern-day conditions nobody could any longer guarantee the right to work, free health care and education. It was essential to renounce a futile declaration of these. The following rights were proclaimed in the new Constitution instead: to freedom of labour, the free choice of occupation and profession; the receipt of free, guaranteed, extensive medical assistance established by law; and free secondary education.

Another important mechanism making the Constitution practicable is the fact that it has direct effect – in other words, is directly applicable, irrespective of the existence or absence of legal acts in force. This has become a widespread and generally recognised practice in the world. All the norms of the Constitution are today working and genuinely defending Kazakhstani citizen's rights.

The Constitution, moreover, now provides strong guarantees of constitutional rights. Whereas citizens' rights could previously be limited by the state or by any of its representative bodies, Article 39 of the Constitution now stated that the rights and freedoms of an individual and citizen may be limited only by laws, and only to the extent necessary for the protection of the constitutional system, public order, human rights and freedoms, and the health and morality of the population.

The Constitution also instituted a bicameral Parliament. Discussions regarding the need for this had long been under way, but had not been carried through in the 1993 Constitution. The functions of Parliament were given clear definition in the system of apportioning unified state power, envisaging its focus on legislative activity. This legal arena, it goes without saying, is set within a definite constitutional framework, and yet broad-based and fully capable of regulating social relations with laws.

All the prerogatives of the highest representative body adopted in international practice (the approval of the state budget; the ratification or rejection of the Parliament's programme of activity; the provision of consent to the Prime Minister's appointment; the expression of a vote of no-confidence in the government; the chambers' hearings of the dispatches of Members of Parliament, and referrals to the President on their dismissal) are assigned to Kazakhstan's Parliament by our Constitution. Moreover, the Parliament is subordinate, like all the other branches of power, to the spirit and letter of the Constitution, which establishes and regulates its competence and the fundamentals of the legislative process.

The new Constitution established new approaches to defining the status of Parliament and its powers. Heading the system of executive bodies, directing their activity and independently taking administrative decisions, Parliament carries the entirety of responsibility for the state of affairs in the economy and social sphere. What's more, during the course of the all-nation discussion, the norm providing for the immunity of members of Parliament was excluded. The argument was that no state official should be beyond the realm of criticism, especially representatives of executive power.

Before the adoption of the 1995 Constitution the process of establishing a rule-of-law state was only just gathering force, and so guaranteeing an efficient judicial and legal system was no less important than resolving economic problems. The old judicial system we had inherited did not help the implementation of the courts' intended function, and paralysed private business initiatives. The absence of a civilised system of administering justice and genuinely independent judges made it harder to execute the laws.

All this made it essential to introduce drastic reforms to the judicial system, in the course of which the general and arbitration court systems were joined together. The arbitration courts were abolished as, to all extents and purposes they were special courts, while the parallel judicial system operated only for the consideration of economic disputes between members of the legal profession. The status of the courts and judges was fixed in the legislation, consolidating the legal guarantees of administering justice.

The mechanism envisaged by the Constitution for forming a judicial body also helped the just and objective administration of justice. A significant role in this was assigned to the Supreme Judicial Council and Board of Justice.

Instead of being appointed by election, local courts were to be appointed directly by the country's President, guaranteeing the judges' genuine independence from influences at a local level. The judges of the Supreme Court are elected by the Senate of Parliament on the President's behalf.

The Constitution also established a Constitutional Council, replacing the former Constitutional Court. This decision was difficult to come by, but there were objective grounds for it. Before taking it, I had a meeting with all the members of the Constitutional Court and Supreme Court, and other legal experts. Guided by the Supreme Court's three-years' experience of functioning in our country and considering reports on similar bodies worldwide – as well as a series of flaws endemic in the functioning of the Constitutional Court – the proposal was made to reform constitutional legal procedure.

Three types of reform were proposed. The first was to keep the body's old name but assign it the functions of a Constitutional Council. However, this was somewhat illogical. The second proposal was to join all the judicial functions (including that of constitutional supervision) in the Supreme Court. But such a resolution of the issue would have entailed a certain devaluation of the importance of constitutional supervision, which the Supreme Court would have undertaken on in the same way as other matters.

With a presidential form of government in place, the Constitutional Council is the optimum model for a body policing constitutional law. It not only guarantees that the laws of the

Constitution are enacted, but also acts as a kind of additional filter for legislative acts. In addition, it occupies a detached position away from the political fray. The last few years have shown the Constitutional Council to be successfully carrying out its function of defending constitutional rights and freedoms.

The Constitutional Council has frequently acted as an arbiter in disagreements between state bodies, arising from the passing and interpretation of laws. Its resolutions have been a considerable support in much complex political decision-making, for instance, regarding the Laws *On the introduction of changes and addenda to certain legislative acts of the Republic of Kazakhstan on faith issues and the activity of religious associations, On the mass media, On the activity of international and foreign non-commercial organisations in the Republic of Kazakhstan* and a series of others. In response to my appeals, the Constitutional Council pronounced these laws incompatible with the Constitution. I am entitled to lodge objections to the resolutions of the Constitutional Council, but I have not done so as I have agreed with its decisions.

A considerable achievement of the new Constitution has been the recognition of the institution of local government, set up to enable people to make independent decisions on issues of local importance. The importance of this lies in the fact that a person's day-to-day life actually takes place in a specific town, district, village or *aul*, where he resides and works. This being so, every citizen should have the opportunity to go about his business and use his initiative within the framework of local government, which should have a substantial legislative base.

Another argument broke out in the final days prior to the draft's publication in the media. The French specialists who had been helping us with the work suggested introducing an article on the President having the right to dissolve Parliament at any time. Although this idea enjoyed considerable support, on my insistence a milder formulation was included in the draft, stipulating the specific judicial grounds for the premature cessation of Parliament's powers. This, along with the provision for the President's impeachment, is a vital element in the system of restraints and balances guaranteeing the stability of the state and society. After all, the main aim was to create a system in which the different branches of government could work together in harmony.

The 1995 Constitution

The Adoption of the Constitution, 1995

After the draft of the new Constitution had been published in the media for an all-nation discussion, you could say virtually the whole country set to work on it. Every day a summary was made of all the suggestions flooding in from all over Kazakhstan – several files of them. Everything published in the press also had to be taken into account.

The discussion was not unanimous, it has to be said. By no means everyone supported the proposed draft Constitution. There were quite a few critical assessments in the press. The idea of adopting a new type of constitution and its constructive aspect were not immediately appreciated even by specialists in jurisprudence.

Just a few days after the draft Constitution's publication, six judges of the Constitutional Court functioning at the time issued a statement in the media – including a raft of foreign publications – according to which the proposed constitutional model did not provide grounds 'for recognising the Republic as a fully-fledged democratic, rule-of-law and social state', while the distortion of the principle of apportioning power called into question 'not only the presidential but the republican form of government as a whole'. However, the other half of the Constitutional Court judges totally disagreed with their colleagues' viewpoint, and also issued a statement to that effect in the media. Such a confrontation inside the Constitutional Court vividly illustrated the vigorous discussions being conducted in society as a whole.

Over 3,345,000 Kazakhstanis in all took part in the discussions of the draft Constitution, contributing 31,886 suggestions and comments which resulted in 1,100 amendments being made to the draft, and 55 of the 98 articles under discussion being changed, and also a new section and a number of new articles appearing in the Constitution.

In view of the suggestions being sent in, an increasing number of amendments and addenda kept being added. As a result, we calculated that a total of 18 versions of the Constitution's text were drawn up.

When work on the draft Constitution was almost complete, I signed the Decree *On the holding of an all-nation referendum on 30 August 1995* on 28 July 1995, No. 2389. In particular, this Decree resolved:

'1. To hold an all-nation referendum on 30 August 1995.
2. To submit to the all-nation referendum the draft of the new Constitution of the Republic of Kazakhstan with the question formulated as follows: "Do you accept the new Constitution of the Republic of Kazakhstan whose draft was published in the press on 1 August 1995?"
3. To officially publish in the mass media on 1 August, 1995 the draft Constitution, supplemented and amended to take into account the all-nation discussion of it. To also send the draft Constitution to the Central Election Commission of the Republic of Kazakhstan.'

Source: Archive of the President of the Republic of Kazakhstan

The day before the draft's official publication I instructed the working-group members B. Mukhamedzhanov and K. Kolpakov to personally read through the proofs of its text prepared at the publishers, and check that everything there was in order. At about half-past two that night they telephoned to tell me that it was all fine. Then I instructed them and N. Shaikenov to sanction the proofs and gave the order for the draft to be printed. Next morning the draft of the new Constitution was published in the republican media.

After the draft's publication I held a press conference and spoke about the main provisions of the future Constitution and then answered journalists' questions. What I most wanted to get across to all Kazakhstanis through the media was that the new Constitution would definitely pave the way for our country's stable development in a climate of inter-national concord and civil peace, and for carrying out political and economic reforms in the years to come.

Only after gaining the people's support was it possible to embark on constitutional reform. This was what lay behind the decision to step up work on the text of the new Constitution. I was bombarded by a squall of criticism. At this critical moment I was given support by the Assembly of the Peoples of Kazakhstan who suggested choosing the option of a direct address to the people without waiting for the formation of a parliament. I am sure now this was the right decision.

The 1995 Constitution

I had my doubts, I have to admit. On the one hand, it was an objective, valid way of addressing the issue: given the political crisis caused by the resignations of the Parliament and Government, it was essential to strengthen presidential power in the interests of preserving stability. On the other, a President is a person just like everyone else, and I felt uneasy about the personal implications of addressing the issue in this manner. Opinions began to be voiced about my being afraid of an election. And yet the objective sociological research data available offered convincing proof that if the issue had been merely about my keeping my presidency, it would have been worth my while actually to opt for an election. Just then, the gulf between me and the other possible contenders for the post of President was virtually insuperable. An election, moreover, offered a choice between two or three candidates, whereas the question put at the referendum was: 'Nursultan Nazarbayev – yes or no?' I would be standing openly for election with all the odds stacked against me: the hardships of the transitional period, the deterioration in living standards, the resentments that had mounted over all these years, purposeful criticism and downright incitement.

We had got through the difficult phase of forming Kazakhstan as a state, but now once again had to choose how to live from here on in. This was a question of economics, and politics and many other areas of social life. I studied the numerous proposals of politicians and public figures, theoreticians and practitioners, and then turned to the people for support.

Given the historical context, the question put to the referendum was essentially about maintaining stability both for the state and society as a whole. The referendum was to answer questions of key importance for the whole country, namely, whether the policy we had been conducting all these years was correct. Would the people of Kazakhstan give a vote of confidence to the president to continue with it?

The month flashed by. Finally, on 30 August 1995, an all-nation referendum was held on adopting the new Constitution of the Republic of Kazakhstan in accordance with the aforementioned Decree. The referendum was observed by around 1,000 representatives from 19 public associations. Also present were foreign observers from Hungary, Egypt, Canada, Poland, Rumania,

Tajikistan, Ukraine and other countries besides.

A total of 90.58 per cent of the voting public took part in the referendum, of whom 89.14 per cent voted for the adoption of the new Constitution. The new Constitution of the Republic of Kazakhstan was adopted on the basis of the vote. It was a triumph. The high level of voting was an indication of our citizens' support for the course we had proclaimed in the country's Basic Law.

I felt an immense sense of gratitude. Every politician has his hour of glory when he gets his people's full support and gains tremendous satisfaction from the fact that he has done his duty. All those years of doubts and anxieties, and sometimes emptiness all around you, when the circle of like-minded colleagues seemed infinitesimally small compared to the huge mass of problems and endless pile of tasks, both great and small you were landed with – all of these now proved not to have been in vain.

The 1995 Constitution truly became an expression of the entire people's will, and the Kazakhstani people themselves turned into the co-author of the Basic Law. At the press conference on the referendum's results on 1 September 1995 I congratulated all Kazakhstanis on this historic event in the life of our young sovereign state. By voting for the draft of the country's new Constitution, our co-citizens had made a choice of great importance both for the country as a whole and for every individual citizen. It was arguably the first time in Kazakhstan's history that its future was in its people's hands and they were voting for it.

Not only are the principles of the state enshrined in the Basic Law, but so, too, are the decisions taken that have a direct effect on the life of our citizens and every individual. These are issues concerning their freedoms, rights, and obligations in respect of society. In the final count, it is about the future prospects of every individual and family, and the country as a whole.

I then answered journalists' questions. Some of them had the usual 'catches' to them but since the people of Kazakhstan had just voted for the new Constitution so unanimously, I found responding to them easy.

So when BBC correspondent Krivenko asked whether too much power had not been conferred by the new Constitution on the country's President, I replied that the President of Kazakhstan had far less power than the President of France but this, after all, did not make France an undemocratic state. The *Economist* magazine's correspondent Mac Williams wanted to know whether the running of the referendum had been controlled by government officials. It fell to me to remind him that the referendum had been watched by over 1,000 observers, including foreigners, and no serious violations had been noted.

One of the journalists asked me briefly to sum up the results of the experience we had acquired between 1991 and 1995. In my reply I compared the work of a politician expecting results from his labours to the work involved in growing a tree and a crop of potatoes: 'You plant potatoes in spring and by autumn you've already got a crop to pick. But you need five or six years to get apples from a tree. During the past few years nobody has told us how you can do it all quickly, nobody in all post-Soviet space has managed to do it all quickly. But we've managed the main thing – to keep calm in our homeland, the Republic of Kazakhstan. We haven't allowed bloodshed. We have begun running our own finances, we have begun running our own economy, and we know which way to turn for a better life. During this time we have gained trust worldwide. Investments are now being made in Kazakhstan.'

It would be wrong of me to say that there had been no errors at all in the design of the state, in the reforms, in the documents we had approved. However, it's probably only those who do nothing who don't make mistakes. A politician's work is rather like that of a watchmaker, the only difference being that the latter stops the watch before repairing it, whereas the politician has to repair it while it is still showing the time. That's what makes it difficult.

The official presentation ceremony of our country's Constitution took place in the residence of the President of the Republic on 6 September 1995. On this ceremonial occasion the Chairman of the Central Electoral Committee Yuri Kim read out the resolution on the results of the all-nation vote on adopting the new Constitution and presented the original text of the country's new Basic Law to me. I then signed the Decree *On the Constitution of the Republic of Kazakhstan* and 100 original texts of it. I handed the first original text of the country's Constitution adopted on 28 January 1993 over to the State Archive for safe keeping.

In my speech to the assembled Government members, public figures, heads of diplomatic representations and media officials, I congratulated everyone on the adoption of the country's new Constitution and stressed that it marked the start of a new phase of our development and presented us with a host of new issues to be solved:

How to integrate our economy into the global economic market? If we failed to, we were bound to end up as a peripheral country, and an inveterate outsider.

How to induce people used to meagre but guaranteed state rations to grasp the nettle and show initiative? You see, unless a person realises he is responsible for his own destiny and that of his family, he will never achieve real prosperity.

How to design a strong, modern state organisation as the main tool of radical social reforms?

How to preserve the original culture of every one of the peoples of Kazakhstan while avoiding isolationist extremes? We must understand that passivity, like intolerance, causes cultural stagnation.

How to cultivate in society the ideals of spirituality, inter-national concord and civic peace?

How, finally, to curb criminal activity and establish the supremacy of the law at all levels of authority in society, without resorting to repressive measures?

The 1995 Constitution – the 'foundation' of new Kazakhstan

When the foundations of modern democracy were being laid some two hundred years ago, US President Thomas Jefferson, who was not a supporter of frequent changes to laws and constitutions, wrote that 'the laws and human institutions should go hand in hand with intellectual progress.' Two centuries later, this concept is just as relevant today.

I can proudly say that the Constitution adopted in 1995 became a powerful driving force for carrying out reforms in Kazakhstan. It is in many respects thanks to its provisions that in a short period of time we have achieved tremendous positive results in the young state's economy and policy-making, and inter-national stability.

With the adoption of the current Constitution we got the green light to carry through economic reforms in Kazakhstan. The

Supreme Soviet that had governed, figuratively speaking, everything and nothing, was replaced by a professional bicameral Parliament whose laws over these past few years have changed the country's face.

The 1995 Constitution gave a new impulse to the economic reforms, and provided for the setting up of an effective normative legislative base and legislative field for Parliament and the Government to work within that met and continue to meet the modern demands of market relations. The Constitution provides for the equal protection of both state and private property.

The current Constitution proclaims the genuinely state-guaranteed rights to freedom of labour and freedom of entrepreneurial activity; to receive free, extensive medical assistance established by legislation; to a free secondary education; to freedom of religion. Also guaranteed is the right to receive on a competitive basis a higher education; to social security in old age, and in the case of disease, disability or the loss of the breadwinner. Today these constitutional rights are consolidated in the specific norms of laws and part and parcel of people's everyday lives. The Constitution has strengthened basic individual rights and freedoms, providing for the equal rights of all our country's citizens, which enables fundamental democratic principles to be inculcated in society's political life.

In other words, the Constitution formulates both the essence and substance of citizens' constitutional rights, freedoms and obligations in keeping with the principles of a modern market economy, which in turn provides the opportunities for satisfying the multifaceted interests of the individual, subject to his specific contribution in the course of his work. A necessary basic level of free social services is also guaranteed by the state. Economic freedom, ideological and political diversity, every one's equality before the law – these are the basic priorities of Kazakhstan's development.

The democratisation of the political regime has significantly broadened the range of social opportunities afforded the individual by the state. This has resulted in a substantial strengthening of the role of individual and civil rights and freedoms in the national legal system, their traditional legal guarantees receiving new input. After developing the conditions for fully executing the requirements of the UN international package on civil, political, economic, social and cultural rights, Kazakhstan has ratified these crucial documents.

New legislation has been developed on the basis of the Constitution. Updated constitutional law has been introduced. Civil law regulating the relations of private ownership, civil society and free entrepreneurship has received further development. In keeping with the principles firmly established in the world community, substantial amendments have been made to the laws governing civil legal procedure, criminal legal procedure and criminal justice.

A new hierarchy of social values to be protected was defined in criminal law and found expression in its principles. The Criminal Code was to be formed on the basis of them. Since it was a highly complex and responsible matter, I personally worked out nearly every article of the draft law along with working group leader I. Rogov and B. Mukhamedzhanov. It should be said that the Criminal Code won the international legal community's very high praise.

It should also be added that a correctly defined criminal law policy is one of the means of guaranteeing the development of a rule-of-law state. In our country, it ensues from the Basic Law which proclaims an individual, his life, rights and freedom as its highest values. Rejecting harshly repressive means of dealing with lawbreakers, the state is instead establishing judicious forms of accountability for them, and thus making criminal policy more humane and the punitive justice system more liberal. As a result, whereas not so long ago Kazakhstan came third in the world after the USA and Russia in terms of prisoner numbers per 100,000 people, it is now much lower down the same index, in 24th position.

However, in view of globalisation and the transformation of crime which is taking on ever more ominous aspects, the question of responsibility for all infringements of the law and, in particular, for the most dangerous types of crime is becoming increasingly topical.

The complex issue of capital punishment currently being addressed is presenting a social and legal dilemma that is polarising public opinion. For the time being, a moratorium on its application is in force. We know this problem becomes particularly acute at pivotal moments in a state's development, when its society's spiritual life also becomes more active and a reappraisal of social values takes place.

It would not be an exaggeration to say that we have so far managed to achieve quite good results. Our main achievements include internal political and inter-national stability, macroeconomic stabilisation, total control of inflation, the establishment of an effective financial and credit system, the normalisation of ownership relations, and the gradual introduction of privatisation. Industrial production has begun to grow steadily and agriculture is reviving. Nowadays we have reason to say that our Constitution and laws are not only people-oriented: they also activate a person's creative, constructive energy and stimulate his entrepreneurial initiative.

Kazakhstan's economic success shows that economic liberalisation in a transitional period requires a sufficiently tough political structure, professional human resources and discipline in society. This makes it possible to carry out complex, frequently unpopular but absolutely essential economic reforms and guarantee political stability.

Setting out to establish a real presidential republic in 1995, I was aware that with this template of development in place the country would be easier to manage, and that the positive results of the onerous economic reforms were bound to be felt before too long. The President's increased personal responsibility in the course of the reforms called for a parallel increase in a whole range of powers. From then on Parliament no longer became involved in the appointment of the heads of ministries and departments: instead, they were appointed by the country's President. The Cabinet of Ministers was simplified as a collegial body. The Prime Minister appointed by Parliament on the President's recommendation was invested with the powers of 'the country's chief crisis manager'. Later on, collegial councils such as the Economic Policy Council, the Board of the National Bank, the Board of the National Fund and the National Council were to acquire a legal form. They now have more specific orientation and are all under the direction of the Head of State and their membership is not restricted by the representatives of the executive branch of power.

The strengthening of the vertical of power in the centre envisaged similar actions taking place in the provinces where *akims* continue to be appointed by the President while the institution of the President's representatives in the provinces was abolished. The role of provincial councils that had been reformed as provincial *maslikhats* was also reduced. We consciously undertook a number of unprecedented measures, knowing that we would return to a resolution of these problems once we had got through the economic crisis and embarked on the next phase of democratic reform.

I realised that strengthening executive authority, particularly in the provinces, would have a whole series of systemic shortcomings. The main one was, and still is, corruption. When control over the representative bodies in authority is slackened, the appointees from the centre often exceed their official plenary powers. Aware of how hard it is to keep an eye on everyone's activities, they often forget they are supposed to be serving the people. As a result, no sooner had the reform programme begun than the President's administration was inundated with complaints about provincial officials' arbitrary conduct. Through force of habit people addressed their complaints to the 'Central Committee'.

Corruption began penetrating other areas of state life, knocking economic policy and the country's development strategy off course. In view of this, I made an appeal to the citizens of the Republic for their support in a decisive fight against it. At the time, lawyers were divided in their opinion regarding the need to pass a law aimed at eradicating the causes of corruption. However, it was necessary to act resolutely and fast and so, on my instructions, work began on the draft Law *On fighting corruption* which was passed in June 1998. Incidentally, we were the first in the CIS to pass such a law. A programme for fighting corruption was worked out and acountability for corruption-related violations of the law strengthened.

A constitutional norm is effective as long as the laws passed in accordance with it are applied and observed by all the subjects of social relations and, first and foremost, state bodies and officials. I am convinced that a citizen in a rule-of-law state should be protected not by the President, not by a regional leader and not by a minister, but by the Court. Without a just and honest court, a proper legislative base, there can be no stable and civilised society. A healthy economy that underlies such a society can only be created once a market legal regime has been established and the Constitution and laws are being strictly observed by the state apparatus, all citizens and legal entities. Every aspect of this work is important: creating a proper legislative base; strengthening the Court at the apex of the legal pyramid, watching over the Constitution and the protection of the rights and legal interests of individuals and legal entities; and also forming a high-quality judicial system subject only to the law, where judgements are passed rigorously and quickly, and only competent and conscientious personnel are employed.

Each new phase of the political reforms must be closely coordinated with the level of development in the economy, civil society, and political and legal culture. The strengthening of the courts was only the initial solution to the problem, and now that the main reforms in the economic sphere are complete, we need the economic successes to be accompanied by a similar liberalisation of the political system.

Here I once again wish to stress that there is one crucial prerequisite for any political reforms to take place, and that is the formation of a middle class. Only a stable and flourishing society is capable of creating a stable political system.

> '...Before a society can successfully use such a (Western) democratic system, the people must achieve a high standard of education and economic development, create a substantial middle class, and people's life must cease to be a struggle for survival...
>
> The middle class will not emerge without a sustainable economy which cannot exist without a sufficiently strong and wise leadership capable of getting the country out of freefall.'
> Lee Kwan Yew, *Singaporean History: From the 'Third World' into the 'First'* *(1965-2000)*

With regard again to the state's role in its citizens' daily life, we must complete work on decentralising state management. This, in the first instance, consists of limiting the power between the levels of state management, elevating the role of the maslikhats and improving the system of inter-budgetary relations. Once state management has been fully decentralised, we must embark on the process of forming a system of local self-administration. In the period between 2005 and 2007, we shall be addressing the urgent need to introduce the system of appointing the *akims* of towns, regions and other lower-ranking officials by election, and also officially rating their activities.

Having completed these tasks, we shall be able to return to the deferred and more serious phase of liberalising the political system and elevating Parliament's role. A number of problems at a constitutional level will have to be resolved for the political status of the country's Parliament to be strengthened. We shall have to opt for an increase in the numbers of deputies in both Chambers of Parliament. Parliament's function should not only be to approve the state budget, but also to have a real role in controlling the course of the budget's execution.

A new system of forming the Government will possibly have to be worked out in the course of the constitutional amendments. In so doing, we shall clearly have to look into the question of forming the Government by the mechanism of a parliamentary majority.

Kazakhstan's entry into a new phase of its development calls for the close examination and implementation of appropriate reforms in state management, the political system and, possibly, the Constitution. Our ultimate goal is to create the optimum model for our country's political and state system. Obviously, by modernising state management and implementing political reforms we shall help strengthen our society and raise Kazakhstan's authority and prestige in the global arena. This will enable Kazakhstan to become one of the centres of international politics and dialogue between civilisations, and if stability and integration in the Central Asian region.

All these and numerous other amendments will enable us to achieve our goals. After all, we are a young country that has only just begun a new phase of its development. Even after so many years, looking at the Constitution lying on my desk, I still hark back to the events of that time: how enthusiastically we worked on its draft and how heatedly we discussed its various articles and how anxious we were when we submitted it for the all-nation discussion.

During my breaks from work, I open the Constitution, reread its articles and satisfy myself that we acted correctly at the time. Kazakhstan's present-day successes in state-building and economic reform are the best confirmation of this. Guided by the Constitution's key provisions, we implemented transformations of vital importance for the country's destiny: we built a market economy and laid the foundations for a democratic society.

In recent years, all the conditions have been created for the development of the most crucial institute of democracy – parliamentarism. The professional bicameral Parliament, providing for the representation of diverse interests, has successfully withstood the test of time. And we were the first in Central Asia to decisively embark on this course of action. Others then followed us, making use of our know-how.

The system of the executive vertical in conjunction with optimised administrative and territorial organisation, along with other consolidated component areas of the state system, have all enabled Kazakhstan to emerge from its systemic crisis and start dynamic growth, and now announce accelerated socio-economic and political modernisation.

No political disagreement has escalated into a crisis since the Constitution has been in force. All disputes are decided within the framework of constitutional procedures. The system of reciprocal relations established between state institutions has become traditional.

The topicality of inter-national relations and their influence on the competitive advantages of various countries are not only of relevance to events and dates in our country's history. As an analysis of the past decade of world history shows, the radical changes in the planet's national and racial make-up were a major factor of the last quarter of the 20th century.

Let's have a look at what is happening across the globe. The overwhelming majority of states in the modern world are multi-ethnic in composition, and one ethnic group makes up 90 per cent of the population in only 12 countries of the world. It is no coincidence that the Kazakhstan model of inter-national relations has won the highest appraisal of the UN, OSCE (Organisation for Security and Cooperation in Europe) and a number of other authoritative international organisations. All the key development issues of the national groups have been advanced in a three-tiered regulatory system. The first level consists of the activity of the groups themselves. We have comprehensively supported the legitimate aspiration of all the national communities to further their culture. There are now several dozen national cultural centres in Kazakhstan.

Secondly, we have created a unique instrument of inter-national relations in the Assembly of the Peoples of Kazakhstan. No other country in the world today has a similar authoritative and representative national policy instrument.

Then there is state policy in the language sphere. We were able not only to confer on the Kazakh language the position of official state language, but also to resolve the issue of its full use in all areas of public life. Nowadays teaching in over 50 per cent of the country's educational establishments is conducted in Kazakh. One should not forget that Soviet national policy had the most destructive consequences for the state language in Kazakhstan. However, unlike many other countries, we have gone about this process in a dignified manner without any language discrimination.

Political pluralism and a multi-party system are provided for in Kazakhstan. Major national parties operate in the country, including those in opposition, who all have an influence on the political process. There is also no doubt that such a crucial segment of a civil society as non-government organisations has grown noticeably stronger in our country. Whereas a decade ago there were about 400 of them, there are now over 5,000. What's more, the NGOs interact with the authorities as active, equal partners within the framework of the Citizens' Forum that has been set up on my initiative. And, revealingly, it is the NGOs that have now started taking the lead in these relations.

Cardinal changes have taken place in the dissemination of information. Freedom to express one's opinion and criticise the authorities has genuinely been established in the Kazakhstan media, and citizens now have the right to alternative sources of information. The country now has over 2,000 publications of the most diverse political orientation, including some radically opposed to the government. And of all the mass media only 20 per cent are run by the state.

In many other countries of the world, our Constitution is not congealed dogma. We need the know-how we have accrued using the Constitution over the past decade to solve internal problems and also respond effectively to the new challenges of the modern day. Strict adherence to the Constitution is the basis for the state's successful development and civil concord in society. Learning to live by it – this is the greatest lesson in democracy: a lesson all of us are obliged to learn.

It is our duty to honour the Constitution and respect it as we do our country, our history and our achievements. Unless we show respect for the Constitution and consistently observe its norms, it will simply be impossible for us to secure social concord, order, peace and tranquillity – and, it follows, a prosperous future for our country.

The Constitution has laid the foundation for our freedom. It has consolidated all the various successes and acquisitions that brought us independence. Our Constitution has given us what matters most. The right to choose, to create one's own life, is the most precious gift of all.

Our Constitution is not a mirror image of reality, but a representation of how society and the state ought to be. That's why its potential is by no means exhausted: the legal norms and principles of a fundamentally strategic character enshrined in the Basic Law reveal their true worth as the state and society develop and the necessary political, economic and social conditions take shape. And I believe that in some 15 or 20 years' time our society will fully conform to the standard of developed democracies, a two- or three-party system will be running smoothly in Parliament, and over half of society will belong to the middle class.

As I have already mentioned, this Constitution has given new impulse to our economic development. Kazakhstan's economy is established as the driving force of progress – from the design of the new Constitution to the change in Kazakhstanis' way of life and, most importantly, mind-sets. And oil, the 'black gold' of Kazakh land, has at this stage become the life blood of our economy.

Oil and gas have become our main resource and acted as real start-up capital from the very first days of independence; and within the next 15-20 years Kazakhstan is also going to become a top supplier of hydrocarbons to the world market. Our mineral resources have become an object not only of envy but also of claims that might well have cost us our independence. In my next chapter I want to describe exactly how we managed to subdue this wild beast, ever mindful that we cannot afford to relax for an instant and deceive ourselves that we have it under control.

3

THE BATTLE FOR THE CASPIAN AND THE OIL BOOM

'The Oil Fountain of the Century'

During, before and after my time as Secretary of the Central Committee of Kazakhstan's Communist Party, responsible for the economy and industry, I visited the Caspian region numerous times, but never again would I experience what I did that summer of 1985.

This episode became a pivotal moment, and not just for me personally. The attention of the entire top leadership of the USSR was also focused on the small Guriev region at the time.

It all began with a fire at one of the oil wells in the Tengiz field. On 23 July 1985, while drilling was under way at a depth of 4,467 metres, a gigantic fountain of oil suddenly started gushing out of Well T-37. The gushing oil soon got out of control and burst into flames. Not only was the rigging totally destroyed, but the pressure grew so intense that it pushed the drill out of the well. It took over 400 days to bring the fountain of oil and gas under control. The column of fire blazed at a height of 250 metres, jettisoned at 900 atmospheres of pressure. Eight billion cubic metres of hydrogen sulphide were released into the atmosphere, and the material costs exceeded US$1 billion, not counting the damage to the environment and people's health.

All the fauna and flora in the vicinity were destroyed by the vast qualities of sulphurous compounds released into the atmosphere. Attracted by the blazing light of the fire at night, birds dropped straight out of the sky, scorched by the flames and poisoned by the sulphur. The gigantic fireball engulfed the fire-fighters working near the well mouth. Sadly, there were also casualties. One of the members of the paramilitary fire-prevention unit was sucked into the blazing inferno and burned to death. All the fire-fighters involved received various degrees of burns. The temperature in the vicinity of the well was so intense that the top-quality fire-resistant suits were only effective for a matter of minutes. The sand in the barns nearby melted into multicoloured liquid glass.

Top experts from all over the USSR and abroad were called upon to suppress the fire. In keeping with the protocol in those days, the country's militarised fire-protection units, including the then top-ranking Poltava unit from Ukraine and Karshinsk from Uzbekistan, were mobilised to deal with the extremely complex operation of suppressing the fountain. The emergency work at the wells was supervised by First Vice Minister of the USSR Oil Industry I. Igrevsky, chairman of operation headquarters for accident control at the Tengiz T-37 well.

The USSR Ministry of Oil Industry was unable to get the conflagration under control because it lacked the necessary equipment to deal with fountains of such force. Failing to come up with a solution, at one point the Ministry considered the option of an atomic explosion to suppress the fountain. No mention was even made of the people living in nearby *auls*. However, we managed to intercede in time and prevent such a terrible option from being carried through.

It took around two months of constant work to tame the gas and oil fountain. Subsequently, oil workers would refer to it as 'the fountain of the century'. A substantial role was played by the hydro-pressure equipment designed by oil-workers at Guriev's Petrovsky Factory, which was used to suppress the fountain and get the flow of hydrocarbons under control.

The next phase of the work involved lowering pipes into the well and pumping down heavy liquid. This operation also required special equipment – high-pressure prevention systems with a single control. As the necessary technology could not be found in the USSR, the decision was taken to consult specialists from the American company Chevron and the Canadian company Otis, and make use of their American and Canadian equipment. Thanks to the combined efforts of these companies' specialists and Soviet oil workers, the pipes were lowered and the fountain at last eliminated.

The fountain at Well T-37 was an indication of the immense potential of the Tengiz field and first sign of the substantial oil deposits in Kazakhstan's section of the Caspian shelf. And it was already clear that there was no modern technology available in the USSR to develop such fields.

The History of the Development of Caspian Oil
Oil has played a key role in Kazakhstan's history.

By definition, oil is 'a complex compound of liquid hydrocarbons, gaseous and other substances'. Several thousand products are derived from it, and as D.I. Mendeleyev himself noted, 'if you heat a stove with oil, you might as well heat it with banknotes.'

The first evidence of oil in the territory of Kazakhstan was discovered long ago. However, it was only at the end of the 17th century that genuine interest began to be shown in it by Tsarist Russia. Throughout the 18th and 19th centuries Russia sent its leading topographers, geologists and mining engineers to Western Kazakhstan.

In 1892, the first applications were made by Russian entrepreneurs to explore different sections of the Western Kazakhstan region, starting with the areas of Dossop, Karashyngul and Iskene.

> 'The Emba-Caspian Association headed by Russian entrepreneur S. Leman drilled at a depth of between 38 and 275 metres, at oil well 21 in the Karashangul field (now Atyrau district). They got their first oil fountain at Karashungul in 1899, while drilling at a depth of 40 metres at Well 7, but only about 20-25 tonnes of oil were extracted daily.
>
> This event was regarded as the start of the history of Kazakhstan oil extraction and development at the Dossop, Makat, Iskene and other fields. Various associations and societies were set up, including some foreign ones, to carry out exploratory work, drilling and the extraction of Caspian oil. Incidentally, one of the first oil explorers working at the time in Kazakhstan was the illustrious Swedish industrialist Alfred Nobel.'
>
> *Encyclopaedia of Kazakhstan Oil, 1999*

The oil industry's infrastructure began to develop as oil output continued to increase annually. The first oil pipeline was constructed to carry the raw material from the oil fields to the port of Guriev, and then on to Baku by sea.

However, the world was changing, and everything, including the young oil industry, was soon to endure some gruelling trials. Our people were to face tremendous upheavals and tragedies: the national liberation movement of 1916 led by Amangelda Imanov, the October Revolution of 1917, and the great famines of 1921-22 and 1931-33, when we lost as many as 40 per cent of our entire population.

Once the Soviets gained power, the oil industry was nationalised and all the companies dissolved. The Board of the Oilfields, later turned into the Embaneft Trust, was set up on their foundations in 1920, for the industrial development of oil in the Ural-Emba region.

Kazakhstan's oil became a serious topic for discussion in the first years of World War II. The threat of losing the oil wells in the Caucasus and interruptions to the supply of ammunition to the Red Army forced the Soviet leadership to transfer part of the oil production, and later the processing, to Guriev.

'The German command made serious miscalculations in respect of the supplies to their troops, particularly, in the provision of combustibles and lubricants. In the first months of 1942, German troops began conducting the so-called Blau operations whose main objective was to capture the USSR's oil regions of Maikop, Grozny, and Baku. A special brigade of 15,000 oil technicians was organised to re-establish the captured oil wells. During operations, however, the German troops only managed to capture Maikop (9 August 1943), whose infrastructure had been deliberately destroyed by the retreating Red Army.

Exactly how important the USSR's oil regions were to fascist Germany was confirmed by one single fact. In the winter of 1943, Hitler refused to transfer a large unit of troops from the Caucasian line of advance to Stalingrad, despite repeated calls to do so from the German High Command.'

Daniel Yergin, *Extraction*, 2003

1943-45 saw the construction of Kazakhstan's first oil refinery, the Guriev OR, which was to become a trailblazer in this new branch of the economy in the Caspian region. The industrial extraction of hydrocarbon raw materials in Kazakhstan can also be traced back to this time.

The real breakthrough in the development of the oil industry, however, came at the end of 1979, with the opening of the Tengiz oilfield in the Atyrau province, one of the fifth largest oil deposits in the world, and the gigantic oil and gas condensate deposit at Karachaganak in the Western Kazakhstan district.

And yet, even with such rich mineral resources under its earth, Kazakhstan never really felt it truly owned them. All the enterprises of the oil industry were managed by ministries in Moscow. The USSR's top party leadership would not allow us to extract and process the hydrocarbon raw material independently, and reacted jealously to all our initiatives. We depended on the centre for everything, from the transport for the products and equipment, right through to the training of the personnel who came to us from all over the USSR.

With Mikhail Gorbachev's rise to power in 1985, perestroika began.

The oil industry and, indeed, the economy as a whole needed to resolve issues such as resource management and increased scientific production capacity, the elimination of heavy physical work and setting up of an effective production infrastructure. All these could help increase its competitiveness and, subsequently, prevent it from collapsing in the years that followed.

However, the announced course of reform failed to address all the problems that had come to the fore. This was, first and foremost, because the reformers tried to make do with half-measures while the entire economic system, and not just the oil industry, required radical restructuring. The Soviet leadership lacked the resolve to tackle the main cause of the imbalance in the economy, and get rid of planned pricing, thereby doing away with surplus demand and restoring the inner stability of the economic organism.

The Soviet phase of economic reforms resulted in a reduction in production output, increased inflation, a rise in the budget deficit and a decline in people's living standards. The general crisis could not help but affect the oil industry as well. This was when the opportunity was missed to conduct large-scale, step-by-step reforms to transform the planned economy into a market one.

The Battle for the Caspian and the Oil Boom

Politics in the Soviet Union always took precedence over economics. And so, when the combined authority of the leadership of the Soviet Union and Supreme Soviet of the Russian Federation paralysed state management in the country, it was this lapse of an essentially 'political' character in the system that brought the entire course of economic reforms to a standstill. This made the crisis of the entire Soviet system even worse. The end result was the disintegration of the USSR.

Oil as the Foundation of Economic Independence

As part of the USSR with its dominant centralised planning and rigidly fixed prices, each of the Union republics occupied a particular place in the division of labour. Kazakhstan was fundamentally a supplier of raw materials, foodstuffs and military production.

We were living in Iron Curtain conditions, and all our trade was inside the USSR. All industry, energy, transport, oil and gas pipelines, communications and trade were oriented towards the needs of the entire nation. And yet there was, for example, no direct transport links between the west of Kazakhstan and the east.

All economic and political decisions on Kazakhstan's activity were taken in Moscow. We were able to manage only 7 per cent of our industry while the other 93 per cent – and the infrastructure – was under Moscow's management; 75 per cent of our trade was with the Russian Federation and 15 per cent with the Ukrainian SSR, so the potential for export was extremely narrow.

In the oil industry Kazakhstan was given the role of producer and supplier of marketable oil in the Soviet Union's pipeline system. What's more, the oil and gas enterprises' functions were restricted only to operations at the deposits. Issues concerning the economics of oil projects, marketing and export of oil and gas, Moscow kept for itself.

Despite the oil industry's potential, in the first years of independence Kazakhstan encountered some fairly serious obstacles in the prospecting, working, extraction, refining and transportation of oil and gas. The industry suffered from a considerable shortfall in technology, machinery and equipment, in investment capital and in experience of working with Western oil companies. What mattered most was not the total volume of oil output but the expertise in selling it on world markets. However, at the time of independence our management was not sufficiently progressive and forward-thinking to compete successfully in the world market. The internal transport system set up in the Soviet period did not meet the demands of a sovereign state, and access to international markets was limited. After the collapse of the USSR a large section of the oil pipeline remained in Russia's territory, which seriously reduced the effectiveness and profitability of the work of a single oil and gas section in post-Soviet space. Environmental issues that had been inadequately addressed in Soviet times now became very pressing.

I realised that to develop our oil reserves in a really effective manner we needed wide-ranging cooperation with major world oil companies with considerable expertise in areas such as geological prospecting, extracting and refining hydrocarbon raw material, and its transportation. Before gaining its independence, Kazakhstan had gradually started getting down to talks with the oil industry's heavyweights.

Yes, it was tough. We had no experience of conducting foreign talks. We learnt 'as we went along' – during the negotiating process. The principal questions I always asked was: 'Does this contract comply with international standards? Will it go against Kazakhstan's future interests?' We lacked expertise and authority. We needed fresh, innovative ideas and people with experience of working in crises.

It was very difficult. A lot of people, both inside the country and in neighbouring countries, were against attracting foreign investors. We were accused of selling out our homeland and told we would end up like Nigeria which, having failed to manage its oil resources effectively, had begun to depend on foreign oil companies. Nevertheless, we appreciated the importance of the oil and gas industry for the new republic's economic and social development and the state's strategic security. With this in mind, we made an even greater effort to develop in 1992 a well-considered and promising plan on the subsequent development of Kazakhstan's oil and gas industry.

There were a host of difficulties, particularly of an unforeseen kind, but we still succeeded with our main strategic objective and increased oil production rates. After the collapse of the Soviet

The Battle for the Caspian and the Oil Boom

Union, oil production had fallen from 25 million tonnes in 1991 to 20 million tonnes in 1994, but from then on it began its rapid rise.

While the Soviet Union was still in existence, over 75 oil deposits were discovered in the Atyrau province with known reserves of around one billion tonnes. After gaining independence, we succeeded in working 39 of these deposits with reserves of 846 million tonnes. In addition, preparatory work was carried out at seven deposits. Exploratory drilling was due to get under way at another 25 or so deposits.

Notes on the largest deposits:
1. Kashagan (approximately 1,648 million tonnes overall known extractable reserves of oil;
   969 billion cubic metres of gas);
2. Tengiz (approximately 237.3 million tonnes overall known extractable reserves of oil;
   637.3 billion cubic metres of gas);
3. Karachaganak (approximately 1,318.7 million tonnes overall known extractable reserves of oil; 684.4 billion cubic metres of gas).

Source: Ministry of Energy and Mineral Resources of the Republic of Kazakhstan

After gaining independence, Kazakhstan encountered a series of huge problems, including issues in respect of attracting investors to the oil extraction industry, the driving force of independent Kazakhstan's economy.

We were still facing a lengthy battle with Moscow over the Caspian's rich raw materials. The oil lobby in Russia put tremendous pressure on Boris Yeltsin to get him to convey the ownership of the Tengiz oilfield to Russia. I had many disagreeable conversations with Yeltsin about this.

At a meeting in Moscow Yeltsin once said to me, 'Give Tengiz to Russia.' I looked at him and realising he was not joking, replied, 'Well, if Russia gives us Orenburg province, after all, Orenburg was once the capital of Kazakhstan.' To which he retorted, 'Do you have territorial claims on Russia?' 'Of course not,' I replied. He burst out laughing and so did I.

Russia had neither the means nor the technology to work such a complex oilfield. If Tengiz had gone to the Russians, they would have closed it down, and Kazakhsan might have remained their economic hostage.

The Chevron contract, Kazakhstan's first major success, had repercussions for the future development of the Republic's entire oil industry. A landmark for all subsequent investors, it truly became the 'contract of the century' and the economic cornerstone of our independence. However, it was preceded by years of lengthy negotiations which I would like to describe.

'The Contract of the Century'

At the end of the 1980s and start of the 1990s Chevron was already holding talks with the USSR on the Tengiz oilfield, but the Soviet leaders were doing their uttermost to block foreigners' access to the development project. Russia's oil lobby knew about the Tengiz oil reserves and were reluctant to let them go.

At the time there were about 60 oil wells in operation at Tengiz, with an annual output of around 3 million tonnes of oil. Output could have been increased 15 times over, but there was an urgent need for vast financial investment and innovatory technology. At that moment Moscow had neither, and so the leaders of the Communist Party's Central Committee were forced to reconcile themselves to the idea of attracting foreign investors. It was then a question of choosing them.

Of all the would-be investors – Japanese, English, American and Italian – Moscow decided upon the American company Chevron. An agreement was reached securing not only investments in the Tengiz oilfield, but also the establishment of various joint enterprises which were to fill the USSR's internal market with high-quality oil-processing goods.

There was no doubt that a strong lobby on Moscow, from inside the country and from without, was involved in this choice. Moscow was ready to do anything to strengthen its already collapsing central authority. A protocol was even signed in 1988 between the USSR Ministry of the Oil and Gas Industry and Chevron on their intentions to set up the joint venture, Sovchevroil, to develop the Korolev oilfield. This document was signed in strict confidentiality without our knowledge. Shortly afterwards, however, the USSR finally collapsed, the republics gained their sovereignty, and a year later Moscow was forced not only to involve us in the talks with the Americans but also take our terms into account.

The first official talks with Chevron executives were held in June 1990. A protocol on proposals was signed between Chevron and Kazakhstan's production association Tengizneftgaz, then part of the USSR Ministry of Oil Industry system. According to this protocol, Chevron was to carry out a feasibility study on the Tengiz and Korolev oilfields and hold talks on a potential agreement to form a joint venture with Tengizneftgaz.

After the signing of the protocol I paid my first visit to the United States, staying for around three weeks, and visiting New York, Washington and Chevron works in California and Louisiana.

Around this time I became acquainted in Moscow with a professor of economics of the University of San Francisco, an American of Korean extraction by the name of Chan Yan Beng. He arranged for me to talk to economists, financiers and legal professionals and gain their expertise. Through these conversations I learnt in detail about the US economic and financial systems and the laws enabling investors to make investments, and the actual way investments were made. Chevron put these theoretical studies to the test in practice. It was a good start to the continuing study of a new subject.

Dr Beng now heads the Kazakhstan Institute for International Economic Law, the country's leading higher-education institution, which meets all the latest educational requirements.

The feasibility studies and draft agreement on the setting up of a joint venture had been drawn up by Chevron and Tengizneftgaz by the end of the first quarter of 1991. The studies and agreement were to be examined and approved by a group of experts from the USSR's Gosplan. But then complications occurred, and not just of a technical order.

As is well known, the political situation in the USSR deteriorated sharply in 1989-90. In the summer of 1991, Boris Yeltsin came forward as a candidate for the post of President of Russia and engaged in an open stand-off with the ex-General Secretary and incumbent President Mikhail Gorbachev, and the leadership of the Soviet Union's Communist Party. Supported by the likes of Yegor Gaidar, Yeltsin criticised in particular the proposed joint venture between Chevron and Tengizneftgaz, arguing that it was not in the country's interests. Gaidar set about analysing the agreement. Once the solution to a problem, Tengiz was turned into a political game. At the height of this brouhaha a third commission was set up which also criticised the terms of the proposed deal.

By mid-1991, it became clear that the project was not getting anywhere. We then took decisive action. As a member of the Presidential Council under Mikhail Gorbachev, I persuaded Moscow to hand over the authority for holding talks to the Council of Ministers of the Kazakh SSR on the basis that Kazakhstan's government would be able to get more favourable terms. The Soviet leadership agreed, and on 23 July 1991, at the Permanent Mission of the Kazakh SSR in Moscow, I informed the Chevron representatives that new draft terms were to be discussed at the talks.

I had spent most of the previous night in new Union treaty talks with Gorbachev and the leaders of the other Union republics. Exactly a week later I met with Gorbachev and Yeltsin, and attempted to reconcile the feuding parties and put the finishing touches to the proposed Union treaty. The following day I also met with US President George Bush Snr in Moscow to sign the Start-2 treaty on nuclear threat reduction. We had a detailed discussion about the progress in the Chevron-Tengizneftgaz talks and agreed to support the project.

The US President was interested in the issue, and Gorbachev had spoken to him about it in their talks. I described all the complexities of the oilfield to them in detail, such as the lack of technical transportation in view of the high sulphur content and so on. They were pleased with my explanations. I recall George Bush asking me if I was oil expert by training. 'No, I'm a metallurgist,' I replied, 'but life has made me get to know all the branches of the economy.' During my visit to George Bush Snr. in 2006, he recalled this occasion and said he remembered me from then.

This was a correct decision at a critical moment for Kazakhstan. Three weeks later the USSR ceased to exist as a state. After the collapse of the Soviet Union we held all the Tengiz talks as an independent subject of international law. However, differences of opinion over the agreement emerged straight away.

It should be said here that I was obliged to make an in-depth study of the subject of the talks. At moments like these a knowledge of the facts and details became a decisive element. We were well aware that the destiny of future Kazakhstan was being decided at the negotiations table. The dialogue was conducted with steely resolve and incontrovertible arguments which we formulated as follows.

First, how to evaluate what had already been done at the Tengiz oilfield? Chevron proposed calculating the expenditure to date at a rouble rate greatly in our favour (35 per cent lower than the usual exchange rate). However, even this tempting proposal could not be agreed to, as the sole cost of the newly imported equipment at Tengiz was put at US$850 million dollars and we had also spent around 1.5 billion roubles on the oilfield's development. And so we proposed that an independent valuation of the costs be carried out.

Secondly, there were issues concerning the project's investment plan. Who should take the credits? Which funds should be used to finance the development? We insisted on Chevron's substantial, direct participation rather than just that of the joint venture set up with them.

Thirdly, we were opposed to the original division of Tengiz's territory into sectors for exploration and development. Chevron considered an area of 23,000 square kilometres as the minimum whereas, to put this in perspective, the whole present area of Atyrau province is only 118,600 square kilometres. This was unacceptable to us and we insisted on 2,000 square kilometres.

Fourthly, we proposed setting the American share of the profits at 13 per cent maximum, and Kazakhstan's at 87 per cent, thereby revising the Union's terms in respect of the shares in the joint venture, which had been set at 38 per cent for the Americans and 62 per cent for the USSR.

Fifthly, the royalty rates. Chevron was insisting on 7 per cent, whereas throughout the world royalties were then set in keeping with a project's profitability, at an average rate of approximately 17 per cent.

Sixthly, the political risk level. The Americans were assessing it at a level several times higher than that of investing in Latin America and Africa.

Seventhly, we were proposing increasing payment for the use of the land, and increasing bonuses from US$50m to US$100m, and increasing payment for the use of the resources from US$10b to US$25b. The sum total under dispute was approximately US$17b.

The talks became deadlocked as a result. Chevron was unwilling to make concessions in response to our main demands, but we were ready for this turn of events. Choosing the right moment, we staked our all. At the end of March 1992, the Kazakhstan side was obliged to announce that if Chevron did not make concessions, we would break off talks and open up an international contest for the Tengiz oilfield's development. In actual fact, we did not have the legislation yet in place for holding such contests.

I realised that compromise was an important condition for success. We knew that Chevron also wanted a compromise. And before making this compromise, we clearly defined the limit to which we could make concessions without causing our country harm. We had got our calculations right, and a short while later Chevron agreed to our terms. Of course, we also had to make small concessions. Hence, for instance, the area for exploring and developing Tengiz oil was increased from 2,000 to 4,000 square kilometres.

On 7 May 1992, a cooperation protocol for setting up the Tengizchevroil joint venture was signed between the Government of the Republic of Kazakhstan and the Chevron Corporation, in accordance with which as of 1 January 1993, the 'Tengizchevroil' joint venture would start further developing the Tengiz and Korolev oilfields.

Then, at the end of May 1992, at the invitation of US President George Bush Snr. I paid my first official visit to the United States of America. During my visit I had meetings with President Bush, Secretary of State James Baker, Defence Secretary Dick Cheney, Treasury Secretary Nicholas Brady, Agriculture Secretary Edward Madigan, US congressmen, and the Managing Director of Chevron, Kenneth Derr. As my personal experience shows, from the very start of talks it is very important to establish personal, friendly and confidential contact with partners, which is what we did during our first visit to the USA.

During this visit we signed a number of bilateral agreements, including a constructive agreement on the Tengizchevroil joint venture on developing Kazakhstan's Tengiz and Korolev oilfields, which experts referred to as 'the contract of the century'.

The Battle for the Caspian and the Oil Boom

On 6 April 1993, the Agreement on establishing the Tengizchevroil joint venture, containing the principal parameters of the future contract, was signed in my presence and with Kenneth Derr's participation, at the House of Friendship in Almaty. That same day I signed the Decree *On the activity of the Tengizchevroil joint venture.*

The following information was released by the global news networks: 'According to the contract, the shareholding of Kazakhstan and Chevron in the joint venture was on a 50:50 basis. The American side was to be responsible for all expenditures incurred in the oilfield's development and construction. The signed agreement has a term of 40 years. The area for joint activity is 4,000 square kilometres. The initial financial investment is US\$1.5b. Overall investments – US\$20b. The oil will mainly go for export. Overall revenues over four decades will constitute approximately US\$210b, as against expenditures of approximately US\$83b including taxes and royalties; 80 per cent of projected revenues will go to Kazakhstan. Over the four decades the target at Tengiz is to produce 775 million tonnes of oil, 32 million tonnes of propane gas, 55 million tonnes of a broad fraction of light hydrocarbons and 96 million tonnes of sulphur.'

No sooner had the contract been signed than a barrage of criticism broke out. The American press laid into Chevron for taking on a risk-laden project, and Russia's press criticised us for selling out to the Americans.

However, all this criticism was unfounded. The risk level and Kazakhstan's uncertain future aside, Chevron had become a trailblazer or, as the Americans put it, a pioneer, for which it was fully rewarded in the years that followed. According to the latest results of 2005 alone, Tengizchevroil (TCO) produced 13,657,000 million tonnes of oil. Along with the oil, the venture obtained 4,067,000,000 cubic metres of gas.

What's more, in 2007, TCO planned to complete the construction of second generation units – a new gas-refining plant, and system to pump natural gas back underground and increase the wells' output. This will increase oil production by approximately one million tonnes per month. Upon the second generation units' completion, the overall increase in output will be 11-12 million tonnes of hydrocarbon raw material per year. Once these units start working at full capacity, output at the Tengiz field will reach 25 million tonnes per year.

Looking back, one can say that cooperation between the young republic and Chevron helped significantly reduce our country's investment risks. The contract of the century gave a positive signal to other major oil companies who were then only contemplating investing in Kazakhstan. However, the precedent of Chevron was insufficient to attract further foreign investments immediately. Companies needed legal guarantees for investing in Kazakhstan. We could offer such guarantees only two years later when the Law *On oil* was passed by a presidential decree.

The Law *On Oil*, 1995

As soon as we started developing our state, we encountered problems over not having an adequate legislative base. This was the case in many areas of our state's life. The deficiency was most felt in one of the economy's key sectors – the exploitation of natural resource.

In Soviet times everything was owned by the state and so there was no need to formulate serious agreements on exploitation rights. To conduct geological prospecting works or develop oilfields, enterprises were allotted a specific area by a resolution of the Ministry of Oil and Gas and then started the necessary oil operations. So there was no sense in establishing all sorts of legal relations with the state taking account of all the enterprises' or natural-resource users' interests. The legislation in effect at the time mainly regulated the technical side of the mutual relations.

Practice showed that not having a legislative base to regulate operations was a negative factor holding back investment in the republic. In the initial period of independence, the usual way of developing the country's mineral and raw material resources with investors was to set up joint ventures between the foreign partners and domestic enterprises intending to operate the oilfields. The contract to set up a joint-venture in the territory of the Republic of Kazakhstan was the basis for cooperation. It was, therefore, the Kazakhstan enterprise that was entitled to exploit the mineral resources. As a joint venture stakeholder, the foreign partner acquired co-rights over the exploitation of the mineral resources. Such a form of attracting foreign investments was widely used virtually all over the CIS.

Foreign investors with sizeable funds to invest naturally wanted more cogent guarantees. In the absence of adequate law, either the ratification of each agreement in Parliament or their approval by presidential decree were feasible. I had to take personal responsibility for each and every contract. Likewise, any addendum or amendment to the contracts, which could easily arise during a long-term project lasting many years, could only be made by presidential decrees. Such an unwieldy procedure, lacking a legislative basis that conformed to international standards, was not conducive to attracting wide foreign investment in the oil and gas industry.

By mid-1994, on my instructions, the Government started developing the draft law *On oil*. The Ministry of Fuel and Energy Resources set up a working group made up of representatives of various state bodies, scientific, legal and financial institutions, industrial representatives and others. During the initial stage of its work the group encountered considerable difficulties, as it had to work out a modern draft law that was both acceptable to foreign investors and effectively protected state interests. The hardest thing of all was getting round people's conservative mind-sets. For decades society had been going about its work against a backdrop of total state ownership. It was essential to get used to the concept of private property and prepare a law that would protect not only state interests but also those of the private investor.

In view of the fact that the law was establishing the legal foundations of mutual relations in one of the most crucial sectors of our country's economy, where the interests of the Government, various enterprises, groups of people, and foreign investors well and truly intersected, it became the subject of lengthy discussions in the Supreme Soviet.

By the time the final version of the draft law was ready, the Supreme Soviet had already been disbanded, and the Law *On oil* became one of the 140 key laws forming the foundations of the economic reforms I approved by a presidential Decree with the force of law, on 28 June 1995, No. 2350. And thanks to this decree we began a new chapter in the history of the development of Kazakhstan's oil.

The law confirmed that the oil underground was state property, and after being extracted to the surface, its ownership was defined by the legal acts concluded between the Government of the RK and the resource user. The law made provision for several different types of contract for conducting oil and gas operations in our country: concessional, one involving tax and royalty payments, another in the form of an agreement on production sharing, and also service contracts.

According to the law, the financial risks during the carrying out of geological exploratory works were placed on the investor. Thus, in the event of oil deposits not being found, the investor was not to be reimbursed for any expenditure incurred. What's more, the contracts also indicated the minimum volume of geological exploratory works for the investor, their physical dimensions and financial costs having been calculated by an appropriate state body. If this minimum was not met by the end of the term of exploratory works, the investor was to pay the outstanding amount of the estimated cost of these minimum works to the state budget.

The law set out the state's liabilities in respect of the contracts and provided sufficient guarantees for investors for them to no longer request for the agreements on natural resource exploitation to be approved by presidential decrees. The enactment of the law greatly reduced Kazakhstan's so-called 'country risk' compared to other post-Soviet countries. Having legally approved rules of the game, the foreign oil giants could boldly invest in the development of Kazakhstan's oilfields without fearing that the interests of the parties entering into the contracts would be infringed in any way.

The Law *On oil* played its historic role in the matter of increasing the country's economic prosperity. Thanks to this law, our country's policy in respect of natural-resource exploitation became more transparent and predictable. Our authority and image strengthened with every passing year. One after the other, the foreign oil giants gravitated towards our country.

'Kazakhstan really understands what great opportunities lie ahead of it for making effective use of its oil reserves.

...Oil reserves must be used effectively, they must be integrated into a programme of economic development. And

The Battle for the Caspian and the Oil Boom

I am confident that this is the direction Kazakhstan will certainly be moving in.'
From Vice President of Perseus LLC Robert Holbrook's speech at the Eurasian Media Forum, Almaty, 24 April, 2004

Nowadays many consider this a fact that only stands to reason. Back then, however, we realised that society would regard such difficult decisions in a variety of ways. Many accused us at the time of selling off our homeland and our children's future. But instead of getting embroiled in a futile polemic, we resolved to define clearly the state's guarantees in relation to foreign investors. We lacked the capital, let alone the modern technology, to develop our oil reserves. We started working with the foreign oil companies as partners ready to conduct long-term, profitable business in Kazakhstan.

The enacted law became the basis and impulse for the subsequent development of the oil industry. However, while we were able to give legal guarantees on matters relating to the development of the oilfields on dry land at a republican level, issues relating to the exploration and extraction of hydrocarbons at sea required Kazakhstan not only to pass legislative acts but also enter into inter-state treaties.

The Legal Status of the Caspian Sea

From the very outset the indeterminate legal status of the Caspian Sea acted as a kind of brake on the development of the oil and gas industry on the Caspian shelf. It caused several major companies to merely 'indicate' their presence in the Caspian in anticipation of better times.

We were naturally dissatisfied with the geopolitical and economic situation that had arisen as a result of this issue. As history would have it, until 1991 this expanse of water of considerable geo-strategic importance had been an object of reciprocal relations only between the Soviet Union and Iran. After the collapse of the USSR, the situation in this region grew even more complex. By that time five independent states were involved in the process: Azerbaijan, Russia, Iran, Turkmenistan and

Kazakhstan. A review and definition of the Caspian Sea's status was therefore required to meet the demands of the time and take account of the positions of all the countries of the Caspian region.

The issue became increasingly pressing because in the difficult times of 1992-93, all the Caspian countries considered that exploiting the sea's rich natural resources would substantially improve their economic, social and political position. However, unless the sea's legal status and the national sectors of the littoral countries were clearly defined, it would be impossible to start exploratory and drilling work and attract fully participating foreign investors.

It was obvious that one day the sea's hydrocarbon reserves would rival major oil regions like the North Sea and Gulf of Mexico. This being the case, the problem of the sea, from its very outset, went beyond regional dimensions and acquired a global significance.

That is why, directly after the USSR disintegrated and Kazakhstan gained its independence, our foreign policy department initiated talks between the Caspian countries on the sea's legal status. It was one of the most important problems requiring my constant attention. We had identified our principal objective of securing Kazakhstan's legal right, which would be acknowledged by all the states of the Caspian region and international community, to exploit the natural resources in the Kazakhstan sector of the Caspian.

I had to hold difficult talks with the leaders of the great states, who were conscious of their power and hoped for considerable concessions. I always made it clear that while I might concede on matters that affected only me personally, whenever they concerned the people and country, I would suggest finding an alternative solution that would satisfy both sides. So it was with the talks on the sea's status.

However, despite our considerable input, the first meeting of the interested states' representatives only took place in Moscow in October 1994, when Iran advanced the idea of setting up an organisation of regional cooperation between the Caspian states. The Kazakhstani delegation was the only one among the five present to submit a draft convention on the Caspian Sea's legal status which was not, however, examined in detail 'owing to lack of time'.

The Battle for the Caspian and the Oil Boom

But this was the first meeting, and even this made it notable. The talks had at last got off the ground. Then, in May 1995, another meeting took place in Almaty, after which we succeeded in speeding up the process and making it more organised.

The talks proceeded with great difficulty because of the disparity in the littoral countries' initial viewpoints on regulating the sea's legal status. I would here like to briefly describe how these countries' positions evolved.

Kazakhstan wanted to extend the application of certain provisions of the 1982 UN Convention on maritime law to the Caspian Sea, with due regard for the latter's specific features as a single ecological system. Its seabed and resources were to be demarcated along a middle line, and territorial sea and fishing zones of agreed dimensions set up across its water. The rest of the sea and its surface were to be open only to cargo ships belonging to the littoral states, and to free navigation and fishing on the basis of an agreed quota system. Landlocked states of the Caspian region were to enjoy freedom of transit through the territory of Russia and Iran by all means of transport to access other seas and the Pacific.

Russia considered the Caspian a sea of common usage on the basis of a condominium which was to extend to all types of natural resources, including those of the seabed. Within the framework of Russia's initial position, each Caspian state could only have a narrow 10-mile littoral strip at its disposal and own exclusive rights to explore and exploit the mineral resources of the seabed within these confines. As for the resources outside this zone, according to the Russian proposal, they were to be in combined ownership and managed by a specially organised Committee in charge of the seabed, consisting of representatives of the five littoral states.

Russia consistently stressed the need to strictly observe the Caspian Sea's legal regime which had been ratified in Treaties between the Russian Federation and Iran (Persia) on 26 February 1921, and the USSR and Iran on 25 March 1940. The Russian side rightly pointed out that extending the application of the 1982 UN Convention on maritime law to the Caspian Sea would entail recognising the Volga-Don and Volga-Baltic channels as international waterways. Moreover, Russia declared this contradicted its laws and also made the Caspian Sea accessible to other states, contrary to Russian interests in the Caspian.

107

The Kazakhstan Way

Had the Russian idea become a reality, the littoral states would have had to renounce their sovereign rights on exploiting the natural resources on most of the seabed contiguous with their territory. What's more, such a decision would have resulted in the closure of the consortiums already in existence and made it harder to attract foreign investment to explore and exploit the Sea's resources. And, finally, I would like to note that the condominium idea would have been hard to carry through as there was no precedent anywhere else. Modern international law proceeds along the lines of dividing the seabed's resources between the countries concerned.

I told the President of Russia, Boris Yeltsin, all about this when I tried to persuade him to change Russia's view on the Caspian Sea's legal status. The first result of our talks was the signing in Almaty on 27 April 1996, of a joint declaration of the Presidents of Russia and Kazakhstan in which both sides recognised the other's rights to conduct works with a view to exploiting mineral and biological resources.

Subsequently, analogous documents were signed by myself and the Presidents of Iran and Azerbaijan confirming the principal elements of the Caspian Sea's legal status and principles of activity at sea.

On 6 July 1998, an agreement was signed by myself and Boris Yeltsin in Moscow on demarcating the seabed of the Caspian Sea's northern section with a view to exercising sovereign rights on mineral resource exploitation. What made this agreement new was principally that the parties undertook to divide the seabed of the Northern Caspian between Kazakhstan and Russia in accordance with a modified middle line, definitively renouncing the idea of a condominium. As a result, on 13 May 2002, a protocol constituting an addendum to this agreement and fixing the coordinates of the modified middle line was signed with incumbent President Putin in Moscow.

Meanwhile Azerbaijan had been staunchly upholding the 'inland sea' option and the need to divide the area of water, seabed and the sea's mineral resources into national sectors with the demarcation lines as state borders. The option they were proposing was an example of so-called rigid demarcation. In this instance serious difficulties would have inevitably arisen in providing normal conditions for trade, navigation and fishing, as well as conserving and rationally exploiting the other bio-resources of the sea, and ecological cooperation.

After taking account of these factors, the Baku leadership gradually came round to Kazakhstan's suggestion, as can be seen from the agreement between Kazakhstan and Azerbaijan on demarcating the Caspian seabed signed on 29 November 2001, by myself and President of Azerbaijan Geidar Aliyev, and its protocol on 27 February 2003. The trilateral agreements between the Republics of Kazakhstan and Azerbaijan and the Russian Federation on the demarcation juncture point of the contiguous sectors of the seabed, signed in Almaty on 14 May 2003, completed the process of demarcating the seabed of the Northern Caspian.

During the visit of the President of Turkmenistan, Saparmurat Niyazov, to Almaty on 27 February 1997, I succeeded in persuading him to sign a joint declaration stating that 'until there is an agreement with the states of the Caspian region on the status of the Caspian Sea the parties will adhere to the demarcation of administrative and territorial boundaries along a middle line'. Thus Ashkhabad also showed solidarity with Kazakhstan and Azerbaijan on the main contentious issue.

Despite this common position adopted by the aforementioned countries, Iran, as a country of the Caspian region, is still insisting on the division of the Caspian Sea into five equal parts (20 per cent of the surface each) between the five states of the Caspian region which would mean changing existing borders. This has made the Convention on the legal status of the Caspian Sea impossible to sign, Iran's goal being to increase its territory at the expense of the region's other countries.

A summit of the heads of Caspian states was held in Ashkhabad in April 2002. An unexpected result was Saparmurat Niyazov's proposal to set up a Council of Presidents of the Caspian countries. His idea had originally come from the Iranian side. The idea behind it was that the Council would sit once a year to resolve issues of concern for the various Caspian countries.

This proposal was decisively turned down by President of Azerbaijan Geidar Aliyev. In the intervals between sittings he informed me that this was their way of turning the issue over to a talking-shop instead of resolving it. He then made the reasonable comment, 'How will it look if you and I are in the same council as Iran when it has had an embargo applied to it by the world community?' Geidar Aliyev was wise, sober-minded, and always calm. I still have the warmest regard for him.

The proposal was also turned down by Kazakhstan, as establishing such an institution would have meant merely replacing the existing practice of multilateral consultations rather than completely solving the issue. We still went ahead and planned the next meeting of the heads of Caspian states, only this time in Tehran.

The concluding document (Declaration) of the heads of Caspian states was not signed principally because of the Irano-Azerbaijani divergence of views. The heads of the Caspian states recognised the need to delimit the Caspian Sea into national sectors along a middle line modified on the basis of separate agreements, with the exception of Iran.

At any rate, the foundations for a successful conclusion to the process have already been laid. Recalling the aphorism that 'war always smells of oil', (originally coined at the turn of the 20th century, ahead of its major geopolitical conflicts), we will keep trying to consolidate the efforts of all the Caspian countries – efforts directed towards making the Caspian a sea of friendship and cooperation.

Such an issue as the Caspian Sea's status should not be resolved in a hurry. I am confident that the process will take maximum account of the interests of all five countries of the region. After all, such relationships have become so significant in the world that the process of economic globalisation has become a mechanism, dictating its own terms in the global market and assigning roles almost like directives to one country or another in the international labour division of labour.

After the first sign of there being incredible oil reserves on the Kazakhstan shelf of the Caspian Sea, most experts and analysts became quite reticent and mainly gave sceptical forecasts. So far these pessimistic forecasts have not been justified. The discovery of the major Kashagan deposit in the Northern Caspian has marked the start of the development of the Kazakhstan sector and finally delineated Kazakhstan's potential place among the world's top oil exporters.

The Battle for the Caspian and the Oil Boom

Kazakhstan's Place on the World Oil Map

One can have lengthy discussions on which comes before the other: politics or economics. However, probably everyone will agree that nowadays oil is an issue where policy is clearly determined by the needs of the economy. And not just by needs, but urgent energy provision issues.

According to all the forecasts and estimates, global demands for oil and other forms of fuel are only going to grow. According to US Government-commissioned research, the US, the world's top oil consumer, currently imports six out of every seven barrels they use, and by 2020, the figure will be even higher. By 2030, China whose rapidly growing economy makes it the world's second largest importer of oil, will require imported oil to cover as much as 80 per cent of its needs.

New centres of economic development are emerging, and also new regions with higher and ever increasing energy needs. According to experts, the most dynamic increase in energy consumption rates is going to be in China, South and East Asia, Africa, and Latin America. What's more, their oil consumption growth will be linked not to their consumption of internally sourced raw materials, but to an increase in crude oil imports from other parts of the world, and this signifies an increase in the global demand for energy.

This, albeit to a lesser extent, also concerns Europe, where hydrocarbon reserves are going to run out, and economic growth of 2-3 per cent per year and the transition to natural gas will guarantee a more moderate increase in the demand for oil. Moreover, it is expected that after 2010, there is going to be a significant slump in the production of hydrocarbons in the basin of the North Sea.

Thus, oil will remain the main source of global energy for at least the next three decades. The need to maintain world stability and economic stimulus for further industrialisation and technological progress relies heavily on new energy sources being found in the countries possessing such natural potential. A careful study of the soaring demand for energy, the impending exhaustion of sources currently being exploited, the deteriorating political situation in the oil-producing regions and the increase in the planet's population appear to show that there is nothing to prevent these countries entering the world community. In fact they can no longer remain on the outside, even if they so wished: the price of 'black gold' is, both literally and figuratively, too high.

All this goes to show that integration is inevitable. However, this certainly does not mean the role every country is to play in the international division of labour has been designated from the very start.

Every country joins the integration process with various kinds of baggage of its own: manpower, industrial and technological capability, cultural wealth or natural resources – or a combination of them all. And taking stock of each of these countries' potential, the world market dictates its terms of acceptance to them. Each has to pay membership dues – contributing what it can to the integration economy at the given time. However, after paying its dues and joining the world market, the new member can either stick to the niche allotted to it by the global economy, or – depending on the extent of its contribution – attempt to radically change its disposition and move a step higher in the hierarchy of national economies.

Given the way things have shaped up, the global economy has already, strictly speaking, decided upon Kazakhstan's membership dues to participate in the integration economy: access for leading international companies' to our natural resources, and, principally, hydrocarbon energy sources and non-ferrous metals.

No wonder, then, that from the very first years of our independence we have devoted very serious attention to the development of the oil and gas sector of our economy in particular. You see, for us oil and gas are not only a fuel energy and strategic resource. They are the fundamental principle that will enable us to deal more quickly with the complexities of the transitional period and make up for the damage caused by the disintegration of the united and integrated Soviet Union.

However, once again let me state that the role we are first due to play in the process of the international division of labour is by no means disastrous and permanent. It is a question of what, in real terms, our transitional economy can offer the world community at the present moment. And it should not be forgotten that our current level of economic relations does not allow us, whatever niche we occupy in the world market, to look for other ways of using our potential.

The Battle for the Caspian and the Oil Boom

I am not afraid to say that objectively our state has virtually unlimited development potential. In order to use this potential and take up a suitable place in the world arena, we first have to comply with a whole series of rules, as well as implementing political reforms.

During the first phase of setting up our economy we made use of our potential to export energy and metals. During the next stage of our development, while relying on the export potential of our natural resources, we shall endeavour to place our economy on a new footing, drawing on high technologies and innovations, a developed processing industry, and the utilisation of raw materials.

But just now we are only completing the first stage of our economic development, a stage when our current and short-term position in the world arena is that of a country oriented towards the export of natural raw materials. This is a reality we would be short-sighted to ignore, if only because Kazakhstan in this respect really does have something to offer the world community.

Thank God this is so, and the world is interested in us. The whole issue for Kazakhstan is solely about making rational use of the resources available, for the good of the country and its people.

Kazakhstan is rich in natural mineral resources, most of which have still to be exploited. No wonder there was a saying in Soviet times to the effect that 'Kazakhstan's resources represent all the elements of the Mendeleyev table.' We haven't developed even a hundredth of all the precious resources underground. At present, our country is twelfth in the world in terms of its confirmed oil reserves (not counting the insufficiently accurate forecasts for Caspian shelf reserves), and fifteenth, in terms of gas and gas condensate. Kazakhstan has approximately 3-4 per cent (not counting the Caspian shelf's energy resources) of known and confirmed global oil reserves. The hydrocarbon reserves of Kazakhstan's continental area presently constitute 2.8 billion tonnes of oil and 1.8 trillion cubic metres of gas.

At the time of declaring its independence in December 1991, Kazakhstan's annual production rate was 25 million tonnes of oil, and around 8 billion cubic metres of gas with relatively large predicted oil and gas reserves. By carrying out our programme to develop the known reserves of the Caspian shelf, we are presently on the way to becoming one of the world's top hydrocarbon producers. Together with the reserves of the Caspian shelf, Kazakhstan's hydrocarbon resources are put at around 12 billion tonnes of crude oil and 2-3 trillion cubic metres of natural gas, deposited in producible sectors with an area in excess of 1.6 million kilometres, in addition to the already available reserves.

> 'A country with a population of 15 million, occupying a vast territory in the Central Asian steppes, Kazakhstan is becoming an increasingly important player in the world energy resources market. With the largest reserves of crude oil in the Caspian region, Kazakhstan produces 1.2 million barrels daily, and exports 1 million. By 2015, the country's government hopes to increase production rates to 3.5 million barrels daily, thus equalling Iran's output. American and Russian companies, and these countries' governments, are vying for access to Kazakhstan oil.'
>
> Peter Baker, *The Washington Post*, USA, 29 August, 2006

All this goes to show the promising prospects of the economy's oil sector, and also, therefore, Kazakhstan's capability in taking up a quite prominent position in the world energy-resource club. Thus, I believe that in the near future the Kazakhstan oil sector will be able to play a major role in world economic development in both economic and political relations.

Kazakhstan now has a relatively well-developed infrastructure for the transportation of oil and gas from the production areas to pipeline systems able to secure the onward export of hydrocarbons. The Caspian Pipeline Consortium (CPC) is one of the major pipeline providers.

The Caspian Pipeline Consortium was created to construct and operate the Tengiz-Novorossiysk pipeline, which has a total length of 1,510 kilometres. The aim of this project is to transport crude oil from Russia and Western Kazakhstan and export it through the new sea terminal on the north-eastern Black Sea shore.

The Consortium was initially founded in 1992 by the governments of Kazakhstan, the Sultanate of Oman and, sub-sequently, Russia. In 1996, we were joined by a number of private oil companies operating the development programme of the Kazakhstan sector of the Caspian Sea. 2001 saw the commissioning of the first phase of the pipeline, capable of carrying a total of 28 million tonnes of oil per year. Oil was first pumped into the CPC pipeline on 26 March 2001, and a trial loading of the first tanker was carried out at the CPC terminal in October of the same year.

The idea of constructing the Tengiz-Novorossiysk pipeline came about at the beginning of the 1990s. After the disintegration of the Soviet Union, Kazakhstan's vast oil reserves were land-locked as the country did not have an outlet to the ocean. The route across Russia was selected because preliminary estimates had shown it to be the shortest and least expensive development option. Top-level talks were held with Russia from 1994 onwards. It took six years to talk the Russian side round to building the oil pipeline.

All in all, one could write a separate book about the numerous talks with Russian Prime Minister Viktor Chernomyrdin, the leaders of the Russian Federation Ministry of Oil and Gas, and, finally, with Boris Yeltsin himself. One day our Prime Minister Nurlan Balgimbayev came to us and said, 'That's it! Totally rejected and sabotaged! I reckon the issue's never going to be resolved.' I entrusted him with drawing up a brief, clear summary that anyone could understand, clearly setting out all the figures and showing how much money Russia would be losing in terms of potential earnings from the transportation of oil across its territory in the event of its refusal to take part in the pipeline construction project.

Boris Yeltsin was in the Kremlin hospital at the time. I visited him there and after a two-hour conversation the deal was done.

The first agreement on the pipeline consortium was signed by representatives of the Republic of Kazakhstan and Sultanate of Oman in Bermuda on 17 June 1992. The Russian Federation joined up to it at a later date. The agreement stipulated that Russia and Kazakhstan would hand over all their existing pipeline assets to the consortium and Oman would finance the project. The parties would have an equal shareholding in the consortium. Oman, however, was unable to attract sufficient finance. The technical and economic feasibility study of the investment project, drawn up in 1995 by a Russian Federation state-run team of experts, was dispatched for revision. The main problem was that the agreement was being drawn up at an inter-state level, without account being taken for the privatisation process only just under way and, consequently, the interests of the main companies in charge of oil production in the Caspian. This was also evident when the European Bank for Reconstruction and Development refused to provide Oman with finance guarantees for the project.

At that moment in time neither Russia nor Kazakhstan had an adequate legal base for carrying through a project of such a kind. First and foremost, there was the issue of free currency circulation, without which the project's financing could not be opened. On 19 April 1997, I signed the Decree *On the Caspian Pipeline Consortium* pertaining to the issues of the project's currency regulation. Following on from it, a similar decree was signed by Boris Yeltsin on 24 April. These decrees had the desired effect, but a whole series of normative legal acts then had to be enacted for the consortium to function properly in both countries.

Our Karachaganak, which celebrated its 25th anniversary in 2004, is one of the world's top oil and gas condense deposits, with reserves totalling over 1.2 billion tonnes of liquid hydrocarbons and over 1.3 trillion cubic metres of gas. Production got under way in the oilfield in 1979, five years after its opening. However, it was unable to function and develop self-sufficiently as it relied totally on the processing capacity of the Orenburg Gas Processing Plant (OGPP), to which it was linked by a 130-kilometre-long pipeline.

After gaining independence, Karachaganak, along with its problems relating to hydrocarbon processing and transportation, also had to contend with very serious ecological challenges such as oil pollution caused by accidents at the wells, the so-called 'Lira objectives' – six cavities made by underground nuclear explosions in Soviet times for condensate storage – as well as derelict warehouses full of drilling detritus and derricks.

Considerable investment was needed to eradicate these problems and proceed with the project's development. In 1992, the Republic's government announced a competition to encourage top foreign oil companies to tender for the right to develop the Karachaganak field. As a result, an Agreement on the Principles governing the Division of the Production output (APDP) was signed in March 1995 between the Republic of Kazakhstan and an Agip-British Gas alliance.

Within the term of this Agreement, from March 1995 to the end of 1997, US$293.5 million were spent on the project's development. After the signing of the Treaty on the Caspian Pipeline Consortium's reorganisation and other documents relating to it in

The Battle for the Caspian and the Oil Boom

December 1996, there appeared genuine prospects for the setting up of an effective transport system which would allow the export of hydrocarbons from Karachaganak to international markets. It also gave impetus to the process of preparing the Definitive Agreement on the Division of Output (DADO) for signature. During the course of the talks between representatives of the contractor and the Republic's ministries and departments, a definitive draft agreement was drawn up and then signed in November 1997, coming into force on 27 January 1998, with a 40-year term.

The Kashagan field in the North Caspian was also declared to be another of the largest oil deposits discovered over the past 30 years. Its extractable reserves are put at 10 billion barrels. The opening of this field has put Kazakhstan alongside the world's top-ranking countries in possession of significant hydrocarbon resources. The discovery of such large-scale oil reserves has attracted the entire world's huge interest in the Caspian region and increased its investment attractiveness.

In order to proceed with a survey of the oil and gas potential of the Kazakhstan sector of the Caspian, the decision was taken in 1993 to establish an international consortium. Mindful of the complex technical conditions involved in working in the Caspian and the high demands on the ecology, a careful selection of oil companies was made during the initial stages of choosing the membership of the first maritime consortium. These included companies with the most advanced technical and technological expertise in working in complex fields and meeting the most stringent ecological demands: British Petroleum/Statoil (Great Britain/Norway), British Gas (Great Britain), Shell (Netherlands), Agip (Italy), Mobil (USA) and Total (France).

The Consortium's principal responsibilities were to conduct geological and geophysical exploration and ecological monitoring; calculate the impact of the geological and geophysical works on the environment; develop the Caspian region's industrial and social infrastructure, train Kazakhstani specialists; and finance scientific research projects. The overall investment in the international Consortium's works programme was in excess of US$218 million.

It was thanks to our oil and gas sector that we have been able to carry through our initial economic development. In the future, it will be essential for us to develop complementary sectors and transfer the economic centre of gravity to them, turning them into the driving force of our economic growth.

'Black Gold' – an Asset or a Curse?

Since the 1990s the Caspian basin has been one of the most important regional hubs of multilateral relations where many countries' economic and geopolitical interests have begun to intersect. This explains the acute – sometimes apparent and at other times concealed – diplomatic struggle for influence on the countries of the Caspian region.

Kazakhstan had to put up with stiff competition in the region while at the same time creating its institutions of state power. We now have a highly professional foreign policy department, a mobile, modern army, and our own experts in key areas. But at that time we had none of these, nor any experience of conducting major international talks.

> 'Central Asia where the Great Game for supremacy was conducted in the 19th century between the British Empire and Tsarist Russia, is now, thanks to its oil and gas resources, becoming the first strategic battlefield of the "multipolar era" between the US, China and Moscow.
> China (currently increasing in global importance), Russia (awash with oil), and the US have locked horns in their struggle for resources and influence in Central Asia, a region which has regained its global strategic importance after five of its states gained independence from the Soviet Union in 1991. Central Asia is becoming a strategic battlefield.'
> Frederick Kempe, *The Wall Street Journal*, USA, 16 May 2006

The oil industry itself has been transformed since independence. The challenges facing the state in the oil sector have grown more complex. Thus the State Development Programme for the Caspian Sea's Kazakhstan sector until 2015 sets out two fundamental goals to be achieved by the oil industry. Firstly, to develop oil production operations and set up the best possible network of oil pipelines.

Secondly, to create our own oil-refining and oil-chemical industry. This programme was the logical continuation of the first phase of implementing the State Development Programme for the Caspian's Kazakhstan Sector, approved in 1993.

Our policy to get our oil and gas resources into global economic circulation currently consists of attracting foreign oil companies to explore, produce and develop the oil and gas deposits. Foreign investors are expected on fixed terms not only to provide adequate financial backing to develop the oil and gas works, but also to organise their production, refining and transportation, from start to finish.

Thanks to Kazakhstan having earned a reputation for being a reliable and predictable investment object, we can present our demands to foreign investors. We have won international authority and our own credit history, and it is therefore quite natural that our wishes are met with understanding by our foreign partners.

'It's a natural process. Kazakhstan has grown strong and wants to get real revenues from its natural resources. And if we want to keep working successfully from now on, we must do so by devising compromises in respect of the fiscal regime for the new oil and gas projects.'

From the speech of General Manager of ExxonMobil Kazakhstan Inc. James Taylor

at the 11th plenary meeting of the Council of Foreign Investors, Kenderley,

5 June, 2004

According to Chevron experts, once the Caspian Pipeline Consortium is working at full capacity, Kazakhstan oil will start successfully competing on the Mediterranean, and Northern and Western European markets. We will be able to move into the North American markets by using tankers with a 200,000-tonne capacity. And, of course, the Atyrau-Samara pipeline with a capacity of 15m tonnes per year will allow us to move into the markets of Eastern and Central Europe and the countries around the Baltic Sea.

At the same time, we should not limit our development to already existing directions. Kazakhstan is going to adhere to a multi-vectorial strategy in respect of hydrocarbon exports and investigate a variety of projects to develop arterial systems for the transportation of oil. We are now actively working on other pipeline systems. Discussions are taking place on the pros and cons of the Aktau-Baku-Ceyhan and Kazakhstan-Turkmenistan-Iran projects. And the Atasu-Alashankou project is already under way.

An agreement between China's and Kazakhstan's national oil companies to embark on the construction of an oil pipeline was signed during my visit to China, in May 2004. The pipeline construction work started on 28 September of the same year when the first joint was welded. And the first oil from Kazakhstan reached China on 25 May 2006. We will be able to export as much as 20 million tonnes per year via this arterial oil pipeline linking Atasu (Kazakhstan) and the border point of Alashankou (China). It was also envisaged for this pipeline to form the basis of a larger project – a 3,000-kilometre long pipeline from the Caspian to China.

With all this in mind, it should be stressed that the feasibility of these projects is going to depend in many aspects on the state of the global energy supplies market and actual results of the oil and gas deposit development projects on the Caspian shelf.

When speaking now of Kazakhstan's successes in this area, one simply has to say that oil wealth has been the key to our economic success. Some may regard this as a pretext for a subjective appraisal of Kazakhstan's successes and, possibly, a subject to arouse envy.

And yet, world history shows that oil can damage a state's economy and general development. Suffice it to say that of the 36 states classified as low-income and high-debt countries, 27 are mineral resources exporters.

That's why, paradoxical as it may sound, a profusion of oil dollars brings with it potential danger in the form of increased public spending. Take, for instance, countries like Nigeria, Venezuela and Saudi Arabia, where public spending increased precisely because of the influx of oil sales revenues. The present king of Saudi Arabia told me during our meeting in 2004 that he is now getting Arabs to do the work previously done by foreigners. After all the state benefits they had received, the Arabs had got out of the habit of working. The benefits have now been halted because they pampered the nation and engendered parasites.

A similar strategy to increase state public spending was adopted, in particular, in Venezuela and Nigeria in the mid-1970s. With a view to creating social prosperity, these countries opted for a sharp increase in spending in the state budget (to an average of 74.5 per cent and 32.2 per cent, respectively). This increase had been made possible by substantial oil sales revenues. Increased spending certainly helped expand their employment structure, service and goods sectors, subsidise consumption and housing construction, and reduce taxes. But when oil prices subsequently stagnated, state spending started to exceed their oil-export revenue.

Foreign loans were then taken to continue financing the social programmes and that, in turn, led to an increase in foreign debts. In the period between 1976 and 1982 alone, the average annual increase in these countries' debts was 45 per cent. It was this misguided and short-sighted decision-making of politicians that brought about a deficit in the payment balance and budget, virtually bankrupting the state and causing increased social tension. The abundance of free money has led to a decline in these countries' competitiveness and economic dynamism and this, in turn, has resulted in their continued dependence on oil exports.

Even Norway with its diversified economy increased public spending as a result of discovering oil in the North Sea, and then encountered the problem of 'Dutch disease'.

On the other hand, in countries of the East Asian region, and particularly Japan, the lack of natural resources has actually forced the bureaucratic elite to wake up to their country's vulnerability. Fear of losing economic and, consequently, political independence has jolted them into focusing their efforts on the country's domestic potential earnings from competitive, exportable goods.

We must therefore bear in mind that oil sales earnings are not a stable source of state income and may in the future lead to a whole range of other difficulties, such as the infamous 'Dutch disease' and the elementary unsustainability of resources. I know countries with precisely these characteristics.

Incidentally, as far as Kazakhstan's rich reserves are concerned, one should not be dazzled by the incredible-sounding figures. Yes, our reserves are confidence-inspiring, but given the constant increase in world oil consumption rates, how long is our future really secure with them? For instance, according to data from British Petroleum's annual company report 'World Energy 2005', based on current production rates and oil prices, world supplies are expected to last another 40 years. What's more, Russia's oil is expected to last for just over 21 years. Saudi Arabia, a kind of oil World Central Bank, has another 42 years' of oil supplies. Iran has supplies for another 89 years. According to this same report, given the large reserve levels and its relatively low current production rates, Kazakhstan's supplies should last another 83 years. But an increase in production rates would quickly bring the number of years down.

It is essential for Kazakhstan to learn to live without the oil dollars and not get hooked on them. It's very important not to give in to the temptation of spending funds not generated by production and automatically raising wages instead of economising for a rainy day. The National Fund set up back in 2000 with precisely these functions in mind is one of the main instruments for tying up excess liquid assets and reducing inflationary pressure.

On 1 November 2006, the assets of the National Fund of the Republic of Kazakhstan were in excess of US$12 billion, in absolute terms consisting of 1,586 billion tenge. The highest percentage of Fund revenues were from the above-plan revenues of organisations in the raw-materials sector. It is worth mentioning that the Russian Federation's Stabilisation Fund was set up on 1 January 2004, following the example of our National Fund.

I would also like to say a few words about the fact that the National Fund really can be called the 'fund of future generations' in so far as, by selling oil, our mineral wealth which also belongs to our children, we do not have the right to waste it on some kind of short-lived measures and on sorting out present-day problems. We can only spend part of these funds on domestic construction and development programmes, refurbishing the home we are leaving to our children and grandchildren.

In the next few years, for instance, Kazakhstan needs to invest heavily in its infrastructure, primarily, in the north-west and south-west. We must complete the Western ring road from Kyzylorda to Aktau and Atyrau, and from Uralsk to Aktiubinsk. The strategy adopted in the country to develop transport and communications envisages the construction of highways from the European part of Russia through the west, south and north of Kazakhstan as far as China. Railways are to link Western Kazakhstan and China. Reconstruction and building work are to be carried out on airports, electricity lines and stations.

The Battle for the Caspian and the Oil Boom

By increasing transport mobility in the regions, we shall be able to bring our people even closer together. We shall also be able to give the people and businesses of these regions proper access to the country's financial and educational centres such as Almaty, to the industrial developments of Central and Eastern Kazakhstan, to the agricultural heartlands of Southern and Northern Kazakhstan. And so, if intelligently and prudently invested, the oil revenues will enable the country to become stronger and more cohesive.

All these measures will make it possible in the very near future to regulate the output of the competitive goods and services essential for the massive-scale development of the Caspian shelf. In the long-term we will be switching to, and efficiently using, hydrocarbon raw materials and developing the oil and chemical industries as a whole. When the concomitant infrastructure development programme of our ports, airports and terminals gets under way, Kazakhstan will advance onto a new growth trajectory where oil will be financing the development of high-technology products.

A number of documents have been drawn up with a view to further increasing this potential, including the aforementioned 'State Development Programme for the Kazakhstan sector of the Caspian Sea', which envisages creating the right conditions for the comprehensive development of the Caspian shelf. The objective elaborated in 'The Strategy for industrial and innovatory development until 2015', which I approved in August 2003, is to achieve the country's steady development by diversifying the economy, moving away from its emphasis on raw materials orientation, and doing the groundwork for the eventual transfer to a service and technology economy.

I can already state that we are successfully moving in this direction. However, looking back to the first years of independence, not everything went so smoothly. In those days we had to hold talks independently with trans-national oil companies headed by the sharks of the oil business. We urgently needed new ideas, approaches and, most importantly, personnel unencumbered by old Communist party methods of working. But in those days they were pitifully few and far between. This was why I sought gradually to replace the old guard with young managers. However, I admit this was no easy task for me, and I had my doubts. But I could see no other way out.

Mindful of the importance of the oil and gas sector, at a time when we were involved in active talks with investors, I put forward a proposal to Parliament concerning the appointment of Nurlan Balgimbayev, the incumbent Minister of Oil and Gas, an experienced oil professional and energetic personality, to the post of Prime Minister. His contribution to getting the above-mentioned works done in the initial stages of the Caspian Pipeline Consortium's construction programme was considerable. Unfortunately, he was in office when the crisis struck South-East Asia and there was a decline in living standards, and he had no alternative but to resign.

Over the years a new generation of oil professionals has grown up before my very eyes. Many of our personnel have worked at oil companies with global names and studied at the top institutions of learning of the oil business, studying foreign languages and gaining excellent management skills. I personally have had a hand in their education, mentoring them in every possible way. As a result, many of them have gone on to senior state positions.

Thanks to the oil resources available and large number of oil companies wanting to develop them, we have all gained plenty of experience of holding talks. As far as this is concerned, here is one piece of advice I want to give our newly appointed managers. While your opposite number in any talks tries to anticipate your next move, he will be thinking about how to change or even neutralise your plan of action. It is very important to devote attention to details during the talks but without getting in their thrall. Any number of minor victories may be overturned by one major defeat. Our financial dependency on Russia at the turn of the 1990s might have been just such a major defeat.

The introduction of our national currency, the tenge, heralded one of Kazakhstan's first major victories. Exactly how we succeeded in defending our financial independence will be explained in the next chapter.

4

THE TENGE – SYMBOL OF OUR INDEPENDENCE

The Economic Crisis of the 1990s

One morning in June 1989, a week after being elected First Secretary of the Kazakhstan Communist Party's Central Committee, I flew to the city of Karaganda with a group of members of the Kazakhstan SSR Council of Ministers. As our government plane taxied towards its stand, I caught sight of the Karaganda district's top officials waiting by the gangway to greet us. The tension that had gripped the city for the past week was visible in their grim expressions. The entire Soviet Union had been caught up in the miners' strikes, and Karaganda was the latest city where the miners had walked out. In those days, all the mining in Kazakhstan was under the USSR Ministry of the Coal Industry, and so Moscow had to deal with any problems, while the republic was rarely called upon to intervene. The day before, however, I had received a phone call from Mikhail Gorbachev informing me that my intervention was needed to smooth things over there.

Karaganda is a city very close to my heart. It is where I started my career. The republic's industrial centre developed and expanded right before my eyes. I personally knew virtually all the directors and chief engineers of the city's enterprises. You could say that the Karaganda district was a miniature replica of Kazakhstan. A great many circumstances had contributed to its becoming the home and workplace of people of nearly all the republic's nationalities. Mining is such a tough job that over time it forges high-principled, strong characters. With its onerous past, multi-national Karaganda – home and workplace of many political prisoners and their descendants – had nurtured numerous outstanding, strong characters. After the events of 1986, aware that any serious discontent in Karaganda might spread throughout the republic, we were doing our uttermost to protect fragile inter-national concord.

125

The Kazakhstan Way

Pondering over the causes of the strike, I had already made my mind up on the plane that we would drive straight to the square where the miners were holding meetings. Directly after our arrival we had a short meeting at the airport and listened to the local party leaders' disturbing reports. First Secretary of the Karaganda party's district committee Lokotunin suggested going to the residence where I would be staying. The crowd of miners was apparently very agitated and it would be best to wait for the representatives from Moscow. I particularly remember him saying, 'Who knows what the miners may get up to next! Let's wait till they've calmed down a bit and maybe dispersed to their homes.' Sensing that it was going to involve more than just a simple meeting, I insisted on going straight to the square without calling in at the district administration headquarters on the way.

In the very centre of the city, in Sovietsky Prospekt, we were awaited by a large crowd of disgruntled and angry miners. Exhausted after long hours of meetings, many of them were sitting silently in their mining overalls, just their eyes shining out of their grimy faces, as they banged their helmets on the tarmac. Some of them had come here straight from the coal face, and the soot on their faces added to the grimness and tension of the meeting. The atmosphere was extremely strained and the scene alarming. The miners' trade-union leaders were refusing to negotiate with the district's leadership and demanding Nazarbayev in person. So here I was, going straight to the meeting in person.

They moved back to let me walk through to the rigged-up wooden stage. I answered their questions for several hours. We started the discussion with the basics. The main causes of the strike were the non-payment of wages, a consequence of not sending off the raw materials, and no coal meant no money, failure to provide safe working conditions and empty shop shelves. To channel the talks in a useful direction, I asked the miners to choose their own representatives. The talks then moved to the Karaganda coal works administration headquarters, where they continued until the next morning in the presence of the ministers responsible. By then, at my request, Vice Chairman of the USSR Council of Ministers Doguzhiyev and Minister of the Coal Industry Minister Shadov had arrived.

During the many hours of talks we managed to come to a compromise and satisfy the most pressing demands of the miners' collectives. Similar talks were going on in all the mining towns of the Karaganda district – Shakhtinsk, Saranya, Abai.

The strikes were stopped. Subsequently, Moscow asked for a detailed report of the talks so that the Kazakhstan method could be used in other regions of the Soviet Union. It could hardly be called a 'method'. To tell the truth, given the tense situation, I had expected worse, because all the new enterprises in the USSR that used our coal were halting production.

However, despite all the Kazakhstanis' patience during these dreadful ordeals, the discontent among the workers' collectives throughout the country continued to grow. Although we managed to sort out the conflict with the miners fairly quickly, it was clear we were hostages to the developing situation.

The situation worsened with every passing year. The Soviet Union was ineluctably moving towards disintegration. First the putsch of 19 August, then the Belovezhskoye Agreement between Russia, Ukraine and Belorussia made the disintegration of the USSR inevitable. But that is a separate subject.

The next two years were terrible for us. In 1992, the country's economy went completely off the rails because of hyperinflation, the prevailing non-payment of wages and pensions, the cessation of commercial ties between enterprises, the shortages of consumer goods and cash. All these matters had been overseen from the centre by the Union ministries which had now ceased to exist. A whole series of linked mutual settlements and goods supplies were lost. Now it is hard to imagine the empty shop shelves and huge queues for bread, baby food, salt, sugar and cigarettes, but back then it was a bitter reality.

The break in financial links and interaction between the former Union republics made the economic situation even more complex and this, naturally, began to have an impact on ordinary people's lives. The failure to resolve problems and the shortages of cash in Kazakhstan resulted in delays in the payment of wages and pensions, and so on. The reason for the shortage of cash was the State Bank of Russia, Gosbank, being in charge of issuing roubles, and, strictly speaking, all financial resources being allocated only from Moscow.

I repeatedly asked Moscow to increase the amounts of cash we were being allocated to a level that would enable us to at least partially resolve the problem. In response I received assurances that the matter would be settled as soon as possible. However, our petitions often went unnoticed. And the high inflation rate in those days meant that by the time the delayed wages were paid out, they had already lost part of their value. With every passing day the problems continued growing like weeds, and we had to work flatout.

All this caused social instability among most of the population which, in turn, resulted in strikes and demonstrations. I often had to go out to towns and *auls* and pacify people and explain what was going on. I called upon people to be patient and spoke of the measures that were being adopted and about the difficulties that lay ahead. People had faith in me. I always tried to carry out all my promises. It was essential to carefully pick the right words and even intonation in conversations with people, especially at that difficult time when the 'great common homeland' was disintegrating before our very eyes. Everyone's nerves were at breaking point.

Sometimes I recall how people would first start yelling and kicking up a fuss and then gradually begin listening to my explanations. Once they had begun to understand what the problem was and how we were tackling these issues, they slowly calmed down. And someone would shout from the crowd, 'Nursultan Abishevich, got any cigarettes?' I did not smoke but I always kept a packet of cigarettes on me for such occasions. Then I started taking more cigarettes with me so that I could hand them out during my conversations with people. There was a bizarre period when cigarettes were being sold in metre lengths because the factories had run out of cardboard packaging. It's amusing to recall it now but what could be done then? Sometimes handing out cigarettes really defused the tension and our conversation eventually served some good.

We had to buy money in Russia to pay wages, pensions, and benefits. Until the first half of 1992 we received money from the Central Bank of Russia free of charge. However, once the budgets were divided up, we ended up having to purchase it. But as Kazakhstan did not have sufficient funds in its budget for these purchases, money at once became a deficit commodity in the country. We borrowed roubles (you could say, on credit) and then Russia announced we were US$1.5 billion in arrears with repayments to them. Only in the course of the settlements over the Baikonur Cosmodrome several years later were we able to write this debt off.

The payment system functioned through the single channel of a correspondent account at the National Bank of Kazakhstan in Moscow. Kazakhstan would send its payment documents to the National Bank in Almaty, as it did not have a single commercial bank linked up to the foreign banking system. And although there were about 200 commercial banks in the country, they were all small and none was represented in Moscow or the other Union republics. They did not even have correspondent accounts at Moscow's commercial banks. Payments between Kazakhstan and Russia ceased almost completely on account of there being no links between them. There were instances when it took over half a year for transfers and payments to go through. After running smoothly for decades, this payment system fell apart almost instantly. The entire burden of the transfer system was handed over to the National Bank, which could not yet cope with all the inter-republican and international settlements.

But life still went on. The supplies of equipment and goods kept going and the sums involved were vast. Piles of correspondence from all over Kazakhstan kept arriving at the National Bank's head office with requests for transfers, but it was very difficult to stem this flow. All inter-state settlements of the countries of the former USSR were paid in roubles, and monetary and credit policy was entirely the responsibility of the Central Bank of Russia and Ministry of Finance.

Not only payments but also the entire savings system of the Soviet Union was totally focused on Moscow. All savings accounts in the Savings Bank (Sberbank) were kept at the USSR Central Savings Bank there. In other words, all the money we put in Sberbank was immediately taken away to the capital. Whenever people wanted to withdraw savings, the required amount had to be requested from Moscow. That's why the people who lost their savings at the time should realise that the money that went missing from their accounts had remained in Moscow instead of being returned to Kazakhstan. The Government of Kazakhstan had nothing to do with it. And so, failing to get our citizens' savings back from Moscow, we were forced to cancel these debts ourselves.

Russia's Reformers

As part of the Soviet Union, we could not remain detached from the events taking place in Moscow. Even before the August putsch of 1991, the antagonism between the Union and Russian governments was incandescent. The Baltic republics and Ukraine were pouring oil onto the flames by refusing to transfer their taxes to the Union budget and embarking on independent economic development programmes instead. What's more, it was evident that the Union ministries and departments were in a state of utter turmoil, and all functioning in an inadequate, uncoordinated manner.

'By the time the USSR disintegrated, its foreign debt in convertible currency had risen to US$76 billion, its domestic hard currency debt to US$5.6 billion, and debt in clearing operations had reached US$29 billion. Its gold and currency reserves had declined sharply, and for the first time in the state's history its gold reserve had dropped below 3000 tonnes (289.6 tonnes on 1 January 1992). In the ten months of 1992, the shortfall between currency receipts from centralised exports and payments for centralised imports and clearance of foreign debt amounted to US$10.6 billion. To cover this deficit, the last Union government sold part of its gold reserve for US$3.4 billion and spent a total of US$5.5 billion of the hard currency funds of its enterprises, organisations and local authorities deposited at the USSR Vnesheconombank.

The republics of the former USSR began introducing virtual substitutes for money (coupons, purchasers' cards, multiple-use vouchers and so on) and in a number of cases (Ukraine, Estonia, Latvia, Lithuania) preparing to introduce national currencies. This increased the money mass in circulation and pushed it out into the territory of Russia, aggravating the complex financial situation there.

Virtually all types of goods were in short supply. There was a sharp deterioration in the correlation between people's cash savings and stocks of goods (five times that of 1970 and over double that of 1985). The stocks of goods in the retail trade reached an all-time low.

The total paralysis of all management groups and systems

resulted in the virtual collapse of food supplies. Thus, in January 1992, grain resources (excluding imports) amounted to approximately 3 million tonnes, whereas the country consumed 5 million tonnes of food per month.

Meanwhile, ships carrying imported grain stood waiting to be unloaded in Russia's ports because of a shortage of hard currency to pay for the transportation and shipping freight. Lines of credit were not opened because over recent years the former USSR's reputation as a first-class borrower had been totally undermined.

A strict rationing system was introduced in towns all over the country. The shops were restocked with all the basics like meat products, animal and vegetable oils, cereals, pasta, sugar, salt, matches, alcoholic beverages, cheese, dairy produce, tobacco and confectionery and so on.

In most cases, by the end of 1991, the monthly food allocation per person was as follows: one kilogram of sugar, half a kilogramme of meat products (including pre-cooked products), and 200 grams of butter. And even these allocations exceeded resources and supplies were not guaranteed; coupons were exchanged for goods only every few months, and that involved waiting in huge queues...'
Economic Policy Essays of Post-Communist Russia (1991-97), 1998.

The Russian Soviet Federative Socialist Republic (RSFSR) Government looked more energetic against the backdrop of the dwindling Union apparatus. However, it also lacked inner unity, as the subsequent events of autumn 1993 and the first Chechen war in 1994 were to prove. A wave of populism and demagogy in the RSFSR Supreme Soviet brought into Government a hotchpotch of politicians and economists of the most diverse views. There, too, you came across rampant monetarists who relied on the 'market's invisible hand', and outright nationalists who believed Russia would regain its former might as soon as it had rid itself of the 'subsidised' republics which were putting a 'serious additional strain on the economy undermining its [Russia's] scope for social and economic regeneration'.

At that time two rival programmes stood out among the great many strategies and other programmes the Moscow academic establishment is still famous for: the '500-Day Programme' of Grigory Yavlinsky's group and Yegor Gaidar's *Strategy of Russia in the transitional period*, later known as *Programme 91*.

The '500-Days Programme' was the first in what is now the former USSR to introduce the principle of an individual's right to private ownership. The programme acknowledged the right to free economic activity, the growth of incomes and social guarantees. The entrepreneur was declared to be the economy's cornerstone. The republics' right to economic sovereignty was also acknowledged. The concept of an integral economic space was introduced for the first time.

What made Yavlinsky's programme stand out was that it was oriented towards the preservation of the Union. The republics' economic sovereignty may have been acknowledged but mutual relations were based on the equal rights of the centre and republics. The preservation of a single hard currency union was envisaged while the Union budget was to be formed on the basis of per capita GNP.

The programme's ideas and optimism made quite an impression on Kazakhstanis. Mindful of the internal political situation and state of the economy, I expressed my support for the Union being reformed as a confederation of independent republics. While the programme was still being developed, we incorporated numerous means and ways of interacting with the centre within the ideology of a broad-based independent engaged republic. Grigory Yavlinsky had also been appointed Deputy Leader of Russia's Government as my economic adviser. During 1991-92, his group worked productively with the Kazakh SSR's Cabinet of Ministers. They were professionals, and I have to say they helped us to plan our course of action amidst the general chaos.

The programme of Gaidar's Institute of Economic Policy primarily envisaged Russia's political and economic independence from the other republics. Gaidar's group confidently based their arguments on the fact that Russia, as the 'leader of economic reform in the territory of the former USSR', should carry out independent, rapid and comprehensive reforms and 'the other republics could not help but follow suit later.'

They openly put the interests of Russia's economic development before preserving the Union. Clearly, they could not have conducted such a policy without Boris Yeltsin's support. You see, it was envisaged from the very start that Russia would have an independent monetary policy, its own national currency, own pricing, fiscal and budgetary policy. In their opinion, the principles and mechanisms, both existing and planned, of Union relations had no future. Independent reforms meant a whole plethora of inter-republican problems and the complex process of coordinating the republics' interests could be ignored. Kazakhstan's aspiration to preserve the Union on a confederate basis was regarded as an opportunity to regenerate its economy at Russia's expense.

'In simplified terms, the republics' interests were served by the template of "an economic union coupled with immediate political independence," which essentially meant socialising Russia's financial and economic resources and privatising the Union's political and legislative legacy. And Russia's interests were served by the template of "achieving economic independence as rapidly as possibly while preserving political union during the transitional period."

In political and economic terms, the very logic behind the said stage in recent history made Russia the leader of economic reform in the territory of the former USSR. Russia possesses the overwhelming share of the former USSR's export potential, and so only it can take responsibility for the foreign debt, which therefore enables it to lay claim to the gold and hard currency reserves, property abroad and foreign states' debt to the Soviet Union. Russia was becoming a natural leading partner of the Western states and international financial organisations.

Russia has a highly capacious domestic market, and potential to export material resources easily reoriented to developing countries. This binds to it the foreign economic policy of the other republics, which mostly do not have such potential. Finally, Russia controls the basic components of the inter-republican production infrastructure, possesses the material base and human resources, and is in charge of the transport, communication and energy systems.

The programme of Gaidar's Institute of Economic Policy primarily envisaged limiting the redistribution of resources from Russia by directly financing the army, Ministry of the Interior and other major Union structures and introducing Russia's control over money circulation during the transition to a convertible rouble, and a request was made to support it as the Russian national currency.'

ibid

Unlike Yavlinsky, who proposed gradually forming market relations by step-by-step privatisation and demonopolisation and only then economic liberalisation, Gaidar's programme envisaged 'implementing the full-scale liberalisation of prices and simultaneously introducing a powerful mechanism for macro-economic stabilisation, the basic element of which would be the introduction of the convertible rouble, severing non-Russian currency-supply sources.'

The views expressed by Gaidar and his group had to do with the 'neo-liberalism' that was becoming increasingly popular at the time. I shall now digress briefly. As a leading ideology laying claim to global domination, neo-liberalism began getting more popular with the so-called 'right-wingers' return' – Margaret Thatcher's and Ronald Reagan's electoral successes in Britain and the USA respectively. At the time, the West's leading industrial countries were going through a crisis caused by low economic growth and high inflation. There were obvious problems in the economy connected with the state's inefficiency and the need to reject the concept of the 'universally respected state'. Mindful of this, the right-wingers proposed introducing the so-called 'less state, more market' principle. In other words, the market was regarded as a system that regulated everything itself without any state intervention: everything took shape of its own accord as long as the processes of market self-regulation were not prevented from developing.

After certain reforms had been tried and tested in the West, the ideas of neo-liberalism were transferred to the developing countries of Africa and Latin America via international financial institutions and within the framework of financial aid. One of the conditions for receiving loans was that these countries had to accept a set of prescriptions that included privatisation, reconstruction, optimisation and the state's greatly reduced role in economic regulation.

The Tenge – Symbol of Our Independence

To be fair, it should be said that the effectiveness of these recommendations differed from one country to another. For instance, the African and Latin American countries that had turned their backs on state regulation and opted for economic freedom were unable to secure an acceptable level of social and economic development in their regions. On the other hand, the state's active intervention in the activities of business concerns in the countries of Europe, North America and the Middle East has allowed these countries to provide their citizens with quite a decent standard of living on the basis of rapid economic growth.

In the early 1990s, neo-liberalism quickly filled the ideological vacuum that had developed after the disintegration of the USSR. In the throes of an economic crisis, the former socialist states welcomed these ideas of liberalism as the panacea for all their problems. The practical implementation of the Washington Consensus, in many ways, owed its success to the fact that it had been supported by leading financial organisations such as the IMF, World Bank, US International Development Agency and Inter-American Development Bank – all, in fact, US-controlled. In view of this and a swathe of other reasons (dependency on IMF loans, inexperience, insufficient skills and so on), the prescriptions of the Washington Consensus were all adopted to some extent or other by these countries.

The result of this idea being taken up by politicians of a number of countries, particularly Russia, was that reforms became intensive. A leading role in carrying these neo-liberal reforms out in post-Soviet space was played by the so-called 'Chicago kids' – young liberals like Gaidar who had studied at the University of Chicago, a kind of propagator of neo-liberalism. They totally agreed with the theses of neo-liberal advocates Friedrich von Hayek and Milton Friedman on the market mechanism's capacity for self-regulation and inherent stability, and fluctuations being only due to state intervention.

On 12 June 1990, over a year before the disintegration of the USSR, Russia declared its sovereignty. From whom? The USSR and the Union republics. Who else, after all? That moment marked the actual start of the vast country's collapse. In June 1992, the first President of Russia Boris Yeltsin appointed his economic adviser Yegor Gaidar Acting Chairman of the Government of the Russian

Federation. That's just how definitively the die was cast on Russia's political and economic independence. The next step should have been Gaidar's confirmation as Prime Minister, after he had gained the Supreme Soviet deputies' support. However, the situation in Russia was so catastrophic that its Supreme Soviet did not, in fact, confirm Gaidar's appointment, and at the end of 1992, Viktor Chernomyrdin was appointed to the post.

The new Premier paid a visit to Almaty immediately after his appointment. Our two-hour conversation was conducted in a friendly atmosphere. He sought my advice on a number of issues. The conversation, I have to say, gave me some cause for optimism as far as the rouble zone being kept. Unfortunately, however, my expectations were short-lived.

Meanwhile the economic situation was still continuing to deteriorate. The liberalisation of prices introduced by the Russian Government on 1 January 1992 was beginning to pay off. For its part, Kazakhstan, in a more flexible position, tried to put off price liberalisation until it had managed to carry through measures to reduce the negative effects involved.

Kazakhstan had a whole range of economic links with Russia. However, the prevailing conditions were putting demands on us and we, too, were forced to liberalise prices, with the exception of basic food products. And even these were restricted to a strict list of bare essentials. Otherwise, price disequilibrium might have caused a shortage of fixed-price goods, thereby increasing pressures on the budget. However, we also realised that gradual price liberalisation was fraught with constant inflation expectations. Economic stabilisation could not be expected in such a situation.

The Central Bank of Russia became an example of this erratic economic policy. Owing to its functions not having been precisely fixed, it was subordinate to both the Government and the Supreme Soviet. And this, in turn, affected the extent to which Russia's Government could implement an effective policy to stabilise the economy. This was despite the fact that the Central Bank of Russia had assumed all the functions of the USSR Gosbank (State Bank) and only Russia was in a position to issue money and supply all the Union republics with currency. Russia distributed the cash to the republics not in response to their requirements but as it saw fit. Given the hyperinflation, the demand for cash increased proportionately to the exorbitant growth in prices. Even though Kazakhstan's Cabinet of Ministers was late indexing budget payments, there was such a shortage of cash that debts, even those in respect of fixed wages and pensions, kept on growing.

The situation regarding Russia's unpredictable economic policy was aggravated by the dual power that had resulted from the stand-off between the President and Russia's Government on the one hand, and the Supreme Soviet, on the other. Moscow kept giving contradictory signals to Russia's different regions and the Union republics.

Confronted by huge cash-supply difficulties, we were forced to make special trips to Moscow to 'extricate' cash to pay people's wages with, not to mention the economy's needs overall. These trips went on all through the summer and autumn of 1992.

When it came out in favour of keeping the rouble zone, Kazakhstan, along with the other states of post-Soviet space, had regarded it first and foremost as a means of maintaining financial stability in the region and supporting the still functioning economic and commercial links between individual enterprises, as well as those at an inter-state level. However, in July 1992, Gaidar's team in the Government and Central Bank of Russia unilaterally introduced non-cash transaction systems between state enterprises. The transfer to this system was essentially to allow the central banks of the rouble-zone states to open correspondent accounts at the Central Bank of Russia and for transactions in these accounts to be by so-called 'technical credit' only. Furthermore, in the event of a country's failure to repay this credit, the outstanding balance of settlements became this country's state debt to Russia. This was unfair. It was a case of 'strong man's law' and everyone else involved having to simply put up with these really tough conditions. We had to pay vast sums for various securities. After this new system's introduction, a number of countries – Belorussia, Moldavia and the Caucasian republics – assessed all the difficulties with rouble currency supplies and payments and introduced their own national currencies or substitutes for them.

Another feature of Russia's economic policy at the time was that the said decision regarding the non-cash transaction system was taken without the consent of the remaining rouble-zone states and announced ten days before its actual introduction. Russia's financial system possibly gained something from this but the proposed schedule of mutual settlements between states' commercial units resulted in payments taking up to half a year to go through, documents being lost and various kinds of counterfeit payment documents being circulated. This set off alarm bells for us, making us think seriously about the expediency of our republic's participation in an ineffective, unified rouble zone.

Despite all the difficulties in our inter-relations with Russia, it was not easy for us to opt out of the unified rouble zone. The operations of almost all our enterprises and all our processing and mining industry was tied up to rouble payments. We were reluctant to completely break all the links that had been developed between enterprises. What's more, time and substantial funds were required to introduce a national currency of our own. Let me remind you that when the CIS was created after the Belovezhskoye talks, all the heads of the CIS, including Russia, had solemnly promised that we would all stay in the rouble zone until times improved. And nothing would change.

Apart from issues of an economic nature there was the highly important, purely human factor. A great many Kazakhstani (not only of Russian nationality, incidentally) had families, relatives and friends in Russia and, of course these ties remained despite the Union's disintegration. We did not want to abruptly sever our connections with Russia, but people in Russia were unwilling to understand this. As for our problems and the ways we suggested solving them, we mainly encountered a wall of incomprehension on the part of the key officials of Russia's economic block.

'The first real step in eliminating the rouble zone and approving Russia's national currency and hard currency system – introducing a non-cash transaction system by setting up correspondent accounts of the central banks of the former union republics at the Central Bank of Russia – was actually taken in July 1992 and the remaining measures were introduced over a long period of time. Only in April 1993 was the step actually taken to stop the practice of providing the CIS countries with so-called 'technical credits' for trade with Russia. It was a display of political realism since the currency distribution system demanded considerably more time than initially envisaged, and this work was carried out with substantial difficulties, and in several stages. This had a lot to do with the powerful lobby in favour of keeping the rouble zone, consisting of industrialists from Russia and the other republics of the former USSR, these republics' governments and a broad spectrum of Russia's political groupings from Rutskoi to Yavlinsky. Unfortunately, in the initial phase authoritative organisations such as the International Monetary Fund and European Community Commission turned out to be among those advocating the rouble zone...'

ibid

Kazakhstan was, indeed, in favour of keeping the rouble zone, if only for the time being. We were those 'industrialist' lobbyists from other republics of the former USSR whom Gaidar's comrades-in-arms were describing because we knew full well that we were representing many thousands of enterprise work forces such as KarMet-Kombinat, Kaztsvetmet, and Karugol who were likely to lose their jobs and livelihoods.

Talks with Russia's Government became increasingly difficult, particularly with the reformers who had finally consolidated their grouping in 1992 (Gaidar, Shokhin, Fedorov, Shakhrai and a number of others). Many of them were still euphoric about free Russia's 'great future'. At numerous talks they spoke quite openly about it being to Russia's advantage to rid itself of the burden of subsidised Kazakhstan, and us inevitably ending up 'crawling back' on their terms, without any political guarantees or independence. Getting us to crawl back on our knees was regarded as one of the ways of reinstating the Union on their terms. This was really bizarre, seeing it was they who had destroyed it in the first place.

Even Gaidar's departure from his post as Chairman of Russia's Government did not essentially affect this course adopted by Russia. It was then the beginning of 1993, a year that was to prove the most difficult for Kazakhstan's economy.

Whereas in 1992, the distribution of cash funds from Russia had been carried out more or less proportionately among the rouble-zone republics, in 1993 the officials responsible for Russia's economic block started making priorities of their own objectives, and holding back cash assignments to Kazakhstan, thus directly or indirectly affecting the social and political situation there. By the spring we had stopping receiving any money at all. In May 1993, Russia's government passed a motion to put a stop to the CIS countries' credits.

Then, virtually at the same time as the non-cash mutual settlements were being divided between business concerns, the Central Bank of Russia started printing new 1993-issue banknotes and circulating them in Siberia and the Far East. During talks the Russian side kept assuring us that the new banknotes were ready money or rouble-zone currency, that the interests of Kazakhstan and its needs had been taken into account when the new banknotes were being printed, and that there would be no sudden seizure of Soviet banknotes (issued between 1961 and 1992). We also received assurances that the introduction of the new specimen banknotes would mean that the current requirements of Kazakhstan and the other rouble-zone states for Soviet banknotes would be better met, and once the rouble zone was up and running, the old banknotes would be exchanged for Bank of Russia notes.

Despite Viktor Chernomyrdin's promises to me during the World Economic Forum in Davos in January 1993, Russia did not, in fact, supply Kazakhstan with new banknotes. And this exacerbated the problem of wages being in arrears even further as all the State Mint (Gosznak) factories' production lines were busy printing Russia's new currency.

By June 1993, talks with Russia's Government on the creation of a rouble zone had finally reached a deadlock. It was eventually decided to give up the old idea of the rouble zone and come up with a new plan. However, just then something unforeseen happened or at least, unforseen within the framework of preliminary agreements. Despite there being a special agreement between the member countries of the rouble zone to the effect that if any of them decided to leave the rouble zone and introduce its own currency, it was obliged to give three months' notice to the others, on 1 July 1993, Russia actually introduced its own national currency those same new-style roubles supposedly printed for use throughout the rouble zone.

I remember that Saturday morning of 29 June when Viktor Chernomyrdin rang and informed me of this as an accomplished fact. At the same time, Russia made an announcement regarding its readiness to hold special talks in two weeks' time to consider the principles and technicalities of a collective monetary system based on the rouble, already Russia's currency. It was ready to sign an agreement on practical measures to create a new type of rouble zone and for it then to be ratified by the parliaments of the states involved.

Essentially, they were offering to reinstate the same manipulatory mechanism using the rouble currency, only it would now mean being dependent on Russia's national currency. This step seriously undermined our faith in Russia's leaders and the shadow of 'monetary betrayal' will be hovering over our relations for some time to come.

Despite an agreement being signed within the framework of the CIS on maintaining the rouble zone until the states had introduced currencies of their own, Russia made attempts to eject the republics of the former USSR from the rouble zone from its very outset. I held the view then, and still do, that this was totally unfair. We trusted Russia and believed in our mutual neighbourly relations. This step came like a bolt from the blue for Kazakhstan, as about 30 per cent of the country's population were Russian and we had such close mutual ties with Russia. When setting our future development policy, I used to do all I could to strengthen our relations.

I shall now make a short digression. Within the framework of the CIS, EEP, and Eurasian Economic Union we are currently talking about a common market and our countries' close integration. The final phase of this integration is supposedly to be the introduction of an equivalent or single currency. Essentially, we are intending to return to what we once started moving towards, namely, a single currency zone. Such a zone could have been created back then, in 1991-92. It could have become the basis of our joint development during the period after the disintegration of the Union, and the start of the economic integration and increased competitiveness of the entire region at world level in the present. However, the former 'Union' countries simply failed to reach an agreement. Russia considered it would be better off without us. And the sovereign republics stopped believing in their 'elder brother', possibly, because of all the above-mentioned 'features' of

Russia's economic policy. In my opinion, all Russia's current difficulties in its interaction with the CIS states and their mutual lack of trust and rebukes can be traced back to then.

Strategically, it seems to me, these decisions were wrong and not to the advantage of Russia itself. In 1991, Sergei Tereshchenko became the first Prime Minister of independent Kazakhstan. He was to work in this post during Kazakhstan's most difficult years of crisis caused by the disintegration of the USSR. He used to get particularly exasperated by the attitude of the Russian reformers of the time. Property was being divided up, first and foremost, with Russia. There were cash and goods shortages. He was at the receiving end of masses of criticism. However, he honestly did everything he could. He had to fly to Russia virtually every week to reach agreements – and be let down. And the tenge was introduced during his term of office. To this day I feel grateful to him. It's fine nowadays talking about what was not right in those days, but time dictates its own rules.

It took exactly ten years for the Government of Russia to acknowledge the success of Kazakhstan's economic reforms. Despite the great many exceedingly pessimistic forecasts of Russia's leading economists, Kazakhstan has carried out successful reforms in separate branches of the economy, as recent estimates have shown. In those days Russia's reformers could not have even imagined that key economists would be travelling to former Tselinograd, now Astana, from Russia every month to share know-how with Kazakhstani officials.

'...Which area of Kazakhstan's economic reforms, in your opinion, could be of interest and use to Russia?'

'Virtually, everything. Whichever way you look at it, it's all useful: the housing and municipal economy reforms, and in banking, electrical energy, state service, state finances. The state management reform currently under way at various levels. It's all highly interesting. Getting foreign investments, setting up the National Reserve Fund, the National Bank's monetary policy – it's a very long list and the results achieved by the republic in every area are impressive. They're particularly impressive because Kazakhstan and Russia are countries very similar in many parameters, above all, in terms of their economy, policies, people, common history, culture, approaches to economics and business – in all these areas your experience is extremely useful.'

From an interview with economics adviser to the President of the Russian
Federation A. Illarionov, *Zheti kun* programme, Astana, 31 August 2003

At that moment in time, however, aware of the instability and unpredictability of the developing political and economic situation in Russia, young Kazakhstan was faced with the dilemma of either continuing to set hopes by its neighbour controlling and changing the conditions of the existing rouble zone as it saw fit and remaining a hostage to a system primarily serving Russia's interests, or taking a decisive step towards extricating itself from the rouble 'cover-up', adopting its own currency, and taking on full responsibility for its people's future.

It was a tough choice. Maintaining the stability of the recently introduced currency was one thing, starting to build a financial system from zero, quite another. In those days the state did not yet have enough adequate financial institutions, instruments, or qualified personnel. There was an urgent need for a Ministry of Finance, tax authority, customs department and National Bank to be established. Research had to be done and the budget independently planned and worked out. Furthermore, in those days we did not yet have a legislation of our own, adapted to market conditions. This was the predicament we were in when we had to take cardinal steps to confront the most complex economic problems.

It would be logical to ask why we put up with things for so long instead of introducing our own currency straight away. First, it was because I had faith in the inter-state treaties and personal relations with the leaders of Russia of the day. The rouble zone maintained thousands of links between enterprises and suppliers and could possibly overcome the crisis faster. Secondly, we had neither the know-how to introduce our own currency nor the funds to get the banknotes printed abroad. Nor did we have our own banknote factory. This is the lesson I was taught that our country's future leaders must learn from: heads of state don't have friends, they have the interests of their country and people. An independent state has to rely on its own strengths and be prepared in advance for any

143

difficulties that may occur. In those days, however, regardless of all these problems, I maintained a good relationship with Russia's President Boris Yeltsin. He and I dealt with many bilateral relations issues such as the Baikonur Cosmodrome and division of the Caspian seabed. I do not feel resentment towards any of the other aforementioned officials. They did what they considered right for Russia.

The Introduction of the National Currency

An independent state must have its own currency. This I clearly understood from the very outset.

In the spring of 1992, I set up a secret commission to study the feasibility of introducing a national currency. Only seven people, including myself, knew about the commission. While still attempting to keep the single rouble zone, we started getting ready to introduce our own currency.

The only ones among the country's top leaders to be told about the state secret were Chairman of the Supreme Council S. Albildin, Chairman of the Finance and Budget Committee S. Takezhanov, Chairman of the State National Bank G. Bainazarov, his vice chairman, M. Tursunov, and head of the National Bank's enterprise construction board Kozhamuratov.

At the same time, a group of artists and designers were also confidentially brought together to design the new currency. It was a truly unique situation and innovative project, and the talented people involved were aware of their responsibility and the significance of the historic moment. Under Timur Suleimenov's direction, artists M. Alin and A. Euzelkhanov came up with four different designs for the banknotes and coins, all of which were truly excellent, and of a very highly professional and creative standard.

After a long discussion, it was finally decided to opt for the design depicting renowned figures of historic importance for Kazakhstan – people who had done much for our people and the formation of Kazakh statehood. At the very start of independence this was needed to boost national pride. Only upon gaining independence were we able to pay tribute to these personalities, whose names could not even be mentioned under the Soviet regime.

This calls the following incident to mind. To begin with, the designers proposed a banknote design with the portrait of the First President, that is, me. E. Asanbayev, T. Suleimenov and G. Bainazarov came to show me a 50 tenge note with my portrait on the face side. Eric Asanbayev said, 'Nursultan Abishevich, you are a historic figure, the first president of free Kazakhstan. And that's why we want to put your portrait on the tenge.' To which I replied that it was up to future generations to judge whether I was a historic figure or not. I turned it all into a joke, saying that I simply did not wish my portrait to figure on the currency because apart from certain rulers of African countries, no other living heads of state did. After having a laugh together over the proposal, we ruled this option out.

Every evening I would travel out to the country house where our group was at work. We had a big argument over the currency's name. The short-listed options were 'som', 'aksha' and 'tenge'. We eventually opted for 'tenge' which was taken from mediaeval history when 'tanga' coins were in usage in the Kypchak steppes. What's more, the Russian word for money 'dengi' and 'tenge' have the same root.

However, we had another big problem apart from the design and name. In those days Kazakhstan did not have a banknote factory as all the money was transported from Moscow. After consultations with experts, it was decided to place this very special order with a European country. The choice fell to the English companies Harrison and Sons and Thomas De La Rue, who had vast expertise in this area. The quality of the banknotes, financial side of the contract and confidentiality all lived up to our expectations. Had we come to an agreement with Russia, the costs involved in producing our own currency might have been not only very substantial but also simply unwarranted. However, Kazakhstan had no other option but to place the order abroad. Time has shown that we did not make a mistake. During the printing process, batches of banknotes were secretly delivered to the republic.

As was mentioned in the previous chapter, in September 1993 an agreement was signed between Russia and five other CIS counties on the urgent need to set up a new rouble zone. The document was a mere formality, and even then it was obvious that

Russia had no intention of including any countries in this zone. This was confirmed once again when our representatives were presented with patently unacceptable terms.

In a Decree a month later, in November 1993, I announced the names of the members of the official government commission responsible for the introduction of the state currency. Under the direction of Prime Minister Sergei Tereshchenko, the commission members were first Deputy Prime Minister D. Sembayev, Finance Minister E. Derbisov, Minister for the Economy B. Iztleuov, National Bank Chairman G. Bainazarov, and Parliamentary Committee Chairman S. Takezhanov. They were to meet virtually on a daily basis and had exclusive plenary powers to oversee the entire operation to introduce the currency.

A working group under D. Sembayev was also set up to carry out the numerous complex mathematical estimates involved, such as the number and face value of the units we needed. The commission members consulted foreign experts on all these issues. For instance, the British economist Dr Paine immediately advised us that we needed notes in units of 20 tenge rather than the usual unit, 25, as in Soviet days. He also held the view that the main bulk of the currency should be put in circulation during the first phase of the operation. Then, basing his calculations on the banknotes' eight-month life cycle, he worked out how much money would be needed to replace the worn-out notes. Later on, we were to verify in practice that his forecasts had been totally accurate, both in terms of the quantities of each unit, the sum total of cash in circulation, and inflation.

After mapping out the basic lines along which the state's independent monetary and credit policy should be conducted, the commission and working group members were to work out the principles and conditions for the currency's introduction and also long-term management. Various options were looked at. The first was to introduce three Kazakhstani rouble banknotes in 5,000, 10,000, and 50,000 units that were to be produced in Russia. The second envisaged the three highest banknote units being printed in Russia and then an interim national currency being introduced for 1-2 years until the situation stabilised, in the same way as in Ukraine and Belorussia, followed by the introduction of a permanent national currency. The third option was to introduce the national currency in parallel with the rouble. And, finally, the last option was to introduce the tenge immediately.

We dismissed the first three options as unworkable. It was impossible to subject the public to the double stress and psychological pressure of introducing first an interim currency and then a permanent one a year later. That's why, after consultations, the working group unanimously voted for the last option, fully aware, nonetheless, of all its advantages and disadvantages.

The advantages were obvious. The republic would be able to conduct an independent monetary and credit policy. The several levels of security protection the new banknotes were to be provided with would reduce the likelihood of them being counterfeited. If the national currency was introduced directly, the public would only have to exchange their money once, which was just as well, as the ordeal of exchanging 50 and 100 rouble notes in December 1990 was still fresh in their memories.

The introduction of the national currency had its downsides, too. Not all the technical issues had yet been worked out, particularly in respect of the coins, and the minting process came up against problems from the very start. The newly established mint was simply unable to produce sufficient coins by the end of the year. As a result, the decision was taken by the working group to print paper tiyin on an interim basis and then circulate the full-value coins once the mint was fully up and running.

While work was under way to introduce the tenge, new problems cropped up which we simply had not given much thought to before, such as the choice of a currency regime and course options. Discussions once again started regarding all the pros and cons of the various options and whether to opt for a floating course, a course of controlled floating within a certain range, a course linked to another currency (say, the US dollar) or a basket of currencies. We decided on a controlled floating course on the currency market. The plan was to introduce the fixed rate of the tenge with a monthly devaluation rate of 2-3 per cent in the event of the country's hard currency reserves being insufficient to efficiently manage the currency course. The decision to go for a single currency course was fundamental, but other mechanisms were used to compensate for the difference in the various currencies' real purchasing power during privatisation, with foreign investors participating.

Another choice whose significance we were to appreciate much later concerned the national currency's convertibility. The IMF representatives kept stressing the need for the introduction of full convertibility, as this step would, among other things, guarantee less state intervention in the currency regime, liberalise foreign trade and accelerate the country's integration in the world economy. At the same time, they continued to assert that currency control had proved totally ineffective and there was no sense in even introducing it. While we realised there was some validity to the IMF experts' assessment, we also knew that at that moment in time no Eastern or Central European country had introduced a totally convertible currency, even though they had begun their reforms three years before us. All these countries were, to some extent or other, reinstating currency control measures after their currencies had come under attack from currency market speculators.

Eventually, we decided to opt for the single currency course and partially convertible tenge for current account transactions and the repatriation of profits by foreign investors. Time confirmed this to be the correct option. According to IMF experts' forecasts, the currency course would fall to 150 tenge to the dollar in September 1994, and then to 200 tenge to the dollar in January 1995. In actual fact, the tenge fell at low rates (3-4 per cent per month) and by 1996, had stabilised at a level of 70 tenge to the dollar.

The first sign of our country being able to finance the national currency's introduction and operation was seen on 1 November 1993, when the first data on Kazakhstan's gold and hard currency reserves was published. According to the experts, at the time of introducing its own national currency, a country should have gold and hard currency reserves with a total value of at least three months' worth of imports. Kazakhstan's imports at the time amounted to US$500 million and its gold and hard currency reserves to US$722.9 million. We were more than ready to finance the introduction of the tenge.

Of course, this figure seems risible compared to our current reserves of approximately US$25 billion. However, in those days it was yet another cause for the delay in introducing our currency.

On 3 November 1993, the minutes of a working meeting between delegations of Russia and Kazakhstan were approved by Prime Ministers S. Tereshchenko and V. Chernomyrdin. Russia officially acknowledged that the best way to solve the situation that had developed with the single rouble zone was for Kazakhstan to introduce its own currency and implement measures as soon as possible to strengthen its monetary system.

Considering the sizeable volume of commodity circulation, a proposal of paramount importance for us was put forward, namely, that non-cash settlements between legal entities and individual citizens of Russia and Kazakhstan were to be transacted in roubles or the Kazakhstani national currency, and the procedure of the said settlements was to be fixed by a separate agreement.

The Kazakhstan side insisted on the provision being included that both sides would commit themselves to creating the conditions to enable citizens to exchange Kazakhstani currency and Russian roubles at the market rate.

After coordinating the introduction of the tenge with the functioning of the rouble zone in such a manner, we encountered yet another problem. By the time the commission overseeing the introduction of the tenge was up and running, Ukraine, Moldavia, Azerbaijan, Georgia and Kirghizia had already introduced their own national currencies and Turkmenistan had announced its intention to do so. We were by then gravely concerned that there was no guarantee any of these states would honour an important condition of introducing their own currency, namely, the compulsory surrender of immobilised Soviet roubles to Russia's Centrobank. What worried us was that all this massive amount of roubles, reduced to worthless paper notes after our neighbours had introduced their own currencies, would come flooding into Kazakhstan where until the introduction of the tenge, these roubles would still be legal tender. Alas, very soon our fears were to prove well-founded.

The Decree *On urgent measures to stabilise the monetary system* signed by me on 5 November 1993 was an essential step before the introduction of our national currency. What made such measures so urgent was the sharp increase in the quantity of illegally imported Soviet roubles within the territory of Kazakhstan that had been immobilised in neighbouring countries. This was undermining the republic's financial system by accelerating the already catastrophic inflation rate and lowering people's living standards. To protect state and public economic interests, the banks were given orders to place the banknotes issued between 1961 and 1992 belonging to individuals and legal entities in special accounts that could not be activated until further instructions from the National Bank of Kazakhstan.

By this time I had received a resolution signed by all the state commission members stating that all the necessary preliminary measures had been taken and the banking system was ready to introduce the national currency. Naturally, all the work had been conducted so far in strict confidence. The banknotes were flown in from London in cargo aircraft under the guise of industrial equipment. The Committee for National Security controlled the distribution of the tenge around the country.

We knew how important it was to avoid panic by not alerting the public beforehand. Although the results of most of the talks with Russia had been published and the public realised the introduction of the national currency was now a foregone conclusion, we released no further information on related issues such as exchange terms and conditions, rates and much else besides, including whether confiscation would be involved. And then, of course, there was the timing. I still had to come to a political decision and fix the date for the introduction of the tenge. And I would like to explain this further.

All our neighbouring states had been warned well in advance in an open, direct manner that Kazakhstan would be introducing its own currency. We always understood that, despite their declarations of political sovereignty, all the countries of the former Union were still closely linked, first and foremost, in terms of the mutual knock-on effect of their economies. This meant that when one country introduced its national currency, all the rest had to be prepared for it. It never even occurred to us to act in the same way as Russia had. For instance, one of the countries we discussed the issue of introducing the tenge with was Uzbekistan, an important partner that shared a border, had serious economic links with us, also belonged to the rouble zone, and suffered from similar problems as us. I had agreed beforehand with President Karimov that we would introduce our national currencies at exactly the same time, to the hour, so as not to create problems for each other. And so it was that Uzbekistan introduced its suum on 15 November 1993.

The Tenge – Symbol of Our Independence

Yes, the launch was set for 15 November 1993. The Decree *On the introduction of the Republic of Kazakhstan's national currency* was signed on 12 November, and made public the next day. In the evening of 12 November, I went on television to address the country and inform them of the introduction of the tenge, the very first national currency in Kazakhstan's history.

I felt extremely agitated on that memorable Friday evening because I was to inform all the citizens of Kazakhstan of one of the most momentous, cardinal steps we had taken on our way to building Kazakhstan's statehood. How would the public react? Would they understand and accept the need for this extreme measure? In my address I tried to convey all the significance and historic importance of the step, even though the introduction of the currency was in fact a forced measure, and made the following points:

1. Russia left the rouble zone itself; since 26 July our currency systems have been separate, and the said measure has been necessitated by the fact that we are not being admitted to the new rouble zone;
2. the introduction of the national currency does not signify a rift in business and other links with Russia and the CIS countries;
3. the measure is necessary to strengthen the republic's economic sovereignty and conduct independent economic policy;
4. the republic is in a critical position with cash supplies and the measure is the only way to supply the public with ready money.

Source: Archive of the President of the Republic of Kazakhstan

The national currency, the tenge, was introduced in the territory of Kazakhstan at eight am on 15 November 1993, at a rate of one tenge to 500 roubles.

By this time the new currency's banknotes and coins had been distributed all through the country's provinces and regions. Mindful of what had happened with Soviet currency reforms, the commission decided the exchange should not only take place in secondary-level bank branches: post office branches and enterprises with large work forces were also to be involved in this work.

It was announced that the tenge would become legal tender from the first day of the five-day exchange period and the rouble could be used as legal tender for all five days. In addition, we tried to take steps to avoid a massive shedding of roubles and rush to purchase goods on the day of the announcement.

Four sources of funding were identified for the national currency: the National Bank's gold and hard currency reserves, the republican currency fund, a foreign stabilisation fund (if one was set up by international organisations) and a positive balance of payments. The next major challenge was to increase export volumes and regulate hard currency export earnings.

For the first few years after the national currency's introduction there was a substantial shortage of internal sources providing foreign currency. The drain of hard currency funds from the country was posing a threat to the currency rate's stability. That was why, as soon as the tenge was introduced, hard currency transactions involving capital transfers from residents to non-residents required a licence, while the influx of capital was registered purely for statistical purposes.

The national currency's introduction gave rise principally to new challenges. One of the main ones was to strengthen the use of the tenge in payments and increase confidence in it. The measures adopted to achieve this included the transfer to payment in tenge of export and import taxes, customs and excise duty; banning retail trade in foreign currency; and banning barter transactions by legal entities resident in the Republic of Kazakhstan. All these measures helped stabilise the situation, and get our national currency, the tenge, off to a good start.

Russia's financial crisis in 1998 was 'an endurance test' for the new tenge. The serious devaluation of the national currencies of a series of countries that were Kazakhstan's trade partners resulted in an increase in the value of the tenge in real terms and that, in turn, reduced the competitiveness of Kazakhstan's exports. The National Bank's substantial currency interventions had only a temporary effect and, what's more, led to a significant reduction in our gold and hard currency reserves. It became necessary to devalue the tenge. In view of all the above-mentioned problems, the decision was then taken to transfer from a controlled floating regime to a free floating tenge exchange rate regime (FFER).

152

The Tenge – Symbol of Our Independence

This was introduced in April 1999, when the financial situation in Russia had stabilised and expectations of devolution had died down within the country. Measures were simultaneously taken to protect individuals' tenge accounts and legal entities' deposits in secondary-level banks, as well as the tenge assets of pension funds. In particular, pension assets were converted into state securities at the former, high rate. The obligatory sale of 50 per cent of export earnings was introduced as a temporary measure. To allow banks to adapt to the new regime, reserve requirements were reduced temporarily from 10 to 5 per cent, and other rules also relaxed.

It should be said that by force of habit many 'experts' were yet again predicting that catastrophic consequences would ensue from the introduction of the free floating exchange rate. Their forecasts that free floating the tenge would cause unprecedented devaluation levels because it had been an artificially supported currency and so on, heightened tension among people who still recalled what had happened during the crisis in Russia. Yes, the tenge exchange rate did fall, but by no means catastrophically, and this actually had a positive effect at the time. The transfer to the free floating exchange rate made it easier to restore the competitiveness of Kazakhstan's exports and renew production growth. As a result, the country's balance of payments improved significantly, its gold and hard currency reserves increased, and its banking system was substantially strengthened.

The transition to a freely floating exchange rate was necessitated by the reduced competitiveness of Kazakhstan's enterprises caused by the influx of cheap imports, from Russia included, and also by the dwindling gold and hard currency reserves essential for further maintaining the fixed course of the tenge. The transition was prepared in advance by working out various possible scenarios for the future development of the foreign economic situation and likely changes in the exchange rate in various hard currency regimes. The international currency fund and World Bank supported our decision, having noted, in particular, that the exchange rate 'should develop under the impact of market mechanisms'.

At the time of its introduction, the tenge was convertible only in current transactions. However, we had set ourselves the goal of making it fully convertible in due course. In July 1996, having met the conditions of Article VIII of the IMF Agreement, Kazakhstan was already able to guarantee the full convertibility of the tenge. In so doing, Kazakhstan committed itself not to introduce any currency restrictions, nor use multiple currency rates of exchange, nor conclude bilateral payment agreements at variance with the article, nor introduce import restrictions for reasons linked to its balance of payments. Payments were also then lifted on the execution of payments and transfers on current international transactions. The freedom of money transfers connected with foreign investments was guaranteed, as were the conversion and purchase of foreign currency on the internal market to non-residents, and individuals were permitted to export a set amount of foreign currency without validating documentation. All this made it possible to aim confidently for the tenge to be fully convertible by 2007 – convertible, that is, not only in current transactions but also capital ones.

Generally speaking, it is already possible to say with total confidence that the introduction of the tenge has gone very well. However, we knew back then that not everyone was psychologically ready for the new currency's introduction and there was a real threat of a negative reaction to it. It was also easy to predict that the stringent currency and credit policy would make new enemies of the national currency, both among our people in general and our deputies in particular.

To introduce the national currency we had had to work out a whole range of measures in money and credit, fiscal, budget, customs and internal trade policies in an exceedingly short period, because we could only have one go at it and time was of the essence.

As our national currency, the tenge has played a significant role in our country's history, and not only as the economic basis of our independence. In a way, the tenge is already part and parcel of our history and a landmark of its time. And I would also like to mention that this year our tenge is going to be changing its look which we have got so used to over the past 13 years. As far as the purely technical side of new banknote designs is concerned, the world's leading currency manufacturers prefer to steer clear of. The principal reason for the change is to take positive action against money counterfeiting. Interpol highly recommends all the world's central banks regularly, say, once every five to seven years, change their currency's design and technical features. Replacing old money with new is common practice the world over. So, 16 different security devices have been used in the new design: a set number and a set level for different denominations. Everything is taken into account when changing a currency's design: new technologies, dies, security devices, trends. That's where the technological side is concerned. But that's not all. Kazakhstan is a unique, multi-ethnic state. Whenever a venerated person's portrait appears on a banknote, the question is always asked why that person was chosen over someone else. Currency should unite people, not divide them, as it is, after all, a symbol of statehood and testimony to a country's might and international image. The designs on the new tenge are to be of things belonging both to Kazakh culture and world heritage such as cave drawings, ancient archaeological finds, and scenes of our wonderful landscape, as well as uniquely Kazakhstani features such as our state emblem, flag and views of both capitals.

The tenge has also inscribed a page of its own in world history or, rather, the history of world currency. The Kazakhstan Mint already has a reputation in the world for being one of the most state-of-the-art enterprises in the field. It is a little known fact that two years ago the Kazakhstan Mint was certified to the ISO 9001:2000 international standard by the TUV CERT certification board. Its representatives regularly take part in coin exhibitions and fairs. The demand for Kazakhstani coins among numismatists is sometimes so great that they are snapped up even before the end of a fair. Unlike the first fair Kazakhstan took part in when a furore was caused not so much by the currency on display as the fact itself that this remote Asiatic country was involved in one of numismatics' top four world events, the interest in Kazakhstani coins is now professional and very high. And this is, first and foremost, due to their design, lack of politicising elements and the superb calibre of the coining.

Onwards into the Future; Back to Integration

With the introduction of the tenge, the country's independent financial system well and truly got under way, and is now considered ready to join the world system of labour division and competition. Subsequently a set of measures designed to stabilise the macroeconomic indices began to be implemented, forming the basis for the start of economic growth in November 1993.

From the very outset we rejected the idea of an interim hard currency and began introducing our own which conformed with the national interests of budgetary, money and credit policy. Since then our currency has generally proved stable and consistently in demand in a number of neighbouring states.

Achieving such results has not been easy. We realised that introducing a national currency was not going to solve any social or economic problems. Furthermore, with no anti-inflation or tight control of monetary spending in place, the introduction of a hard currency might sharply exacerbate these problems, undermining public confidence in the new currency which would then take a long time and considerable effort to restore.

Other countries' experience showed that more stringent monetary and credit, fiscal and budgetary policy would have to be implemented to introduce and support the national currency successfully. As I have already mentioned, this was not to everyone's liking, but we had to learn to live within our means and rely only on our own strengths.

Moreover, in 1992-93, Kazakhstan was actually conducting a less harsh monetary and credit policy than Russia and that, it should be said, was not working in our favour. Happily there is no comparison between the situation 10 years ago and the present state of affairs in the economic systems of the former Union's states. According to independent IMF and World Bank experts, in terms of the rates and effectiveness of its economic reforms Kazakhstan is now ranked among the leaders. It has paid off its debts of US$400 million to the IMF ahead of schedule and paid back a total of US$350 million in Euro bonds on time. This has helped greatly improve our international image. Senior state officials in Russia are now applauding our achievements.

Russia is a vast country with a promising future. We Kazakhstanis sincerely wish our neighbour well. There have been a lot of good and bad things in our common history. Now that we are independent, we want to build friendly, strategic relations with Russia on an equal footing. I am certain this is in Russia's interests as well. This had been officially acknowledged in the agreements between our countries, and Vladimir Putin and I have covered a lot of ground in establishing great mutual confidence.

But not everyone in Russia is the same. Different tendencies are at work there. Previously unknown, ambitious people gained positions of power who knew little about the economic and human ties of Soviet times. Taking advantage of the weakness of the authorities higher up and in the provinces, they acted without regard for the ties between or shared strategic interests of both Russia and her neighbours.

The people of Kazakhstan have not forgotten how some of these people tried to make a 'banana republic' of us. It was their ill-considered statements that made many of our compatriots leave their homes of many years in Kazakhstan in search of a better life in Russia. Sitting in their centres and associations, surrounded by stacks of dusty papers, these blinkered officials are now passively observing the gradual return to the ideas of integration that Kazakhstan put forward back at the start of the 1990s.

I am pleased that nowadays sober reckoning and pragmatism are taking the place of erratic swings in direction and economic snobbery in Russia. I hope that the idea of a Eurasian Union advanced by me in 1994, as well as our states' stake on economic integration, will enable our co-citizens to achieve higher living standards in the long term. Ten years after the disintegration of the USSR, it was possible to trace the evolving views of politicians throughout the CIS in favour of our states' economic integration. The advantages these unifying processes could bring us were patently clear.

I must add that the processes took on a substantial new lease of life with Vladimir Putin's election as Russia's President. In a short period of time he has strengthened authority in the country and accelerated reform, and is doing a lot to combine our efforts towards integration in the CIS.

That's why, in 2003, he and I put forward the idea of creating a Single Economic Space (SES). Work in this direction will allow the prerequisites to be established for introducing a single currency. Key to this process will be measures to increase the effectiveness of cooperation on integration and the economic rapprochement of the countries participating in the currency union.

In this respect we do not need to invent anything new. We have the example of the European Union, which at the time of the USSR's disintegration was engaged exclusively in integration. Countries of the SES simply have to adapt successful European know-how in a well-considered and rational manner.

If the SES does not come about because of Ukraine's position, our efforts will pay off in a Eurasian Economic Union or other organisations. All the participants will come to understand that integration is essential and advantageous for the security and development of all those concerned.

Over recent years, however, the meaning of the term 'integration' has changed so bizarrely that at times not everyone understands what it is really all about. This most likely explains why the potential of the integration we were all in favour of and perceived as an absolute fact has still not been fully realised. Factors both objective and subjective have caused this. If we are unable to use it independently, then we should certainly learn how to interact, cooperate and achieve common goals. We only have to look at the European Union. Regardless of all the differences of opinions (and there have certainly been many), they have still come to a full understanding of integration, as the introduction of the single currency of the euro, the European Parliament and much else point to.

I think I have already said enough about the benefit of the integration processes. It is now time to take real steps towards drawing countries closer. First and foremost, within the framework of the SES. Yes, one has to admit that integration, particularly a currency union, will require our countries to move away slightly from the principles of economic and political independence. However, the results of integration will be of much greater benefit for the state than the wish to be fully independent of everyone else. It is impossible to climb really high without a strong partner's help – it takes a joint effort to get to the top.

In my opinion, because of the bygone 'brotherhood' of Union members with its absolutely unequivocal hierarchy, where relations were based on 'older and young brother' models, it will take a long time for us to opt finally for serious integration. This is despite the fact that we have common strategic economic interests, are moving along a parallel course of reforms, and have opted for institutional changes in the same direction. There are also still systemic problems in the way of integration. First, there is the low level of trust, which could be raised by respecting laws both inside the country and those of inter-state treaties. Secondly, the political regimes of the countries of the SES (Belarus, Kazakhstan, Russia and Ukraine) are all essentially different and, the differences between them are currently much greater than, say, those between the political regimes of the EU countries. This being so, the treaties signed by our countries are still unstable and will depend on internal political tendencies. Thirdly, we have not yet finally decided upon what constitutes the national interests of each of the countries. The problem of identifying an individual country's interests has to be resolved first. Otherwise any integration will be short-lived.

The introduction of the national currency has become a symbol of independence. In order for it to continue functioning, radical market reforms had to be carried out, aimed at improving the country's social and economic development. It is also important to remember that no economic reforms can happen without the key players – proprietors. You see, a class of proprietors is a key element of a market economy. Conducting large-scale privatisation in the country was one of the first steps in this direction.

5

FROM STATE TO PRIVATE OWNERSHIP

Privatisation became the most controversial chapter in Kazakhstan's recent history. None of the former socialist countries found this period of history plain sailing. Unlike Poland, Hungary and the Czech Republic, we introduced privatisation at the same time as we were developing our state institutions. Whereas in Eastern Europe Western investors were prepared to transfer their business and lobby for the immediate sale of state property, Kazakhstan had to deal with its own partners in Russia, where 'bandit capitalism' was rife.

Could we put off privatisation until our state institutions were fully developed? As Uzbekistan had shown, deferring the process of developing proprietors would have exacerbated our economic situation even more. We had embarked on independence with vast enterprises manufacturing uncompetitive and unfinished products for an ineffective military-industrial economy which had sunk into oblivion along with the Soviet state. As Marek Belka, economic adviser to the President of Poland and then the Prime Minister under whom Poland became a full member of the EU, was to admit, by far the most successful Polish enterprises were set up from zero, and in no way connected with the privatised enterprises of the socialist period.

If I were to assess privatisation, I would first say that for Kazakhstan it was a historic process developing competent and enterprising proprietors, who created thousands of self-sufficient points of growth. Privatisation cleared the way for new economic and social relations. By using shock measures, the state made it clear from the very outset that it was not going to be dictated to by the industrial lobby and keep unprofitable enterprises afloat.

Secondly, the mistakes committed during privatisation became an important lesson for us all. After supporting newly-fledged Kazakhstani businessmen during the period of so-called 'PIV' (Privatisation Investment Voucher) privatisation, the state did not develop an adequate legislative basis for the investment funds to function for, or put financial and professional demands on fund managers, or agree the level of their responsibility to investors. Subsequently, the state had to work for a long time to overcome the public distrust and disillusionment caused by the failure of this phase of privatisation.

Three years later, we took these errors into account when implementing pension reform. A state accumulative pension fund was set up alongside the non-state pension funds. A normative legislative base placed the most stringent demands on the functioning and investment of all the pension funds' accumulations. The results did not take long in coming, and today our pension system is the best thought-out and most reliable in all post-Soviet space.

Let's begin at the very beginning. In order to understand the logic of privatisation, one first has to give a general overview of the situation that had by then developed. Kazakhstan's economy was a separate element of the Soviet Union's overall economy and its specific function was to provide the other Union republics with raw materials. So, 70 per cent of all extracted oil, 55 per cent of iron ore, 28 per cent of coal, 46 per cent of heavy metals, 86 per cent of synthetic rubber, and 54 per cent of basic chemical products were transported out of Kazakhstan. At the same time, the republic came 12th out of the 15 republics of the former USSR in terms of per capita quantities of imported consumer goods.

A key role was played in the development of Kazakhstan's commodity exchange through links with the other republics of the former USSR – the source of 84 per cent of all imported material resources and destination of 91 per cent of all exports from Kazakhstan. The largest percentage of imported goods, for instance, was intended for the machine-building and metal-working industries (34 per cent).

Of course, all this was bound to have an impact on the structural development of Kazakhstan's economy, which was oriented, I shall stress again, on extracting natural raw materials and supplying them outside the republic. The contribution of Kazakhstan's mining industry was 1.7 times higher than the average in the former Union; 1.5 times higher than Russia's, and over twice as high as Ukraine's. Over 30 per cent of Kazakhstan's main industrial and production funds were allocated to the mining industries. At that time, over 90 per cent of property in the production sector was state-owned and steadily losing its capacity to be profitable.

Another characteristic feature of the period was the mass theft of state property by the public. We were unable to stop the chain reaction of this pilferage discrediting the very idea of the market economy. 'National property' had no clearly defined proprietor to look after it. The key issue then became the manageability of the processes transforming the state sector of the economy: carrying through the planned dismantling of state ownership and legitimate privatisation of state property as swiftly as possible.

Evidently, the former system of state paternalism had to be broken up as quickly as possible. The transition had to be made from state to private ownership, and from a parasitic view of life with the expectation that everything would be resolved by 'the powers that be' to responsibility and enterprise.

Apart from everything else, it is important to bear in mind that nothing like this had ever happened in Kazakhstan before. It was all entirely new. People were not to blame for the mistrust and misapprehension that everything connected with introducing a market economy was greeted with. That's why it was particularly important to involve as many people as possible in the continuing processes and dispel their misgivings over the new realities.

This was greatly helped by the distribution of farm allotments and country cottage (*dacha*) plots, along with the conveyance of state apartments to private ownership. The complexity of Kazakhstan's situation and the absolute newness of the challenges ahead required extraordinary decisions.

Events were unfolding at such a speed that at times it was not so much a case of managing continuing processes as trying to catch up with them. We had radically to change existing economic relations. Otherwise, it would be impossible to deal with the problems that had emerged.

Enterprises were standing still or running at a loss because their production was failing to find a market. As I have already stated in the previous chapter, consumer goods production was in steady decline. The empty shop shelves reflected the disparity between supply and demand. Tens of thousands of people found themselves without a job or livelihood.

Presidents Nazarbayev and Putin attend the launch of KazSat, Kazakhstan's first satellite, at Baikonur Cosmodrome in June 2006.

President Nazarbayev meets George W. Bush for extensive discussions at the White House in September 2006.

At the General Assembly of the United Nations, in 2007, Kazakhstan's Nursultan Nazarbayev builds rapport with his French opposite number, President Nicolas Sarkozy.

Nursultan Nazarbayev attends the unveiling of a replica of Kazakhstan's Independence Monument at the Kazakh Embassy in Washington DC in September 2006 during his official visit to the US.

Dennis Tito (right), an American, the world's first space tourist, is entrusted by Nursultan Nazarbayev to his Kazakh pilot Talgat Musabayev (left) in 2001.

President Nazarbayev joins José Manuel Barroso, Chairman of the European Commission, on the platform in Brussels on 4 December 2006, in the context of Kazakhstan's geographic presence on European territory.

President Nazarbayev (centre) welcomes leaders of member countries of the Conference on Interaction and Confidence Building Measures in Asia (CICA) at the Second CICA Summit in Almaty in June 2006.

President Nazarbayev delivers his State-of the-Nation address in February 2005.

Attending the opening of a new synagogue in Astana, 'Beit Rachel – Chabad Lubavitch', President Nazarbayev is greeted by Yona Metzger, Chief Rabbi of Israel, in September 2004.

Hydrocarbons beneath and beside the Caspian bring employment to thousands and give Kazakhstan a bright future, transforming the country's economy.

Soon to become a symbol of Kazakhstan's new capital, Astana, first mooted in 1995, the glittering 'Baiterek' – holy tree – monument (by Akmyrza Rustambekov) is seen here beyond foreground construction at the end of the decade.

President Nazarbayev welcomes Pope John Paul II to Kazakhstan in 2002.

Leaders of 'World and Traditional Religions', gathered in Astana in September 2003 for their First Congress, are welcomed by Kazakhstan's President Nazarbayev.

Spanning the globe, President Nazarbayev of Kazakhstan, Prime Minister Junichiro Koizumi of Japan, and the Presidents Putin of Russia and George W. Bush of the USA, are brought together by the G8 summit in St Petersburg in July 2006.

From State to Private Ownership

The rural economy was also in crisis. The collective and state farms oriented towards centralised purchases were left without a market or funds. The total lack of revenues meant there was nothing left in the budget with which to pay wages and pensions.

What the country needed to get the radical reforms up and running was a backbone of proprietors who would become engines of economic regeneration by saving the enterprises they had privatised, and turning them into paying concerns. By transferring former state enterprises into private hands, we sought to free them from state management and intervention. Such private firms and enterprises had to independently establish new economic ties, regulate production output and create new jobs that would naturally lead to a general improvement in the economy.

However, most of the industrial units that needed privatising were in an economic coma. Many required not only investments and new technology but, most of all, competent management which the previous Soviet-style directors were unable to provide. What's more, in the chaos and pervading atmosphere of impunity, many of the incumbent directors of large and medium-sized industrial, service, and agricultural enterprises were primarily concerned about lining their own pockets at the expense of the languishing enterprises and their work forces. Taking advantage of the confusion and unclear situation in the country's economy, such directors openly embezzled enterprises on the brink of collapse. Most worked for Union ministries and came from outside the republic, with no moral obligations to or ties with Kazakhstan. The system by which directors were elected to their posts enabled them to absolve themselves of any responsibility.

I admit that in this situation the republic's government had no real chance of stopping the embezzlement of the property still in state ownership. The lack of adequate laws and precise rules of ownership enabled the 'red' directors to escape responsibility.

Numerous critics are now accusing us of supposedly 'giving away national property' and so on. And, thank God, we did. In the situation that existed it was hard to estimate the true value and future prospects of any enterprise. Many of the industrial enterprises consisted of vast production and administrative buildings with obsolete equipment; most of the enterprises had enormous debts. An incredible amount of time, effort and

163

investment were required to make paying concerns of these enterprises. Swift, effective measures were needed, aimed at stabilising the situation. The embezzlement of property that developed on a mass scale during this period was a supplementary factor forcing the process of dismantling state ownership and privatisation.

In view of all this, we decided to opt for mass privatisation. State property was privatised in four phases, each with its own specific features, aims and challenges. It is impossible to say now whether all these phases of the privatisation process were planned by us in the form they took. More likely, each was a logical continuation of its predecessor. An attempt was made in each successive phase to take stock of all the errors and miscalculations of the previous phases. And there certainly were both.

Unfortunately, many of the expectations linked to the so-called Privatisation Investment Voucher (PIV) Privatisation came to nothing. For instance, the distribution of privatisation investment vouchers, which the public were to invest in privatisation investment funds (PIF) to acquire shares in privatised enterprises, only made it easier for the PIF to withdraw their assets through their own fake firms. This they did by accruing financial liabilities and then paying them off with assets acquired through the privatisation investment vouchers. As a result, the privatised enterprises ended up in the hands of a limited circle of people and the idea of popular privatisation was discredited. If the surnames of the directors of the privatisation investment funds of that period were published now, we would recognise them as quite well-off people. Ordinary people, on the other hand, were unable to get hold of any enterprise shares. Specific individuals have this on their conscience.

To explain how privatisation worked in Kazakhstan and how effective it was, I shall describe each of its phases.

Phase One: Initiative Privatisation, 1991-92
On 22 June 1991, the Law was enacted *On the dismantling of state ownership and privatisation* according to which initiative was to play a key role in the privatisation process, and state authorities

could not privatise an enterprise without first receiving the go-ahead from its work force. Only then were auctions and tenders to take place, or the production and social infrastructure transferred to the work force free of charge.

This law marked the start of the first phase of privatisation (1991-92) and laid the foundations for the development of the first *National Programme to dismantle state ownership and privatise state property in the Kazakh SSR for 1991-92* based on the idea of involving the country's citizens as much as possible in the processes of changing the forms of ownership through their work forces. This programme was based on quite a few compromises.

In view of the exponential inflation rates and people's lack of funds for privatisation purposes, every citizen in Kazakhstan was offered housing privatisation vouchers free of charge as a means of payment when taking part in the housing privatisation scheme.

Each voucher had a face value of one rouble at the time. The number of coupons people received was calculated on the basis of their length of employment, and their dependants received 2,000 vouchers each. The programme not only encouraged people's initiative but gave them hope that during the privatisation process state property would be fairly distributed among the country's working population. The simple mechanism of voucher purchases made it possible within a short period of time to develop a housing market, and ensure the mobility of the population and other essential conditions for developing market relations. Subsequently, housing vouchers were used in the purchase of small-scale privatised property and agricultural concerns. The first phase of privatisation saw a great many leased and collectively owned enterprises being set up, as well as the auction sale of communal property. In such cases work forces were given specific preferential terms.

A service market gradually began to take shape in the republic. The results of the first phase of privatisation encouraged the development of enterprise and the growing stratum of private owners. 4,771 state-owned properties were privatised as a result of this phase. 60 per cent of all retail trade, public catering, consumer and communal services units were privatised, most of which were trade (29.6 per cent) and consumer service units (25.8 per cent).

However, this first phase highlighted the limited potential of the instruments for transforming property ownership with its particular emphasis on collective ownership. A decision had to be taken in the country as soon as possible to transfer from initiative privatisation to a uniform privatisation system.

The Second Phase: Investment Voucher Privatisation, 1993-95

On 5 March 1993, I approved 'The National Programme for dismantling state ownership and privatisation in the Republic of Kazakhstan'. Its adoption may be regarded as the start of the second phase of what was to become privatisation on a mass scale and therefore the most complex period of the entire process. It was to prove an extraordinary process in many ways – in form, methods and speed.

So, a strictly centralised system was put in place to manage and privatise state property, and local administrative authorities with similar functions were discharged. Uniform regulations were introduced to prepare for, and carry out, the privatisation of property. There was now a wide range of privatisation methods: the sale of shares on the stock exchange; auction; commercial tender; investment tender; the sale of property with the retention of lease terms until the sale's completion; the direct sale of units of social significance in rural areas; the sale of non-liquid units without fixing a minimum price; the transfer of enterprises to administrative boards on set investment terms. The variety of mechanisms used to implement privatisation made it possible to take account of both the specific features of privatised industrial enterprises and the public's continuing needs and prevailing attitudes. The choice of method was determined by the size of the enterprise – the number of employees and the basic capital value.

Four types of privatisation were envisioned by the reform: small-scale; mass; on an individual basis; and in the agricultural sector (the agro-industrial complex). We carried out small-scale privatisation within a tight time-scale, selling off over 6,000 properties. This, in turn, greatly stimulated the consumer services, trade and public catering sectors. Thousands of private enterprises of small-scale and middling businesses were soon up and running well as a result of this phase.

The National Programme's main directions were:

- small-scale privatisation (sale by auction and tender of trade and consumer service sector units and industrial enterprises with a total work force of 200 or under);
- mass privatisation (enterprises with a work force of between 200 and 500);
- privatisation of individual projects (enterprises with a work force in excess of 5,000);
- privatisation of the agro-industrial complex.

National Programme for the dismantling of state ownership and privatisation in the Republic of Kazakhstan, 1993-95

The second phase also saw a great many compromises and preferential terms retained for those taking part in the privatisation. For instance, the work force of a unit being privatised were allowed to form working associations made up of at least 50 per cent of the total work force, take part in the auction sale and receive a discount of up to 10 per cent of the sale price.

The broad spectrum of privatisation methods that could be flexibly used along with the compromises and preferential terms on offer enabled the bulk of units in the small-scale privatisation programme to be sold within the time-scale of the second phase. The rest of the still unclaimed units were sold off through a combination of the above methods in 1996, after a series of price reductions. The units in the small-scale privatisation scheme could be purchased with a combination of cash (50 per cent) and housing vouchers (50 per cent). Housing vouchers could be freely bought and sold at National Savings Bank branches. Different purchasing terms were applied to the units that remained unsold at auctions: their asking price was either reduced or not fixed, or they were leased prior to being sold. The method of selling units to their work forces was also used. Leased units were sold with retained lease terms. 50 per cent of the funds from small-scale privatisation sales were kept in local budgets. When state enterprises were auctioned off, the work forces received up to 10 per cent of privileged shares free of charge of the overall statutory capital.

Apart from the purely economic impact, small-scale privatisation also had an effect on society. Literally within the first two years of its introduction, the shelves of our shops and markets began filling up with food products and all sorts of other essential consumer goods. A pharmaceutical products market developed. People gradually stopped feeling afraid of the private sector. The sale of shops and stalls encouraged enterprise growth in these sectors. The new firms emerging often had better technical equipment and management levels than their privatised counterparts. A whole network of vehicle repair workshops also appeared in such a manner.

During this period personal investment voucher accounts were set up free of charge for all Kazakhstani citizens in the National Savings Bank. Every citizen could invest his or her vouchers only in the shares of privatisation investment funds (PIF), through which state enterprise vouchers could be acquired at special auctions.

Voucher privatisation – the most popular phase, in terms of the numbers of people taking part, of dismantling state ownership in Kazakhstan's economy – was implemented along similar lines in other countries with transitional economies such as Poland and Czechoslovakia. During the process the intention was to privatise the bulk of middling enterprises, and provide all the country's citizens with private property (on a voucher basis). Subsequently, this sector of private owners would – it was hoped – pave the way for the emergence of a Kazakhstani middle class.

But the results of this phase can still hardly be rated as socially acceptable. The voucher phase did not, in fact, encourage the emergence of a stable securities market. Attempts to develop the open trading of shares on the stock market widely were unsuccessful: because of the complex economic situation most enterprises were in, their quotation of shares was doomed to failure. Most of the PIFs went bankrupt. The voucher phase did not result in the development of a mass stratum of active, flourishing small-scale and middling shareholders for a number of reasons, including some I have already listed. Hand on my heart, I have to say here that the very idea of voucher privatisation did not live up to people's expectations.

From State to Private Ownership

During the preparations and introduction of mass-scale voucher privatisation, few people thought for a moment that the process was going too slowly. On the contrary, there were numerous appeals for less haste and more caution; there were demands to 'halt mass-scale privatisation, consider the pros and cons and make preparations for it'. Time has also shown that mass-scale privatisation was the right choice for the economy's regeneration.

Parallel work was also under way to turn enterprises into stockholding companies. This process, and the emergence of state equity packages, were intended to facilitate the emergence and development of corporate enterprise management. With this in mind, work continued to promote active supporters of the introduction of a market economy, and financial industrial groups and holdings were set up within middling enterprises and various forms of financial structures. Their endeavours to commercialise and corporatise the market and apply global know-how to working in market conditions were endorsed in every possible way.

The situation meant all but ignoring the procedures of financial and partly physical restructuring, and having to rely on the endeavours of new private owners to complete these procedures in the best way possible. However, so critically acute were the problems – particularly the liabilities – in this phase of privatisation that units were sharply devalued and potentially effective investors discouraged. Another key economic and social effect of mass-scale privatisation was the transition to the sale of state-owned property for money.

Like many other reforms, privatisation involved yet more responsibility for the decisions being taken – and of all these, those concerning unconditional privatisation were probably the most complex. The process of transition to private ownership had to become irreversible. The very logic of the time made this so. Only privatisation of such a kind could act as a guarantee of our market policy for international organisations and foreign investors. The responsibility for taking the decision to cross such a Rubicon undoubtedly had to rest with the head of state. This was clear then, just as it is now. And it was up to me to bear the full weight of this responsibility.

We had been taught that property should only belong to the state (or to 'all the people', as we used to say) but in actual fact it belonged to nobody. And then all of sudden here was this talk of private ownership and the emergence of a petty bourgeoisie. It was quite daunting for everyone. I recall now how scared ministers often were of signing agreements on the sale of major, and at times totally unique, enterprises. Mindful of this, I did all I could to reassure them of my support and protection when carrying through the most radical changes. As a result, we managed to avoid the long-term uncertainty in property reform issues experienced by most of the countries of the former Union. Politicians should always remember that property relations are the very foundations of economics and, consequently, the origin of a society's financial and social stability.

The first money sales of major units such as the Almaty Tobacco Factory, YuzhNefteGaz and ShNOS were revolutionary events in all post-Soviet space. And it was not just a question of reforming the structure of budget revenues. The introduction of private property to Kazakhstanis' everyday life involved, first and foremost, a change in people's mind-sets.

The dynamic of the money sales process gradually improved. However, normal market prices were only achieved in 1997. In 1996-97, receipts from privatisation were already representing around 20-30 per cent of budget revenues. All the enterprises privatised on an individual basis during that period are still our highest tax payers, providing the budget with stable fiscal revenues.

The end of the second phase saw individual projects going ahead to privatise major enterprises of particular economic and social significance. Essentially different, new components were introduced to the reforms in the guise of potential foreign capital. There was no doubt in anyone's mind by then that to continue with its privatisation programme, Kazakhstan would need to acquire foreign capital and establish enterprises with it.

From 1994 onwards, foreign capital investment was permitted in the privatisation investment funds, and from the spring of 1995, foreigners were admitted to the sales auctions of any units where they could pay with hard currency and acquire up to 31 per cent of the privatised enterprises' shares.

Foreign investors were presented with obligatory conditions in respect of the following:

- investments in the main production, terms, output and directions.
- production output growth as per the main output register.
- obligations in the payment of wage arrears, in respect of the budget and suppliers.

ibid

The initial plan was only to sell individual major enterprises to foreign investors. In 1993, there was a list of 38 units. Such urgent measures were needed to tackle the crisis the republic's enterprises were in, as many were on the brink of stoppage and bankruptcy.

The Almaty Tobacco Factory and Shymkent Confectionery Factory were the first to be sold in that period (1993-94) on an individual basis. The American company Philip Morris paid over US$100 million for the Almaty Tobacco Factory, committing itself to invest US$240 million in production, and immediately embarked on its human resources investment programme to increase wages, purchase new housing for its new employees and introduce a number of other benefits. Before it stepped in, the factory had been in a dire state with insufficient funds to acquire raw materials, equipment and spare parts or pay the work force's wages. This was the first achievement and first major source of budget revenue from an investor. I congratulated Prime Minister S. Tereshchenko and Chairman of the State Property Committee Zh. Karibzhanov on this project. Thus the signal was given for everyone to proceed further.

Because of Soviet-style xenophobia, which viewed any foreign presence as tantamount to treason, many people began saying there was no need for foreign investments, and that privatisation should be a strictly internal process in the country. This is what I want to say in response to all these statements: we really did try to carry out privatisation independently, but that made matters even worse.

But why not judge for yourselves?

Just then Kazakhstan's industrial giant, Karmetkombinat, was in a calamitous position on account of its enormous electric power and transport debts, and on the verge of bankruptcy. Things had got so bad that virtually all the metallurgical assembly units had been shut down in the foundries. An urgent search got under way

171

for an investor capable of rescuing the plant. Young Kazakhstani entrepreneurs offered us their services. Jointly with the Austrian company Fest Alpina, they committed themselves to tackling the enterprise's financial problems and introducing a modern management system.

We were glad of their help. As embezzlement at the plant was then rife, at the investors' request I gave instructions to the Government to give them assistance. Specialist military units from the north of the country were sent into the grounds of the enterprise to provide security.

However, the management skills our young entrepreneurs had acquired in the trade sector proved inadequate to manage this major industrial plant's operations and collaborate with serious foreign partners in metallurgy. Miscalculations in the drawing up of metal trading and coke supply agreements in early 1995 resulted in the plant having only three days' supply of coke left and no working assets whatsoever. Wage payments were also six months in arrears. It reached a point where our young entrepreneurs had to simply leave the plant. Less than a month later the help of the installed military units was required to halt more embezzlement – this time by the young investors.

So you see, our young people wanted to take on such major projects and we met them half way. But lacking the necessary expertise and funds, they were simply not ready to. They had taken part in the privatisation process but proved unable to manage the enterprise properly. They did, however, learn a valuable lesson. Kazkommertsbank took over the management of the metallurgical plants, purchased the ShNOS refinery, and then resold it later on.

Another glaring example was our civil aviation. After taking over the management of Air Kazakhstan, our young entrepreneurs got into such a mess that our aircraft started being impounded at foreign airports. Foreign companies refused to let their employees fly on Air Kazakhstan flights because of their poor safety standards. Had it not been for my decision to set up the Kazakhstan-British joint company Air Astana, we would have no airline at all now. I think our managers will with experience, however, learn to do better.

In conditions such as these, only major investments on the part of companies in a firm position on world metal markets could save

172

the enterprise. That's why the metallurgical plant was sold. The new owners of Karmetkombinat, the Indian company Mittal Steel, immediately settled the debts with the raw materials, electric power and transport suppliers, and paid the back wages, and outstanding claims. In total, the investor paid off US$350 million in debts. And in the eight years since privatisation a total of nearly US$1 billion have been invested. Before long the blast furnaces and coke batteries had been repaired and the most important technical lines reconstructed. What's more, a zinc- and aluminium-galvanizing workshop and non-stop steel-casting machines have since been installed, and a profiled iron workshop is in the process of being built.

In view of the extreme economic conditions, the privatisation of these major metallurgical plants engendered a kind of chain reaction, causing the sale of subsidiary industrial assets. Such was the case, for instance, with the sale of the Karaganda metallurgical plant's assets. The problems in providing adequate electric power, heat and raw materials production had to be sorted out for the enterprise to function properly. So, during 1996 the investor had to acquire the Karaganda thermoelectric station, as well as the principal section of the coal mines, and put things right by investing sufficiently in them to ensure a stable supply of energy and raw materials.

The following year the auxiliary coal-mining enterprises KaragandaShakhtUgol were added to Ispat Karmet (as Karaganda metallurgical plant was then called). This coincided with the wave of miners' strikes sweeping across the CIS countries and eventually reaching us, as I have already described. A delay in the solution of these highly serious social and economic problems in such a major industrial region might have had very grave and unforeseeable repercussions for the country as a whole. We succeeded in avoiding this and what helped quite considerably was the fact that the Ispat Karmet had begun functioning normally.

Seeing the achievements of these foreign management teams, managers of numerous non-privatised auxiliary and co-operating enterprises started requesting the government to include their enterprises on the list of units for sale to an investor with good credentials in the region. The government gave the solution of these problems its constant attention. I shall cite several examples.

The privatisation of the open-cast mines Bogatyr and Vostochny in the Pavlodar district triggered a chain of technology sales. In the late autumn of 1996, just before the onset of winter, the coal supply system – an essential component of normal heating and energy supplies – was on the verge of collapse. In these conditions the property complexes of the open-cast mines were privatised by the Eurasian Industrial Group, which had already achieved consistently positive results in sorting out the production in a whole series of industrial enterprises. Before the sale of such socially important, complex works, government representatives made a point of regularly travelling out to the locality to inform the people involved of the situation and the measures being proposed by the government to overcome the current difficulties. So, during the privatisation of the Vostochny open-cast mine, plenipotentiary representatives of the state bodies concerned and investors got the work force together and explained their investment and production programme to them. Guarantees were given there and then in respect of wage payments. By backing up our words with actions, we succeeded in winning the public round.

Indeed, within ten years the Eurasian Industrial Group had succeeded in overcoming the crisis affecting the mining and metallurgical enterprises, stabilised their work and restored their positions in world markets. As for the effectiveness of the measures implemented after privatisation, suffice it to say that US$290 million were invested in the enterprises' financial upgrade and rehabilitation.

And in recent years over US$900 million have been invested in production development, allowing new production capacities to be set up. What's more, the investment process is still continuing, and not just in those enterprises. For instance, US$48 million have been invested by the Eurasian Group in the new capital's development.

Zhezkazgantsvetmet is another success story in terms of opportune financing. In 1995, the enterprise was on the verge of bankruptcy with debts of US$170 million, including US$10 million in wage arrears. The following year the Samsung Corporation was successful in the tender to purchase company shares. They settled the enterprise's debts and invested substantial funds in it. Since then production output has risen to 400,000 tonnes, a record in the enterprise's history.

From State to Private Ownership

Privatisation on an individual project basis, which we approached with caution, was initially implemented in several phases. To begin with, the enterprise was put under a management board. During this period the state was supposed to check the credentials of the interested investor and test its ability to fulfil the investment obligations it had undertaken and provide competent management. The investor was then permitted to acquire a set package of shares. A number of metallurgical enterprises were put under a management board in such a manner.

However, in the course of privatisation a reliable investor was not always immediately forthcoming. For instance, in 1995, the JSC Balkhashmys was sold to the CAM Finance CA company, but the contract later had to be revoked as the investment obligations to the enterprise had not been met. The situation only came right in 1997, after JSC Balkhashmys's property complex had been acquired by the Samsung company. Today Kazakhmys Corporation, a group of non-ferrous metallurgy enterprises, is one of the most profitable in the republic.

Sometimes several phases were involved in the process of setting up new corporative groups. For instance, in the first phase of privatisation a substantial percentage of the shares of the Ust-Kamenogorsk pig iron and zinc, Leninogorsk polimetal and Zyryanovsk mining and coal-processing works were handed over to their work forces. There were still problems, however, getting production up and running normally. First and foremost, it was practically impossible for the then managerial staff to find suitable financial sources to invest in production on such a scale. The situation became easier after a strategic investor – the Swiss firm Glinkor – had come forward. It took some restructuring and merging of the three works for the profitable company Kaztsink to come into being.

Privatisation has taught us a lot, and made us fairly resistant to investment adventurism. One of the lessons we learned was over the privatisation of the Vasilkovsky mining and processing works. The sale by tender of this gold-mining enterprise was organised jointly with the European Bank for Reconstruction and Development (EBRD). As a result, five major companies out of the world's ten leaders in this field declared their interest in tendering. At the last moment, however, a new investor appeared – Placer

Dome Inc – which made the incredibly high offer for the enterprise of US$95 million and consequently won the tender. But the firm ended up only paying US$35 million of the agreed sale price and failed to abide by their investment obligations, and the contract was eventually abrogated. We, on the other hand, had also forfeited the good faith of our investment consultant, the European Bank, and potential solid investors who had warned us against going ahead with the said contract.

During the second phase of privatisation our attitude to foreign partners underwent a radical transformation. Despite the negative characteristics of the investment climate in Kazakhstan at the time (high non-commercial risks and so forth), guarantees provided for the equal rights of foreign and local capital. Something else was needed, however. Within an extremely short period of time the Law *On the state support of direct investments in Kazakhstan* was drawn up and adopted, according to which the system of benefits and entitlements for foreign investments was significantly expanded.

Once this law had come into effect, foreign capital began to play a decisive role in economic growth. As a result, enterprises were able to pay off their debts of various kinds – wage arrears; budget, pension fund, electric power, and transport debts; and debts to suppliers. This also meant that strikes were averted and jobs – the resource any country has the most difficulty acquiring – secured. Foreign partners brought new elements to the enterprises' management systems. Kazakhstani managers, used to an uncompetitive, socialist economy, were given work experience free of charge. Privatisation allowed most of the infrastructure of the social and communal spheres to be kept.

All the hard work that had been carried out since 1991, and the campaign to attract foreign investors, began to produce its first positive results. Thus, GDP for 1995 was 992.5 billion tenge, and industrial production grew to 13.6 per cent: 17.4 per cent in ferrous metallurgy, and 1.9 per cent in the non-ferrous sector. Wages at these enterprises amounted to 16-18,000 tenge, three times the republic's average.

As I have said before, the sale of state enterprises to foreign capital was often regarded as being tantamount to selling off the state, its national treasures and the homeland. To be fair, however, it has to be said that many of the foreign investors had the best potential for buying the state enterprises and providing for their competent management in the years to come. And as I have also stressed before, most of our own entrepreneurs did not have such potential yet. They were unfamiliar with the sales market and much else in a market economy. All this still had to be learned.

The Third Phase: Monetary Privatisation, 1996-98

The third phase of privatisation, implemented in 1996-98, saw the transition to sector programmes in the strategic branches of the economy such as electricity, oil and gas, and also in the social sphere of healthcare, education, science and culture. This was when fully-fledged domestic investors able to purchase major industrial enterprises began to emerge.

At the end of December 1995, I passed a Decree with the force of law *On privatisation*, and in February 1996 *The Programme for the third phase of privatisation for 1996-98* was brought into effect by a Government resolution. The programme's aim was to complete the main privatisation processes as swiftly as possible, and create a stratum of private owners, but this time by means of monetary privatisation – that is, on a payment basis. The dominant feature of this phase of the process was the sale of the privatised unit to the new private owner.

Within three years state packages were set up consisting of partially privatised enterprises and trade, social, cultural and consumer service units that had not been sold previously within the framework of the small-scale privatisation programme. Privatisation on an individual project basis was also continued.

The sector privatisation programmes in strategic branches of Kazakhstan's economy, as well as in healthcare, education, science and culture, were important parts of this phase of the Programme.

'During 1996, the Government sold state packages of shares and the state share of 889 joint stock companies (JSC) and limited liability companies (Ltd) as well as 3,526 units in the social sphere and real estate units, and 27 units privatised on an individual project basis. Budget revenues for this year totalled 31.2 billion tenge.

1997 saw accelerated rates of privatisation, particularly in the energy and mining industries. This process was completed in a number of industries. During 1997, a total of 5,641 real estate units, and 608 state packages of enterprise shares were privatised, and a start was made on dismantling the state ownership of units in the healthcare, education and culture sectors. Revenues from sold and purchased privatisation units totalled 54.5 billion tenge.

In the course of 1998, 513 state packages of joint stock companies and state shares of limited liability companies, 2,716 units in the social sphere and real estate units and enterprises' property complexes were privatised.'

Source: Ministry of Finance of the RK

This phase, like the previous two, was implemented with remarkable speed. Preliminary procedures and the transactions themselves were kept to a minimum time scale. One month was allowed for setting up and holding a tender, and only 15 days for an auction. The main reason for this haste was that illegal privatisation – the stripping of enterprises' principal financial assets and funds – was occurring at an even faster rate.

The managers of many enterprises and organisations were deliberately slowing down privatisation and fraudulently creating the right conditions to make personal fortunes for themselves and their close associates by bleeding the enterprises and accruing enormous credit debts. If these 'commercialisation' processes had gone on any longer, the enterprises in question would have been left with no property to privatise and no hope of functioning normally in the future.

Of course, rapid privatisation was bound to involve massive costs. Enterprises certainly did not always get transferred to reputable private owners. Sometimes owners would strip their newly acquired enterprises to the bone and then vanish into thin air. However, taking account of all the circumstances of this transitional period, it is still impossible to refute the fact that privatisation was completed quite effectively. And subsequently, compared to the results of the privatisation processes in neighbouring states, the pluses definitely outweighed the minuses.

Two main types of property sales were envisioned in the third

178

stage: sales by auction and tender, and direct sales. The latter was to be used only in the case of enterprises that had previously been leased or put under a board of management; 26 of the 66 enterprises contractually put under a board of management were subsequently sold to their management companies (including major enterprises of the ferrous and non-ferrous metallurgy industry).

High initial offers did not always guarantee the results forecast would be achieved. For instance, during lengthy talks the price on 100 per cent of the share package of the Kazakhtelekom company fluctuated between US$2-3 billion and US$60 million. The result was that 40 per cent of the shares were sold for US$100 million to the company, Daewoo. However, after failing to meet investment obligations the buyer later had to sell the package to a domestic investor.

But there was a gratifying element to all this. The resales were evidence of there now being real potential in the third phase of privatisation for attracting national capital to the privatisation of major units.

During the third phase virtually all the electric power generating stations were privatised, and the proceeds from the sales and investment obligations provided the budget with substantial revenues. It was then, in 1997, that we overcame the crisis in energy supplies to industrial enterprises and populated areas in the Eastern Kazakhstan district. The sale of four thermoelectric power stations (Semey, Oskemon, Gorinsk and Ridder) and the transfer of two hydro-electric power stations (Shulbinsk, Oskemon) in concessions to the American company AES Suntree Power averted an impending regional energy crisis.

1997 saw the processes of privatisation gathering momentum in the oil and gas industry. As fairly complex procedures were involved in the valuation of such units, requiring the coordinated expertise of specialists from a whole range of departments, the Government of the Republic of Kazakhstan was instructed to create an Inter-Departmental Commission to work out the conditions and order of enterprise sales in the oil and gas industry as well as establishing the most favourable investment conditions for potential buyers. In 1997, sales agreements in respect of the major enterprises of the oil and gas industry Mangistaumunaigas JSC and Aktobemunaigas JSC were signed with the tender winners, the

Indonesian company Central Asia Petroleum and the Chinese National Oil and Gas Company.

The third phase introduced an innovative approach to the process of privatising unique major units on an individual project basis. The important transition was made from putting enterprises under the management of foreign firms to selling them by tender to foreign investors. It goes without saying that due to a lack of funds Kazakhstanis in this period were simply unable to compete against foreign capital in the tender for major enterprises.

Furthermore, Kazakhstan did not escape the then prevalent serious consequences of agreements for the purchase and sale of industrial enterprise shares being cancelled. This was due to reneging on investment obligations, a deterioration in an enterprise's performance, incompetent management and various abuses in financial and external trade operations.

A total of 94 major enterprises were privatised during the second and third phases, 57 of which were purchased by foreign investors. The transfer of major enterprises to management boards, and their subsequent sale on an individual project basis, allowed new industrial companies to be set up with private and state capital investments. These companies have now found their place on international markets, safeguarding the jobs of thousands of people and substantially strengthening the country's economy.

On the whole, placing Kazakhstani enterprises under foreign management enabled most major enterprises to tackle their financial and production crises and helped them successfully adapt to the harsh conditions of a market economy. The signs of improvement in enterprises' financial and economic state can be traced to this period.

The Fourth Phase: State Property Management
The fourth phase, begun in 1999, featured new approaches to the apportionment of authority between the various levels of state management in the regulation and administration of state property. Thus, a law was enacted envisioning the introduction of changes in over 140 normative legislative acts and specifically distributing the authority of the levels of state management. The legislative base in

the sphere of state property management was also improved.

This phase began with the adoption of the Programme for privatising and increasing the competence of state property management for 1999-2000. The programme identifies the practical results of the previous phases of privatisation, the main one of which being the establishment of private property as the foundation of a market economy. The state retains a presence for itself in strategically important branches of the national economy, particularly those fundamental to it, including industries providing vitally important goods, products and services. In this context, issues to do with improving the efficiency of state property management and controlling the execution of managerial decisions are becoming increasingly topical.

The JSC Samruk National Holding Company is now up and running in the republic. We decided to entrust the development of a business plan for establishing a state holding to a foreign consultancy firm with a track record in setting up similar structures in other countries. Research revealed that the only company to entirely fit the bill was McKinsey, the world's number-one consultancy firm which had been responsible for setting up projects for similar state asset management companies on behalf of governments of developing and developed countries, including Singapore's state-owned investment company Temasek Holdings.

Kazakhstan was represented in the project by the JSC Centre of Marketing and Analytical Research under the Ministry of the Economy and Budget Planning. Within the framework of the project a study was made of the most advanced international expertise of 13 state asset management holdings and agencies in countries of Europe, Asia, North America, Australia and the Pacific.

Before the holding was set up there was a protracted period in which work began stalling and at times completely tailed off. I understood the resistance of our holdings and major companies, which had been perfectly happy stewing in their own juice and doing as they pleased. I repeatedly had to remind the government that the work on setting up the state-asset management holding in the country was not progressing fast enough. In the end, the entire process dragged on for a year and a half.

Eventually, on 28 January 2006, I signed a Decree *On the*

establishment of the JSC Samruk National Holding Company. I set the holding's management the central strategic challenge of increasing the national companies' efficiency by improving corporate management, and thereby increasing the country's economic growth. It is essential we improve the standard of our corporative management, setting an example to private sector companies that will lead to transparency in the financial system as a whole.

Many people now have questions about this, principally to do with the need for such a holding. I have also heard various suggestions regarding its purpose, ranging from 'putting the national companies in order' to setting up a second National Fund or something similar.

It is all in fact much simpler than that. Judge for yourselves: despite the privatisation process, the national companies are still under state authority. This does not in itself contradict market principles because there are always areas, such as market fiascoes and failures, where the state's presence is simply essential. There are other areas where society's well-being is at stake. This is why we left areas such as telecommunications, energy supplies, the railways and part of the mining industry in state hands. Theoretically, this is essential to prevent vitally important branches of the economy being regulated by private individuals and allowing them to concentrate on quality and low prices. But what happened in our country?

After acquiring their national status and, consequently, a set of privileges, our companies disregarded their original functions and started simply working by the same profit principle. Of course, profit itself is no bad thing but, along the way there has hardly been improvement in quality or services accessible to the public. Essentially, national company status means it becomes a sort of legitimate monopolist in its field of activity. In return, being state-owned and therefore operating in society's interests, a company should guarantee acceptable price levels and high quality and invest its profit in achieving these aims. Privately owned firms simply would not operate like this.

Take, for instance, Kazakhtelecom. You must agree it is much more convenient for everyone to have a single provider in charge of technological network integrity across the country. This puts it in a good position to make extremely high profits. However, instead of investing the profit to develop a range of services on offer or lowering delays and prices, the company awards its senior management incredibly high salaries and so forth. And yet there is still no internet access or even telephone service in some rural areas! That's what the national company should be concentrating on. Let me repeat: national means belonging to the nation. These funds belong to the state and, in general terms, to the whole of society. The national companies' activities should be to everyone's advantage. This is why Samruk is being set up and I hope is going to live up to all our expectations.

Key to the fourth phase are the new approaches to apportioning authority between the state bodies in respect of state property management and administration. A vital moment in this programme was the redistribution of authority from republican to communal ownership. For instance, in 1999, state packages of shares and a stockholding in 953 joint stock companies and associations with limited responsibility were transferred to communal ownership. The right to decide upon and implement privatisation was conferred on *akims* of the districts, and the cities of Almaty and Astana.

Furthermore, the programme defined the approach to effective state asset management. So, ten leading enterprises were identified and the state acquired a share in their blue chip stocks. These included joint-stock companies such as Mangistaumunaigaz, Aktobemunaigaz, Kaztsink, Ust-Kamenogorsk Titanium and Magnesium Plant (UKTMP), Sokolovsk-Sarbaisk Ore Mining and Processing Enterprise (SSOMPE), Kazakhstan Aluminium, the Kazkhrom Trans-National Company, the People's Saving Bank of Kazakhstan, Kazakhtelecom, Kazakhmys. In 1999, the privatisation took place of part of the state share package (16.7 per cent) of the JSC the People's Savings Bank of Kazakhstan, and at the end of 2000, of the JSC Mangistaumunaigaz.

To date, the state packages of the following have already been sold: the joint-stock companies Mangistaumunaigaz, Aktobe-munaigaz, Kazakhstan Aluminium, Kazakhmys, the People's Saving Bank of Kazakhstan, UKTMP, to name but a few.

During the fourth phase of privatisation the Government's work was stepped up to increase substantially the budget revenues of money funds from the use of state property. Before 2002, the funds received from privatising state property were treated as state budget revenues, whereas since then they have been used to finance the budget deficit. Since 2003, the funds received from the privatisation of major enterprises have been sent to our National Fund.

Work on optimising the number of the republic's state and communal state enterprises was begun in this period and is still continuing. They can only be kept going in instances when there is a real necessity for them to be run on this sort of legal footing.

Foregoing work experience has enabled a new concept of state property management to be developed. Its main challenges are to implement a complete inventory of state property enterprises, optimise the number of enterprises under management, and provide republican and local budgets with supplementary revenues as a result of the effective use of state property.

On 4 November 2003 the Law was enacted *On the state monitoring of property in branches of the economy of strategic importance*. This envisioned the introduction of a system of monitoring the competence of management in strategic branches of the economy, and its future development and improvement, as well as post-privatisation control.

So, our privatisation produced the results we had expected. Now part and parcel of Kazakhstan's economy, the private sector accounts for around 90 per cent of the republic's overall industrial production. The private sector's future development requires precisely formulated regulations and an adequate normative legal base unencumbered by Soviet tendencies.

Privatisation on the Scales of History

After a painful process fraught with difficulties, Kazakhstan, breaking with traditional core values, made the transition from state to private ownership, from an administrative command economy to well-balanced, rational planning and management and a market system. Only in scholarly articles and books does everything seem plain and simple. In real life, it is an ocean of passions and tragedies, and conflicts of interests between different groups and even generations. Such, regrettably, is the essence of a time of change. And we experienced the heartache of it all.

From State to Private Ownership

Most of our young people have no idea of the titanic effort and stress that went into our successes today. They must realise and remember that it is all the result of the tremendous changes, both external and internal, that have affected us – changes that were brought about by us all, through our sheer will power and perseverance.

Kazakhstan is now a shining example of a country that has emerged from a crisis. According to the experts, it owes its vanguard position in economic reforms among the CIS countries to its most successful choice of a political and economic model of the transitional period: strong presidential power plus swift and energetic reforms. It should be said at once that the reforms had to be implemented from above. Such was the nature of the time: we could not have made a success of it without a strong vertical of power.

This formula helped us build and consolidate an independent state and implement well-defined, logical reforms in the economy and politics, and guaranteed internal stability. It became clear then that had it gone for a parliamentary form of rule, Kazakhstan, with its low level of political culture, would have been doomed to persistent economic and political crises. And for a young state building its independence in the grips of a most vicious economic crisis, this would have ineluctably led to chaos and stagnation.

I shall not hide the fact, however, that the forced transition from state paternalism to economic freedom and enterprise was a most unpopular measure, not only for the public but also for most of the state apparatus. And this task was frequently achieved through resolute measures with hard-hitting consequences for the public. Realising the need for some measure or other, I would sometimes have to win people over and pressurise them to some extent. At others, I had to bear full responsibility for the implemented changes because there was no time to wait for absolutely everyone to be won over and then introduce the reforms in an environment of total concord. If we had waited, there simply would have been nothing – no state or economy – left for us to reform.

The result is plain to see: it is now up to a citizen to make all his own decisions. Altogether, over 90 per cent of the republic's production potential is in the private sector. A stratum of proprietors of small and medium-sized businesses has formed and adapted and is now continuing to expand. And it is these people who are now widely considered as forming the backbone of the middle class, the emergence of which we are doing our uttermost to encourage. Why is this so important for Kazakhstan?

As is well known, this sector of society aspires to success, has considerable purchasing power and makes a sizable contribution to the state coffers. Successful and ambitious, its members have amassed considerable fortunes. Key to middle-class mentality is a sense of responsibility for one's own life, a deep sense of individualism, and an appreciation of the value of professionalism and education as a guarantee of personal prosperity. The middle class are neither billionaires nor paupers but people who provide for themselves. Generally speaking, it's a question of 'I' being stronger than 'we'. This aspiration of an individual to be in control of his life and destiny is reflected in his activities and, consequently, the income he receives.

The emergence of a middle class in Kazakhstan is important because its presence is capable of beneficially changing the existing nature of interrelations within society, both between its strata and between society and the powers-that-be. The middle class is oriented towards stability and is itself a stabilising anchor within any society. It is 'a nation of citizens, a self-ruling majority' who understand that participating in a society's political life is an important mechanism for influencing decision-making in the country.

That's why I am personally devoting a lot of attention to this issue and constantly referring to it in my speeches and elsewhere. The privatisation process laid the foundations for the emergence of the Kazakhstani middle class by enabling people to acquire housing and start up businesses of their own, and, as a result, become owners and entrepreneurs. People were given the opportunity to work and earn a living. Nobody expected instructions or life-saving decisions from on high. People got on with building their businesses and lives. All these changes were necessary, first and foremost, for Kazakhstanis themselves, and they have already been beneficial. The radical economic reforms were greeted by a lack of understanding or downright opposition on the part of our citizens who were afraid of anything new. It is gratifying that a number of the people who left for their ancestral homeland in the 1990s are now returning to Kazakhstan. I'm delighted by this.

From State to Private Ownership

Today we can confidently announce that the main structural reforms in the economy are complete. State-owned property has been privatised, and a business sector set up in line with developed market standards.

Every state with a socialist history introducing privatisation has encountered the problem of dividing state property in a just and effective manner, and of course, not everything went smoothly during privatisation in our republic either. People were simply afraid of the concept of private property. However, during the implementation of each phase of privatisation we pursued public and state interests.

The process of economic reform was not entirely free of erroneous measures, ill-considered decisions and social complications. But it is becoming clear that given the acuteness of the crisis we were in, privatisation could not have been 'just' or 'unjust'. It can only be evaluated in terms of being effective or not. Judge for yourselves. Key areas have been totally removed from the state sector, such as public catering and trade; the light, food and manufacturing industries; various service providers and agro-industrial production. The energy and raw material industries have also been put mostly in private hands. The competitive environment in healthcare provision and education, particularly at a higher level, is undergoing rapid development.

It has to be said that there are still people in favour of redistributing property because they consider it was carried out unjustly. But nowhere in the world has initial privatisation ever taken place justly. No review should or, indeed, will take place. Such are our country's laws, and, what's more, such are development laws. We will never be able to distribute property in a way that satisfies absolutely everyone. Forgive this bitter irony, but we have already experienced what it is like to build an 'absolutely just' society. And nearly all of you know how that ended up for us and the rest of our neighbours in the ex-Union republics. This chapter of history is over. We need to look ahead. We need to improve what we have done and make people's lives better.

Nowadays the progress our citizens – state managers, businessmen and farmers – have made in economic matters is increasingly being commented upon. During one of many interviews about the republic's Independence Day, I was asked one year whom I considered made better managers: people who had previously worked in industry or career managers. I do not have a set opinion on this. Every case is different. However, going by my experience as a professional politician of 20 years' standing, I can say that the brilliant education, high levels of knowledge and healthy ambition many young people have today are not sufficient to make them successful managers, whether in business or state service.

You have seen me over the years giving a great many young businessmen and specialists a free rein. Thirty-year-olds have become government members and ministers, senior provincial officials and managers of departments and major companies. If the truth be known, only a few have succeeded in making a go of it in positions of authority. I am now inclined to think that a manager needs above all to be mature, not necessarily in age but in the way he perceives the world, situations and, most importantly, himself.

Many former plant and factory directors have made good managers in market conditions. As for who is better and who worse, that depends on each individual. Whoever successfully manages his business and people is the better of the two.

While carrying through reforms also aimed at developing a class of private owners, we encountered the need to set up an effective financial system, which was to be, figuratively speaking, the economy's 'circulatory system'. And the process involved in developing a national financial service is the subject under discussion in the next chapter.

6

THE NATIONAL FINANCIAL SYSTEM

In previous chapters of this book I have compared the state to a living organism. I like this metaphor very much. When I set about building Kazakhstan, I frequently used to imagine it as a kind of united body of people living within the same territory, under the same laws and within the framework of the same society as a single, growing, well-formed organism. And to develop this comparison further, if the economy represents the organs that make this entire organism capable of life and keep the country's metabolism going, then finances are the economy's circulatory system.

And so, in view of how important it was for there to be a smooth-running financial system, most of the economic reforms begun in the 1990s and completed later on had to do with this sphere.

It just so happened that we began these reforms at a very complex time. The traumatized public was reacting negatively to everything around it. And the economy, itself traumatized by the collapse of the Soviet system, was going through a real financial storm. The shortage of consumer goods, growth of inflation and devaluation of people's savings and current incomes were all increasing at an exponential rate. It was essential to secure financial stability, bring inflation under control, and set up a transparent, effective and stable budget that would meet public needs and ensure state services and functions were executed with maximum efficiency.

We realised the social cost of the reforms was likely to be very high. And yet we could tell from the way it was in other developed countries that the process of developing a market did not override the social content of the reforms. We endeavoured to carry through the reforms as unobtrusively for the public as possible, but because of hyperinflation this proved very difficult. In such a situation, a delay might result in a complete catastrophe.

What I recall first about those days was the tremendous onus of responsibility we took upon ourselves when we set about these

189

reforms. After the collapse of the Soviet economy it was very hard to get people who had lost their life's savings to trust our country's financial system again. When considering all the reforms, whether in taxation or pensions or any other area, foremost in our minds were our citizens and our responsibility for their well-being.

Many criticise me today, and that's up to them. At times the accusations are verging on the absurd. I know I can ignore this idle talk and unfounded criticism because, believe you me, it is absolutely trifling compared to the burden of responsibility my comrades-in-arms and I lumbered ourselves with. With no experience of similar reform we often took risks. All we knew was that we had to set up an independent financial system from zero, capable of ensuring the normal functioning of the state apparatus and our economy's development.

The reform and evolution of our national financial system took place over a period of time that may be divided into two phases. The first was approximately from 1991 to 1997, when we were confronted with issues pertaining to economic liberalisation and the achievement of general macroeconomic stabilisation. The second phase, dealing with post-stabilisation consolidation and the subsequent intensive growth of the Kazakhstan financial system began in 1998, when the world financial crisis was successfully overcome, and, in my opinion, this phase continues to this day.

Any real attempt to reveal how our financial system developed phase by phase, describing all the implemented reforms, would require a separate book. In this chapter I would like to concentrate on the general reform process, the search for a way of extricating our financial system from the crisis it found itself in, and how it subsequently joined the foremost ranks of CIS countries. There is a separate section in this chapter devoted to the issues in setting up our banking system, the sphere of state finances, pension reform and the establishment of the National Fund. There are, however, many other issues definitely worthy of attention such as the establishment of the Kazakhstan Fund Market, the securities market, the country's state debt management board and much else besides.

The banking sector, taxation and budgetary organisations were the first to undergo reform in the course of setting up our national financial system. In some sense, pension reform and the establishment of the National Fund were a particular source of pride for me. This chapter will tell you all about how it happened, about the difficulties we encountered along the way, and how our financial system came to be recognised by the world community.

First Steps: Economic Liberalisation, 1991-97

Aspiring to achieve the wonderful, distant Communist ideal with its concept of 'from each according to his abilities to each according to his work', the Soviet Union's leadership frequently set up business and production relations for reasons that made little economic sense. And, as a result, with the disintegration of the central planning mechanism – a kind of iron lung for the economically unsound production chains – all the discrepancies and artificiality of the Union's economic system became patently obvious.

That's why, at the very outset of our transition to a market economy, we had to change the actual fundamentals of business activity. To start with, it was essential to transfer economic decision-making on the distribution of financial resources from state level to that of the individual producers. This would give enterprises financial independence and make them responsible for the results and effectiveness of their investments.

The commodity-money relations established during the Soviet period required agreement at central department level in all decision-making, (that is, if such decisions were even allowed to be taken). These unwieldy relations essentially ran along the following lines: any productive or commercial unit would deposit its financial resources in USSR Gosbank accounts or its representations in the union republics. And to use these resources for its own purposes, for instance – for construction, purchasing items and so on – the enterprise would have to agree the said issue with Gosplan, the state planning commission, which, in the event of a positive decision, would transfer the agreed amount to Gosbank for it to release the necessary funds.

Thus, the country's budgetary and fiscal systems simultaneously required solutions to issues in several areas of the banking sector and state finances, areas of fundamental significance for any state. Their successful reform could be carried out only on a coordinated basis.

The Kazakhstan Way

Designing an open market economy required us to implement cardinal changes to the foundations of our economy. I have to say this was very difficult. One such solution was the liberalisation of market relations in 1993: essentially, we decided upon this move towards a market economy at a time of commodity shortages and growing hyperinflation. The introduction of liberalisation immediately led to rapid growth in various financial organisations. A special place among them belonged to commercial banks and organisations performing various forms of banking operations. For instance, by the end of 1993, there were over 200 commercial banks up and running in Kazakhstan. This situation had arisen because of the gaps in the legislation permitting virtually any enterprise or cooperative to set up its own bank. Many of them later became financially insolvent. They were set up solely for the purpose of acquiring speculative income in a climate of high inflation and instability on the hard currency market.

This, in turn, resulted in the first phases of liberalisation being accompanied by a considerable increase in inflation and a reduction in effective demand. Thus, in the period between 1993 and 1995, inflation averaged over 1,200 per cent per year. In 1995 alone, the state budget deficit was around 40 billion tenge, and second-level bank credit rates to enterprises reached 400 per cent per year.

In the initial stage of liberalization, state control was still kept on the prices of certain sorts of commodities. The state used the practice of deliveries for state needs and other restrictions for basic survival purposes. Food and essential commodity prices were fixed. As a result, enterprises suffered losses which could not be recouped even through the favourable compensation rates and policy of extending credit repayment terms.

On top of that, the state was then unable to supply the public fully with essential commodities, which led to considerable shortages. Our economy was narrowly specialised, and in Soviet times many essential goods were simply brought in from the other Union republics producing them. To ensure a supply of essential goods, the Government was forced to take 'commodity (-linked) credits' in the neighbouring producer countries. Sergei Tereshchenko's government obtained a total of over US$100 million of such credits. They were referred to as 'commodity' credits because they were issued to us by the producer countries so that we could acquire what we needed of their commodities (in keeping with their fixed terms) and spend them on the purchase of sugar, tobacco, butter, salami and so on.

Many will quite reasonably wonder after reading this why these credits had to be spent in this way in particular. We had to satiate the market with commodities to diffuse the social tension that had arisen because of the dire shortages. How could there be talk of reform when sometimes our people simply could not buy food? The shops' shelves were empty. It was a terrible sight – imagine going into a shop and seeing nothing there. It had to be seen to be believed.

The Government decided to distribute these credits to our newly-fledged businessmen to support their market activity. We also hoped they would be able to use these funds more effectively than state bodies to purchase food products and medicines for the public, and would pay for the credits themselves. High inflation was devaluing shop revenues which could not cover the amounts of credit. At the same time, some businessmen took advantage of the level of inflation and difference in exchange rates and made money as a result of this government measure. It became one of the first sources of their capital. However, as they were unable to repay the credit themselves, they ended up paying the state.

The root of these problems lay in the fact that we failed to adapt quickly to the consequences of price liberalisation. Kazakhstani enterprises lost their markets and were left on their own to confront huge structural problems. A series of urgent measures had to be taken to create a stable macroeconomic situation.

So, among other things, the state had to suspend the practice of issuing centralised credits and reduce the number of taxes. The financial system required the real price to be restored to credits by reducing the state's role in the distribution of resources. Unprofitable enterprises, which had existed on covert state subsidies in the form of credits, had to be restructured and put in the hands of more responsible, private entrepreneurs. Hence, in 1994, the practice of issuing credits on favourable terms was curtailed and the option of enterprises applying directly to the country's main bank for credits reviewed.

At the time I was afraid we would simply not have enough time for all the problems that needed urgently to be solved. What's more, practically all of them directly affected the public, who were tired and disillusioned, and might easily be pushed over the edge at any moment and over anything. Responding to questions on the reasons for the reforms' success, I sometimes really have difficulty now pinpointing the deciding factor. Some consider it to be the right social environment when people are ready for reforms, understand and applaud their implementation. However, we started the reforms, you could say, with exactly the opposite environment. The disintegration of the Union, loss of savings and accumulations and, most importantly, the loss of faith in the idea and confidence in the immediate future made our people feel abandoned and cheated. And many felt a certain sense of disillusionment and loss of confidence in us as well. But the reforms got carried through – and very successfully, too.

Some academics and experts regard the ground work for the reforms as the most important part of the process. There are plenty of examples of incubation periods for reforms lasting four to five years. Again, however, we had no time for thorough preparations or any long-term research or trials. The situation was changing on a day-to-day basis. Estimates were made in terms of months, weeks and, sometimes, even days. And yet these reforms still had successful outcomes.

I consider the greatest role in the success of our reforms was played by the human factor. I cannot say for certain exactly how, but possibly what guaranteed success was certain features of our people's mentality, their special talent for readily accepting innovation or adapting to foreign imports, and, in particular, the personal qualities of the people who joined the team of reformers at the time.

Thus, by 1999, a solution had already been found to the problem of the vast number of social benefits by switching to targeted social assistance. The transfer was made from the then solidary pension system to a new, accumulative pension system. Budgetary relations and, consequently, the country's taxation system were reviewed and restructured. However, what primarily guaranteed the success of all these reforms was our strong and dynamic banking system, which rightfully enjoys the status of being the best in the Commonwealth of Independent States.

The National Financial System

The Development of the Banking System

Kazakhstan started setting up its own banking system immediately after gaining sovereignty, in December 1990. After having direct experience of all the 'joys' of the cumbersome Soviet banking mechanism, we realised that for a fully developed economy we needed the modern two-level banking system recognised worldwide as the most effective in market conditions. It would allow us to conduct an independent monetary and credit policy, solve the problems of inflation, and meet the financial needs of the state and society. We needed a system where interest rates would reflect true capital value and banks would give credit on the basis of borrowers' financial viability and the economic effectiveness of crediting.

The start of banking reform in the country essentially began with the enactment of the Law *On banks and banking activity in the Kazakh SSR*, in January 1991. The said law provided for the foundations of a two-level banking system to be formed. So, the Republican State bank was transformed into the National Bank of the Republic of Kazakhstan with provincial administrations and branches. The Republican Promstroibank was transformed into the joint-stock commercial bank, Turanbank, and Agroprombank into the joint-stock commercial bank, Agroprombank of the Republic of Kazakhstan; shareholders were responsible for the emergence of Kazakhstan Kommerts bank, which later became known as Kazkommertsbank; Vneshtorgbank became the joint-stock commercial bank, Alembank; the republican Sberbank was renamed the People's Bank of the Republic of Kazakhstan. These are now the major private banks of Kazakhstan, forming the backbone of the second level of our banking system.

So, by the time the tenge was introduced in November 1993, the Kazakhstan banking system had undergone substantial reform: the two-level banking system was up and running, all the specialised banks had been turned into joint-stock banks, and the National Bank had been alloted a number of central bank functions. All this greatly eased the transition to our own national currency.

And yet, despite having been organised as soon as Kazakhstan gained independence, strictly speaking the National Bank was still not fulfilling the classic functions of a country's central bank. Instead, it was still carrying out a number of secondary functions, and, what's more, not everything was entirely clear in respect of its status within the system of state bodies. For instance, during the period between 1991 and 1993, the National Bank was accountable to all the branches of power. The government issued it with instructions, while deputies controlled its activities and gave it additional instructions, frequently requesting their immediate execution. All of them also requested allocations of funds for various needs.

To remedy this problem, in March 1995, I signed the Decree with the force of law *On the National Bank of the Republic of Kazakhstan* in accordance with which the National Bank became independent within the limits of the authority bestowed on it by relevant legislative acts, and accountable only to the President. Since then none of the representative and executive bodies of power has been entitled to intervene in the National Bank's activities. However, just as in all other countries, our National Bank, of course, has to coordinate issues of general state economic policy with the government. Also in 1995, we adopted the first programme to reform the republic's banking system. This programme essentially envisaged the banks financing the economy with independently attracted public savings, the free funds of individual businesses and external loans. Thus, we freed the National Bank from political pressure and functions, which second-level banks could perform much more effectively.

It has now begun to fulfil the direct functions of the country's central bank, carrying out an independent monetary and credit policy and setting up a banking system that meets present-day needs. At different times the National Bank has been headed by G. Bainazarov, D. Sembayev, O. Zhandosov, G. Marchenko, and K. Damitov. They all worked at difficult times and made their own contribution to the country's banking system. I am grateful to them.

The next important step in the development of our banking system was the programme adopted in December 1996, in the course of which the second-level banks acquired international standards of financial accountability. According to this programme, by the end of the year 2000 all Kazakhstan banks were to achieve international standards in terms of sufficient capital liquidity, quality of assets and accounting, standard of management and information collection and dissemination. At the beginning of

The National Financial System

2001, the National Bank was granted powers to supervise banking activities for it to ensure the banks followed this programme's instructions. And so, from 1 July 2001, the minimum amount of statutory capital for newly established banks was set at the fixed level of 2 billion tenge, for regional banks at 500 million tenge, and for other operating banks at over 1 billion tenge.

Normally, major banks like these make up the backbone of the banking system in states with developed market economies, but here most of all the banks' assets are concentrated in only a few of the largest commercial banks. It was this concentration of banking capital that guaranteed the competition between these banks which, in turn, enhanced banking service quality. This special feature of our banking system has been pointed out by many banking sector experts and specialists.

During the reform process we were guided by the simple but harsh market logic of the survival of the fittest. Our financial system had already survived the formation phase when the mere fact that private commercial banks were emerging was welcomed by the state. And now the entire economic system had stabilised, it was definitely time to consider these banks' function level and the quality of the services they provided. Indeed, after the prudential norms had been toughened up by the National Bank, the number of commercial banks in the country was reduced by two thirds, because very few of them were prepared to raise their function level. On the other hand, the National Bank's stringent demands in respect of the banks' accumulation of their own capital and other normatives worked out in the course of the reforms enabled the republic's banking system to survive the repercussions of the April 1999 devaluation of the tenge unscathed, and avoid the sort of financial crisis that occurred in Russia and other countries.

At the same time, however, there were specific features that we took into account as we proceeded with this approach. For instance, we had banks whose activity was mainly concentrated in the provinces where there were predominantly small businesses and agricultural concerns. The vast majority of them were experiencing a shortage of funds. This shortage of liquidity in many provinces of the republic limited the work potential of banks, which were often forced to serve only a limited circle of local clients. After all, it is no secret that the weak spot in the republic's economy was the uneven distribution of financial resources across various regions located a long way from each other. Nor did we escape the bank pyramids of fraudsters who cheated honest people.

Aware that such local banks would not be able to meet the high standards established by the National Bank, from 1998 onwards we started setting up micro-credit organisations, and then credit associations all over the country. Their establishment was aimed, first and foremost, at combating poverty and unemployment. To make banking services accessible to rural communities, the decision was taken to expand the network of post office savings bank branches, thereby providing the banking sector with an alternative means of attracting the private savings of broad sections of the public living in remote areas. Such credit associations were intended to link up to a three-level crediting system made up of banks and organisations providing separate forms of banking services, and also micro-credit organisations.

Subsequently, we took further steps to strengthen the role of the National Bank in the country's economy. First of all, it was essential to sort out the regulation of the financial service providers' activity. At the time, this regulation was carried out by different supervisory bodies. For instance, the banks' activity was regulated by the National Bank; insurance companies by the Ministry of Finance; pension funds by the Ministry of Labour. As a result, the process of coordinating the various segments of the financial market to carry out any general policy in regulating the country's financial system was long-winded and ineffectual.

So, in 2000, the National Bank was given the functions of insurance and banking supervision; in 2001, that of securities market supervision, and in 2002, the management of accumulative pension funds.

It is worth mentioning here that subsequently, in 2004, the functions of regulating the securities market, insurance market and pension system activities were transferred from the National Bank to an independent body, the Agency of the Republic of Kazakhstan (AFN) for the regulation and supervision of financial markets and financial organisations, accountable to the country's President.

It is up to this agency to ensure order in our country's financial market. It has to work within the framework of a large number of provisions and legislative codes pertaining to the pension system, the securities market and all the rest, and, indeed, it does so quite competently. Incidentally, the following data on the results of the AFN's work were particularly gratifying for me. There were 762 appeals of individuals and legal entities recorded by the agency in 2005. At first glance, this may not seem such a lot, but if you remember that most of our people for a variety of reasons usually decide not to raise problems, this number seems quite respectable. For instance, as a result of one such appeal, the Agency dealt with the problem of functioning, or rather, often malfunctioning bank cash machines.

To my mind, in some way this case serves as an example of how all our state bodies should be working. All citizens' appeals should be taken notice of, dealt with and all inquiries fully answered. Given how different life is today, people need to be taught that the state is for people and not vice versa. It's up to Kazakhstani citizens to come and find out about things, ask questions, explain their problems and get answers. And let's start interpreting that erstwhile ironic expression 'servants of the people' literally.

The end of the 1990s can definitely be pinpointed as the period when the upturn in our financial system began, and when it gained public confidence and its first successes were acknowledged by the world community. The same period also saw an upsurge in the country's economy after the crisis it had been through. For instance, in 1997, GDP growth was up 101.7 per cent on the previous year. The favourable economic situation helped the banking sector's dynamic development, a process accompanied by the formation of a competitive market.

Here I would like to note again that the measures taken to increase public confidence were key to our banking system's reform. Nowadays our public use credit of a great many kinds: vehicle, consumer, mortgage and so on. But there was a time when people were afraid of living on credit. And here a considerable role has been played by the measures to get people's accounts insured, which have significantly increased their level of confidence in the country's financial system. For instance, the Kazakhstan Credit Guarantee Fund guaranteeing (insuring) individuals' bank accounts was set up at the end of 1999, its function being to ensure that citizens got their funds back in the event of the forced liquidation of the banks participating in this scheme.

Finally, there is the case of Nauryz Bank, set up with state structural support and then reduced to bankruptcy by its incompetent director. Account holders, including the state, lost their money. The directors went on the run and the Fund had to give account holders back their money.

The Fund is now operating consistently, and gradually making the transition to international standards. The Actuary Centre opened later, in 2001, has won applause from international experts. There is also an Office of Credit Histories and a Fund for acquiring mortgage credits. According to official figures, on 30 December 2005 the Fund supported mortgage credit guarantees of over 5 billion tenge. Twenty banks and mortgage companies in Kazakhstan are currently participating in the mortgage credit guarantee system.

The clearest evidence of the financial system's success is, I consider, not the praise of foreign experts or economic estimates of various kinds but the following fact.

According to official figures, on 1 April 1999, the public held approximately US$348 million in second-level Kazakhstan bank accounts. According to various experts' estimates, citizens' concealed savings ranged from between US$1-3 billion, that is, at least one and a half times more than the sum total in bank and pension fund accounts at the time. The reform we carried out had the effect of encouraging the influx of citizens' savings into our financial system, and at present the reserves of the JSC Kazakhstan Individual Accounts Guarantee Fund in second-level banks of Kazakhstan hold approximately 339 billion tenge.

Recalling those days, I cannot help thinking how easy it is reeling off all these statistics now, when for me personally they stand for a great deal of anxiety and events, some of a curious nature. I like one of them, for instance, very much. During the campaign to attract public funds to banks, Grigory Marchenko, the then chairman of the National Bank, once promised me in public that if this campaign was a success, he would shave his beard off. The agreement was that it would be deemed successful if individual savings accounts in second-level banks reached US$1 billion.

Grigory Marchenko's announcement attracted considerable media attention. On air and in print, many economists and journalists voiced the opinion that Marchenko would be 'going about with an unshaven face for the rest of his life'. Literally two years later, however, on 7 September 2001, he arrived at a press conference, as a number of media commentators admitted, 'looking remarkably youthful, without his graying beard and moustache of many years' and announced that individual savings had reached the US$1.116 billion mark.

It is quite possible that this ingenious bet played just as much of a positive role in attracting public funds to Kazakhstan banks as the usual advertising and information methods. Subsequently, Marchenko made promises on two other occasions to shave off his beard if individual segments of the financial market reached a satisfactory set target. And nobody scoffed at or cracked jokes about his promise any more.

Grigory Alexandrovich Marchenko, a highly skilled professional, voted 'best banker' by the journal *Euromoney*, was brilliant at arguing his case and mostly proved right. I supported his policies when he was the National Bank's Chairman. Not infrequently his candour put him at loggerheads with the government and Parliament, but he always stood his ground.

I want to mention that I first articulated the idea of protecting and stimulating savings at the end of May 1999, during the First Congress of the Republic's financiers. Our economy was then encountering exceedingly severe problems because of having to adapt to the sharp change in conditions in the world's financial and commodity markets. The crisis of 1998-99 forced the banking community to focus its attention on people's domestic savings as an investment resource for economic development, where the shortage of funds essential for its maintenance and development was being compensated by an influx of external loans and foreign investments. In those days I kept a constant watch on this and other problems of the financial system. After all, it is no secret that state and private sector cooperation is much more useful to the economy than unilateral state planning.

Incidentally, thanks to the First Congress, representatives of all the financial market's sections got together for the first time specifically to discuss the development problems of Kazakhstan's financial market. The topics under discussion included expanding investment potential and establishing new financial instruments to enhance shared efforts to resolve global tasks of economic growth and improve public welfare.

At the same time as the accounts guarantee system was set up, the legislation was tightened up on bank secrecy to protect account holders' interests. And so information about the balance and movement of funds in individual accounts is now made available to the investigating authorities only in the event of a criminal case and with the approval of the public prosecutor. What's more, the taxation and customs authorities were excluded from the list of state bodies exercising the right to receive information constituting bank secrecy.

Another clear indication of our financial system's success is the expansion of Kazakh capital into the markets of neighbouring states and the appearance of foreign capital in our financial market.

There was a time when we could not even have imagined such a thing. We simply wanted to keep our own financial system and economy functioning as a whole. In actual fact, though, the results of the reforms have far exceeded our most audacious expectations. The standards of monetisation of Kazakhstan's economy are the highest among the CIS countries, enabling our banks to undertake active expansion into our neighbours' financial markets. Because our banking system is more developed than that of neighbouring countries, our banks are able to offer more favourable rates and conditions, winning the competitive battle with local banks that do not have the same amounts of capital available, or, most importantly, the security and account profitability guarantees. For instance, in Kazakhstan the average annual interest rate is between 10-15 per cent, whereas in neighbouring Tajikstan it is as high as 36 per cent per year. That's quite a difference.

What's more, the stability of the macroeconomic situation, and our people's rising standard of living, make Kazakhstan very attractive for foreign financial companies. Whereas our interest rate may seem low compared to other CIS countries, for Western consumers these rates of 10-15 per cent are unacceptably high. The arrival of foreign banks makes it possible to develop competition in Kazakhstan's financial market.

For instance, the major Czech insurance company Home Credit Group is now in our market, and the JSC Home Credit Kazakhstan was set up last year. The priority direction of the company's operations is consumer crediting. The company is reacting efficiently to the changes taking place in Kazakhstan's credit service market, offering clients and partners optimum conditions for crediting and cooperation. Kazakhstan's most successful commercial enterprises are in partnership with the JSC Home Credit Kazakhstan. They include the top commercial chains Tekhnodom, Evroset, Sulpak, and M-Tekhniks, as well as specialised shops in all the country's provinces and a great many other companies. The network of partners is constantly expanding, and the company is concentrating specifically on developing business relations with reliable, experienced partners.

The growth in the consumer crediting market is attracting new major foreign players to Kazakhstan. Another major financial group in the Euro zone, the French banking group Societé Générale, has now decided to follow the Czech financial group and plans to get into Kazakhstan's retail market by opening a subdivision here.

This may sound odd, but I am simply delighted to have foreign capital here. After all, the time has passed when the high rates were justified by the high level of credit risk. People now have stable incomes and secure financial positions. But our banks are still not ready to move on from this period of high rates. The foreign financiers will raise the level of competition in the financial services market, and society will benefit as a result.

Summing up the results of the banking sector's development, one can say in general terms that throughout the period its development took place thanks to the state's multifaceted support and the large-scale overhaul of the state financial system. It would, therefore, be unjust not to mention the process involved in improving it, especially as cardinal reforms took place in both the budgetary and taxation systems.

The Budgetary and Taxation Systems

As I have already emphasised, effective state policy in the area of state finance had first to be secured in order for the banking system to undergo development. After losing Union budget subsidies and grants (which in 1991 constituted one sixth of our republic's budget) and departmental sources of financing, we began experiencing a severe crisis in our industries and enterprises that had formerly been harnessed to the Soviet system and represented over 90 per cent of the republic's overall production output.

One of the first steps to reform the state financial sphere was the adoption in 1991 of Kazakhstan's own law on the budgetary system, in accordance with which the principles of forming the budgets of the Republic of Kazakhstan were changed and the inter-relations between the republican and local budgets defined. Its underlying principle was the independence of the republican and local budgets.

However, events were developing at such a speed that soon the law no longer met the demands of the time. Suffice it to say, the principle of "different-level budgetary unity", fundamental in setting up an effective budgetary system, had not yet been established, and an additional budget was still being drawn up, treated and passed just like a regular annual one.

As for state financial system management, until 1994, the National Bank and the Ministry of Finance were both involved in executing the state budget, and this joint system did not make for effective control. With a view to improving it, we set about establishing the Treasury's Main Board within the Ministry of Finance. This made it possible from 1996 onwards to conduct all the entry and write-off accounting of aggregate revenues and banking transaction expenditures through a single treasury account. A year later the mechanism of financing local budget expenditure with payment assignments was changed, and financing was effected by means of limits issued in the form of financial and budgetary allowances. This was one of our first steps in improving the country's budgetary system.

Prior to the reforms, the entire budgetary process consisted of the usual processing of budgetary demands followed by the final distribution of exceedingly limited funds between all the budgetary institutions. Virtually no consideration was given during this process to the macroeconomic situation, on the basis of which the budget was to be executed, and no attempts were made to coordinate expenditure with the principles and priorities of economic policy. Thus, the process of drawing up the budget was more about figure shuffling than a discussion of the priorities and programmes the Government ought to be addressing. Even in the final stage of the preparatory process when the budget's final draft was being discussed in Parliament, the debates only revolved around specific items of expenditure. What's more, no attempts were made to link expenditures with programme priorities.

One of the important steps taken in this area in 1997 was the introduction of a new budgetary revenue and expenditure classification in keeping with international standards. This made it possible to co-ordinate the expenditures of budgets at all levels with the execution of the state's programme objectives, improve executive discipline and increase transparency during the formation of a budget.

The year 1999 saw the enactment of the third Law of the Republic of Kazakhstan *On the budgetary system*, which enabled the principle of budgetary system unity to be secured, a uniform standard of state services to be offered the public throughout the republic, and the discrepancies between regions to be leveled out. This law also established inter-budgetary relations: the mechanisms of budget withdrawals and subventions, and the financing of set state functions were delimited from the funds of republican and local budgets respectively. During this phase the main emphasis in the reform was to ensure budget funds were spent purposefully and effectively and prevent the growth of the budget's credit debts. We established in law for the first time that no state institutions were entitled to take on more financial obligations than the total number of budgetary assignments fixed by budgetary legislation for the given financial year.

The budgetary commissions set up on a permanent basis allowed us to resolve the pressing issue of rationalising state expenditures during the formation of the budget for the following year. The state budget was divided into a current budget, on the basis of which the programmes intended to meet the state's continuing needs were carried through, and a development budget including investment spending in the economy – that is, spending on infrastructure development, municipal building, the setting up and development of information systems, science, investments in human capital and so on. Dividing the budget in such a way allowed a full valuation to be made of the cost of the state carrying out its functions, defined in law and aimed at maintaining the networks of state institutions, and the state's total investment contribution to social and economic development. It also systematised budgetary programmes.

The Budgetary Code established to formulate a systemic approach to budgetary regulation made it possible to organise and systematise the functioning norms of legislation and provide them with a more flexible structure. For the first time the National Fund was officially recorded as being part of the country's budgetary system.

This code enshrined the new principles of the budgetary system, guaranteeing its consistency and stability, and revised the previous principles of budgetary planning and approaches to forming the revenue and spending sections of budgets of all levels. It was important that this Budgetary Code provided an appraisal of the budgetary programmes' effectiveness by carrying out the necessary computations, an analysis of the soundness of the budgetary programmes, the course of their execution and their impact on the country's social and economic situation, as well as identifying the budgetary programmes' ineffective directions.

One of the most vital aspects of the budgetary reform was the search for an optimum solution to state loan management. The issue of financing the state budget deficit was particularly pressing, and for the first time we set about laying down in the law the exact limit of state borrowing to cover the country's substantial budget deficit.

The Government had previously financed the budget deficit by borrowing funds from the National Bank. However, the latter's direct crediting of the budget deficit was neutralising our efforts to curb the rate of inflation and maintain national currency stability. That's why the state set about reducing the financing of the deficit with National Bank funds and attracting foreign loans instead. So, in 1997, these loans comprised 81 per cent of the total, whereas in 1994 they had only comprised 55 per cent. The economy's macroeconomic stabilisation also facilitated the increase in foreign borrowing. As a result, by 1998 the republic's government had completely ceased direct borrowing from the National Bank.

Subsequently, the amount of foreign borrowing continued gradually to decrease thanks to economic growth and the relative high cost of these loans, constituting 76 per cent in 1998 and 63 per cent in 1999. The Government's foreign borrowing was effected through four issues of sovereign international bonds: three-year (1996), five-year (1997), five-year (1999) and seven-year (2000). The floating of euro bonds in 1999 and 2000 were particular effective in bolstering Kazakhstan's international image, since it occurred at a time of substantially reduced confidence on international capital markets in developing countries. International experts appraised the second floating in such a manner.

However, as we embarked upon developing our own budgetary system, we came up against the problem of fixing its revenues. During the first years of independence we found ourselves in an impasse on account of an elementary lack of up-to-date legislative acts on taxation issues. In the Soviet period all taxation policy had been formulated outside the republic and we had no relevant expertise in this area. What's more, the sharp increase in the number of established enterprises made business and tax accounting more complex. All these factors added to the urgency of reforming the taxation system itself.

And yet, when referring to the setting of new principles for the budgetary organisation of states, it has to be said that we embarked upon this step in a systematic manner by preparing the rest of the legislative base. It was no easy task. Bills of such vital importance for the country piled up in the Supreme Soviet, and were only brought out for discussion once every six months at best when the situation in the country was literally changing not just daily but hourly – and, more often than not, changing for the worse.

Despite this deteriorating situation, at the seventh session of Kazakhstan's Supreme Soviet in 1991, we enacted a republican package of normative legal acts on taxes, including 14 laws. As a whole, the Law *On the taxation system in the Republic of Kazakhstan* envisioned 16 general state, ten general obligatory, and 17 local laws. The law was one of the first steps in reforming the country's economy.

As well as improving the budgetary system, we conducted work to ensure the taxation system met the demands of the time. The initial step in this direction was the enactment in 1995 of the Law *On taxes and other obligatory budget payments* which increased the taxation system's effectiveness. With the enactment of this, the emphasis of taxation policy was not on increasing the number of taxes but, rather, simplifying them. It encouraged enterprises to increase their business activity and production, and facilitated the introduction of highly effective technologies, long-term capital investment and the attraction of foreign investors.

The law's fundamental principle was that of fairness which envisaged 'vertical' and 'horizontal' equality. In this system all taxpayers' incomes, independent of size and the manner in which they were earned and spent, were taxed uniformly and on equal terms. The advantage of the reformed taxation system was its maximum simplicity, the economic neutrality of taxation and minimisation and compatibility of tax rates. So, the 45 types of taxes and duties and six other types of deductions to so-called targeted funds were replaced by 19 types of taxes and duties.

Depreciation quotas were increased and the method of calculating them was simplified, so as to increase investment stimuli and incentives to renew basic stock and improve production.

However, this law could not fully solve the problems that had emerged during the reforms. It was clear the taxation system was imperfect and required further reform.

The taxation system in effect then worked on the principle of 'selective privileging'. For instance, nine different rates, ranging from zero to 70 per cent, were applied to profit tax (depending on the form of property, industry and type of activity) and over 40 types of privileges in the form of payment exemptions and tax rate reductions (depending on the direction of profit expenditure and the profit's source). The remaining taxes were acquiring an ever-increasing number of privileges. Another example of this system's ineffectiveness was that profits, tax rates were differentiated on the basis of the type of industry and form of property.

By granting the taxation bodies independent status in the same year, we were able to fix the general principles of structuring the taxation system, and the method of raising taxes, and regulate the mechanism of introducing new types of taxes and rate levels. The foundations were thus laid for the current system of taxation administration.

The most important and fundamental change to the taxation system was the introduction in 1992 of what was for us a new tax on additional value (VAT). Its introduction provided the republic's budget with a reliable and effective source of revenue and gave important freedom to the manoeuvre of regulating consumer demand. At the time it served as a means of preventing the inflationary depreciation of budgetary funds as it indexed tax receipts directly with price increases.

Taking account of the subsequent changes to the economic situation in the period after 1995, the new Taxation Code was elaborated in 2001 and launched at the start of 2002. The new Taxation Code's provisions optimally combined the taxes' fiscal and incentivising functions and allowed the basic aim of continuing taxation policy to be effectively carried through: the establishment of a tax system satisfactorily combining the interests of the state and taxpayer.

The adoption of the new Taxation Code marked a further phase in the development of Kazakhstan's tax legislation. This code strengthened the conceptual foundations of the tax system formulated in previous years as well as increasing the effectiveness of the legal mechanisms in the legal sphere. The stability of tax legislation principles and the integrity of tax privilege systems were consolidated by the Code, and the norms of granting privileges of an individual nature to specific taxpayers excluded. In recent years tax rates have been substantially reduced: (personal income tax to 10 per cent and VAT to 14 per cent), and the intention is to simplify and reduce them further. The reform of this segment of Kazakhstan's financial system has played a quite significant role in its general formation and successful development. Our financial system was to win acclaim as the best in the CIS at an international level after we successfully overcame the economic crisis of 1998, which had engulfed the countries of South-East Asia and Russia.

The Economic Crisis of 1998
The economic crisis of 1998 was a sort of endurance test for our young country and its financial system. As a result of global changes in the financial markets, a substantial devaluation of national currencies took place in a whole series of Kazakhstan's trading partner countries. This led to an increase in the price of the Kazakhstan tenge in real terms and contributed to the fall in Kazakhstan's export competitiveness. The negative repercussions of the world crisis on Kazakhstan's economy became more palpable

after the Russian rouble's devaluation. This gave rise to problems linked to protecting domestic commodity producers from the influx of foreign commodities and keeping a steady tenge exchange rate.

The tendency to automatically relate any assessment of the situation in Russia to Kazakhstan caused a flurry of demand for foreign currency on the domestic currency market. To regulate the situation in the currency market and maintain the then fixed tenge exchange rate, the National Bank carried out substantial currency interventions which led to a significant drop in gross gold and foreign reserves. Over US$600 million were lost keeping a stable exchange rate during this period. It was an extremely difficult time for the tenge. To prevent a further slide in the gold and foreign currency reserves and restore the economy's competitiveness, it became necessary to proceed with the tenge's devaluation. You remember well who was against this measure. So, you could say we destroyed yet another myth.

Nowadays one has to put up with claims that the tenge should have been devalued earlier, immediately after the collapse of the Russian rouble. However, I am firmly convinced that at a time of instability in the financial markets of the CIS countries and with expectations of devaluation running high within Kazakhstan, immediate devaluation would not have had the desired effect. Any parity of currency exchange rates fixed as a result of devaluation in such conditions would have quickly lost balance. At that moment the main challenge was not to let the currency market collapse or lose the confidence of the public and economic players in the banking system, which would have been disastrous.

At the time, the National Bank under the chairmanship of Grigory Marchenko adhered to the position that the tenge should not be devalued during a time of crisis. We had sufficient reserves and we were prepared to spend part of them to defuse the crisis. And that is how we dealt with it. Despite the fact that during this period the National Bank lost a significant quality of foreign currency reserves and, to all intents and purposes, contributed to a process that resulted in the banking system receiving high revenues by speculating successfully with foreign currency and state securities, we still overcame the crisis without significant repercussions.

The new National Bank Chairman K. Damitov was seemingly in favour of devaluation. However, he also had his misgivings, as it was a tremendous responsibility for him. I invited him over and we spent a long time discussing the pros and cons, and only in April 1999, once the financial situation in Russia had stabilised and devaluation expectations had died down in the country, did we proceed with the introduction of a free-floating tenge exchange rate.

Thanks to the preparatory work completed prior to the tenge's devaluation in September 1998, the transition to the free-float regime went successfully. A thorough analysis of the basic principles and procedural issues involved helped greatly here. For instance, all manner of scenarios for the ways in which the external economic situation in the world and particularly in Russia might subsequently develop were analysed when deciding about the new exchange-rate regime. The advantages and disadvantages of each option were evaluated in respect of the expected levels of a balanced tenge exchange rate, balance of payments, gold and foreign currency reserves, budget deficit and every segment of the financial market and social indicators. Thanks to accumulated experience and this regime's rapid introduction, the collapse of the currency market and banking system was successfully averted.

As a temporary measure to support the currency market we even carried through the sale of 50 per cent of export revenues from April to mid-November 1999. In so doing, special emphasis was placed on the protection of individuals' tenge accounts and legal entities' deposits in second-level banks, and also the tenge assets of pension funds. A series of indemnity measures were carried through. For instance, bank account holders who kept their tenge deposits for at least nine months after the introduction of the free-float were given the opportunity of converting them fully into US dollars at the exchange rate prior to devaluation. With a view to protecting the pension assets of accumulative pension funds, the Ministry of Finance issued special currency bonds (AVMEKAM) with a face value of US$100 and a five-year term of circulation.

As a result of these adopted measures, the transition to the new currency policy went fairly smoothly and banking system operations remained stable. It took a matter of days for the tenge exchange rate at currency exchanges to stabilise. Introducing free float helped restore the competitiveness of Kazakhstan's exports and revive production growth. For instance, exports for 1998 were in excess of US$6.012 billion.

Introducing free float was a politic measure as well as an economic one, primarily in terms of securing stable economic policy and reassuring the public. Despite various recommendations by international financial organisations, we took as many measures as possible to protect individuals' and legal entities' savings. We granted bank clients the right to convert their accounts at the exchange rate prior to the tenge's devaluation.

The said measures helped avoid an overestimation of the tenge real exchange rate. The results following a year of devaluation revealed a significant improvement in the balance of payments and increase in the state's gold and foreign currency reserve assets and, most importantly, renewed production growth in the economy. The level of the tenge real exchange rate in relation to the currencies of the main trading partner countries achieved three years after the introduction of free float was the same as the one fixed at the end of 1999. I consider the introduction of free float to have been vitally important and fully justified. Foreign experts also concur with this opinion.

'By the time the financial crisis struck Russia in 1998, Kazakhstan was better prepared; the tenge lost only half its value within a year. Thanks to its consistent policy-making, the National Bank has gained the authority of Parliament, the industrialists and the government.'
The journal *Euromoney*, 'The Kazakhstan Miracle', 1 April 2004

As a result of the measures taken, we were able to keep the negative impact of the world financial crisis to a minimum and maintain macroeconomic stability, which duly won the high praise of international financial institutions, as well as retaining foreign bank creditors' and major investors' confidence.

Kazakhstan's economic vulnerability was still, however, a serious problem. Suffice it to say that a year after the tenge's devaluation, we were confronted with the reverse problem of the tenge's re-evaluation, which is now becoming increasingly topical. Thus, despite the apparent strengthening of the tenge, the process of the economy's de-dollarisation is still not taking place on account of the influx of large amounts of foreign currency from oil revenues.

A part here is also played by the banks' substantial foreign loans, and the foreign investments in the economy. This is not bad in itself, but whereas the state used to be more preoccupied with the actual matter of attracting investments, now, in my opinion, we should already be paying more attention to the quality of this investment: where this money is going and what real effect it is having, the terms being applied and so on. As far as the quality of investments is concerned, mention should first be made of the 'long money' – the long-term investments of 15 years and more. Such 'long money' is very necessary for carrying out major investment projects where the term of recoupment and return exceeds the average index in the capital investment market. As a rule, these are scientific development and application projects and new technology and production-line application projects, so essential for our economy.

Many argue that we have funds, such as the assets of accumulative pension funds, that are too restricted by binding legislation. We realise the considerable impact these assets might have if they were involved in our economy. However, this process cannot be hurried. First and foremost, as far as we are concerned, this money belongs to people. That's why it is essential to work out all the issues to protect these accounts and potential projects' criteria.

Our pension system was set up very recently and its greatest achievement to date, in my opinion, is not the extent of its assets and so on but how much public confidence it enjoys. This is the accumulative pension funds' most valuable asset, and perhaps says more about them than profitability indexes or anything else. The gravest consequence of pension funds being unsoundly invested would be a loss of public confidence.

The set of tools for investing pension fund assets are bound to increase, but only when we find an optimum combination of profitability and security guarantees for people's pension funds. I personally am devoting particular attention to this issue because I still recall the shock and rebukes of people who once lost all their savings, and I am particularly grateful to them for, regardless of this, still trusting us and supporting the conduct of pension reform in 1997-98.

Pension Reform, 1997-98

Pension provision is arguably one of those social issues always in a government's field of vision in any state in the world. Kazakhstan is no exception, with its Constitution guaranteeing citizens' rights to social security in old age. One is fully justified in asserting nowadays that the accumulative pension system is the showcase of Kazakhstan's financial system. The country carried out the transition to an accumulative pension system at a time when the former solidary system was no longer able to fulfil all its obligations to pensioners.

In the mid-1990s pension provision issues gained particular acuity on account of the fall in GDP levels, rise in unemployment, rapid rise of inflation, decline in national revenue and acute budget deficit. The result was, among other things, the state's reduced share in the financing of pension provision and an increase in pension payment arrears.

The problems linked to the shortfall in the financing of essential pension spending was exacerbated by demographic processes, namely, that of the republic's aging population – as in many other countries of the world. For instance, weak economies and demographic situations in Germany and France were forcing their governments to introduce measures to raise the pension age and pension contributions.

Something similar was being observed in Kazakhstan. For instance, whereas in 1980 there were nearly 30 pensioner beneficiaries for every 100 employees and pension contributors, in 1997 that number had increased to 73, and in 1998, to 83. Between 1980 and 1997, the percentage of pensioners in the overall population rose from 11.9 per cent to 17.1 per cent. The large-scale migratory processes in the 1990s also played a role here. These were mainly young people seeking to leave Kazakhstan in search of a better life and a better country, whereas pensioners were simply unable to leave because they either had nowhere to go or had insufficient funds.

The pension system's high dependency rate – or, to be more precise, the correlation between pension beneficiaries and contributors – was a result of old USSR pension legislation. The pensionable age was then 60 for a man and 55 for a woman. Moreover, quite frequently retirement pensions were granted at a younger age.

Thus, it was the deformed pension-assignment structure that was determining the growth in state spending on pension provision, constituting 7.9 per cent of GDP in 1996, compared to 5.6 per cent in 1989. Also important to note is that this spending might have been significantly higher, had the state fully indexed pension payments to inflation.

Keeping the solidary pension system of Kazakhstan in the form it had taken until 1998 might have aggravated the crisis in the economy, and ultimately in the republic's social sphere. So I instructed the government to analyse other countries' experiences and come up with proposals.

The Cabinet of Ministers and National Bank proposed adopting the Chilean pension model. This project was heatedly discussed in society and there was considerable opposition to it. There were many misgivings, but we had no other option at that time. The country's economy was simply not coping with the existing conditions.

Why did we go for the Chilean option in particular?

In the mid-20th century most countries in the world came up against the aging population problem: increased longevity and a decline in birth rates. In solidary pension systems, such longevity was a heavy burden on the working population. You see, the taxation load on the economically active sector of the population becomes heavier as their numbers fall in relation to pensioners. Alternatively, there is a shortage of funds and various attempts to cover it, for instance, by lowering pensions, may cause acute social tension in society.

The solution to this situation, which involved privatising the pension system, was found in 1980 by Chile's Minister of Labour José Pinier. In the system he was proposing, every employee was entitled and committed to making private provisions for his or her own future. Instead of a state pension paid out of tax receipts, individual savings invested in securities began to be introduced. Working citizens were given an opportunity to voluntarily transfer to the new system, while it automatically applied to employees starting work for the first time.

As well as solving social problems, conducting similar reform could give additional stimulus to the development of Kazakhstan's economy. Suffice it to say that pension savings could become (as in

Chile) a source for investing in the development, first of all, of the domestic economy through the securities market.

That's why Kazakhstan was the first of the CIS countries to start the planned transition to an accumulative pension system. The Government gave its backing to the concept of reforming the pension system, setting the gradual transition from the principle of generational solidarity, to be retained for the time being, to that of personal pensions as its strategic direction. Essentially, it was a significant step towards forming a new pension system which met market demands.

The main aim of conducting pension reform was to build a financially secure, fair system, adjusting salaries to pensions through a personified register of pension contributions.

The year 1998 saw the adoption of the Law *On pension provision in the Republic of Kazakhstan* envisioning the introduction of a mixed pension system. It also envisaged the retention of state pension provision (the solidary pension system), alongside which the accumulative pension was set up and is still currently developing.

The solidary system was based on pensions being paid out of social taxes and other republican budget revenues, whereas the accumulative pension system is based on deductions of obligatory pension contributions, constituting 10 per cent of an employee's income, as well as voluntary contributions.

During the transitional period to the accumulative pension system, the state committed itself to guaranteeing current pensioners' right to receive pensions, and also meeting its commitments to citizens who had been in employment prior to the start of the pension reforms. The state's pledge to current pensioners was to maintain the size of pension they received from the state pension payment centre, and also index them in line with consumer price growth.

I want to note – the adopted policy, in keeping with the economic practice of the past decade, of consistently raising minimum pensions and indexing pensions in line with inflation, resulted in a reduced differentiation between work pensions and their alignment, regardless of the pensioners' term of employment and former wages.

As the economic situation in the country steadily improved, the insufficient differentiation between work pensions, low level of received pensions and income substitution coefficient acquired particular topicality as factors inhibiting the effective demand growth of this sector of the population. A mechanism for the differentiated increase of pensions was worked out to resolve this problem. It envisaged establishing a link between pension sizes and employment service, the wages forming the basis on which the pension was to be calculated, and the average monthly wage in the branch of the economy from which the employee was to retire.

The state reserved the right to regulate the activities of accumulative pension system bodies: accumulative pension funds, custodian banks and pension asset investment management organisations. The activity of all these bodies became licensed, and legal restrictions on powers to deal with assets were introduced, as were requirements in respect of the openness and transparency of information pertaining to the system's bodies' financial status.

With a view to guaranteeing investment effectiveness, and pension savings' security, and avoiding the depreciation of pension accumulations, a list of the assets to be invested was established legislatively. And, furthermore, voluntary pension contributions from private sources were now allowed. As a result of recent reforms in the country, pension funds may now invest their portfolios directly, as well as through pension asset-fund investment companies. These changes are aimed at eliminating pension asset-management monopolies and reducing administrative expenditure.

The introduction of pension reform has enhanced financial organisations' further development.

Pension assets are involved in the economy's real sector by being invested in the domestic organisations' non-state securities, in (deposit) accounts in second-level banks which, in turn, use these resources for crediting Kazakhstan's economy. Thus, on 1 January 2006, pension asset investments in domestic organisations' non-state securities and second-level bank accounts constituted 218.6 billion tenge.

Implementing pension reform obviously takes time. For instance, the citizens who were close to pensionable age at the time the new pension system was introduced will have little time to accumulate funds. In view of this, the complete transfer to an accumulative pension system in Kazakhstan will take place before 2038-2040.

When I recall the reform that has been carried through, I

sometimes simply say to myself, 'How good that we've managed to do this!' Our people can accumulate funds themselves and in so doing, guarantee a normal old age for themselves. A pension is now made up of three contributors: the state + employer + citizen. Gradually the state will cease to be in the equation. That's why every Kazakhstani must become a participant in an accumulative pension fund if he wants to guarantee a suitable old age for himself. And, what's more, the money accumulating in pension funds can contribute to the economy.

However, I have again returned to an important issue. What matters most is that the state guarantees the inviolability and security of these funds. They must never be in danger. And so, many issues must be considered when these funds are used for investment purposes, particularly the status of the enterprise or firm in question. A draft law on ensuring the security of funds is being drawn up which, by reviewing this issue, will allow pension funds to invest money in reliable enterprises. This, in turn, will stimulate the development of the loan securities market and reduce credit costs.

For instance, the first project we will be investing in is the construction of the Shar-Oskemon Railway. We shall also most probably be investing in oil projects, and the infrastructure under state guarantee, and looking at possible options when carrying out industrial programmes. And then there is possibly housing construction. We are now working very seriously on ensuring that the pension funds provide good interest rates for our future pensioners, and the money contributes satisfactorily to the economy. This is similar to what is going on all over the world.

Returning to the question of investing pension savings and internal investments, I also want to say the following. While reforming the financial system and trying to involve people's funds in the economy, we came up against the problem of 'grey money' which, like pension fund assets, might have become a domestic source of investing in the country's economy. Income legalisation has been an attempt to solve the issue of the emergence of a black economy and capital leakage.

The National Financial System

The Financial Amnesty and Legalisation of Property

During the first years of independence, weak market institutions and the lack of effective legislative acts contributed to the fact that between US$1.2 and US$2 billion were being illegally taken out of Kazakhstan every year. As a comparison, the sum in Russia was US$40-50 billion. In 1999, the Statistics Agency of the Republic of Kazakhstan estimated that the black sector constituted 20-25 per cent of GDP, although independent experts put it higher, at 45-50 per cent of GDP.

Given such substantial sums, we had to create the conditions to return this capital to the country and channel these resources into developing the country's economy. There was an increasing need for an economic amnesty. This was planned exclusively as a one-off to legalise the money of citizens of the Republic of Kazakhstan previously undeclared and taken out of legal economic circulation. The action was essentially intended to exempt people from taxation and legal action if they legalised black capital, which had been earned on a legal basis but not legalised owing to the high taxes. Subsequently, we found ourselves in the position of having to repeat this act, which passed off very well indeed.

During preparations for the legalisation I made arrangements for a fully comprehensive worldwide study to be conducted on the effects (positive and negative) of such actions. Its main conclusion was that the expediency of such actions depended largely on the conditions enabling citizens to legalise their previously covert capital. Kazakhstan's government devoted particular attention to developing conditions that would guarantee highly positive and effective reform.

For instance, a study of the first amnesty in Switzerland showed that it had had a very beneficial effect on the country's banking system and helped sharply improve the investment climate, production levels and the macroeconomic indexes of the country as a whole.

There were also positive results from the amnesties in countries such as France (1982, 1986), Argentina (1987), India (1997) and China, as well as a number of others. After officially declaring their capitals and paying taxes on them, citizens in China, for instance, were allowed to do as they pleased with their money without worrying about tax demands. In due course, several billion US dollars went into the state budget. In Ireland the sum total received from the taxation amnesty exceeded that in the budget and constituted 2.5 per cent of GDP. As the result of a similar amnesty Mexico received over two billion US dollars.

At the beginning of April 2001, the Law of the Republic of Kazakhstan *On the amnesty of citizens of the Republic of Kazakhstan in connection with the legalisation of money by them* was passed. The law worked as follows. Kazakhstan's citizens had to deposit their money in, or transfer it to special accounts (which could not be accessed during the legalisation period) in second-level banks participating in the account security system. After the cash in domestic or foreign currency had been deposited, or the transfers from personal accounts in foreign banks had gone through, the bank issued the account holder with an official document (certifying the sum had been deposited in a special account as part of the legalisation process) confirming the sum total and date of receipt. The sums deposited in special accounts were not counted as taxable income.

The persons who deposited sums of money were exonerated from criminal liability for committing crimes before legalisation. Exemption from criminal liability was, however, only granted for unlawful entrepreneurial activity without a license, for being engaged in prohibited forms of entrepreneurial activity, for false business undertakings and so on.

The force of law did not extend to persons who, before the legalisation of money, already had criminal proceedings instituted against them or were in receivership; or to convicts or persons who had administrative penalties imposed upon them. What's more, its force did not extend to cases of legalising money received as a result of corrupt infringements of the law, crimes against the individual, world and human security, the foundations of the constitutional order and state security, property and the interests of the state service, social security and social order, the public's health and morality, or money belonging to other persons or received as credits.

Confidentiality was a specific condition of the legalisation process. It was established in law that information on the special accounts and sums of money in them was not disclosable, and the presence of a special account could not be the basis for any procedural actions, including the institution of criminal proceedings or application of administration penalty measures. The money presented for legalisation could be seized as state property only in the event of court rulings (sentences) coming into effect, making provision for the confiscation of the property of citizens amnestied in accordance with the present law. The money placed in special accounts in domestic or foreign currency could be withdrawn by the account holder immediately upon the expiration of the term of legalisation.

As a result, in only two months (June and July 2001) the sum total of personal accounts in the banking system increased by over 46 per cent (to 51.7 billion tenge). The sum total of legalised funds was around US$480 million, or over 2 per cent of GDP. Approximately 55 per cent of these funds remained in the banking system in the form of deposits, which helped the substantial expansion of the banks' resource base.

To make effective use of the amnestied funds, emissions of medium-term state securities were reduced from May to June 2001, with a planned increase for July 2001. The terms of the arrangements for issuing the securities of major enterprises, including national companies, were extended so that the initial date of the securities' investment coincided with the end of the legalisation period. At the same time, tax rates in Kazakhstan began to be reduced: from 1 July 2001 VAT was reduced by 4 per cent, and social tax by 5 per cent.

As a conclusion, I would like to add that the economic amnesty in Kazakhstan was a unique action in post-Soviet space. Its aim was to attract additional financial funds to Kazakhstan's economy which had previously been removed from legal economic circulation. Approximately half a billion US dollars were legalised as a result. Although these legalised funds are private and the state has not received a single tenge from them in the form of tax payments, the mediated economic benefit is obvious. The capital now in the banking sector is working for the good of the state and society, and the substantial influx of foreign currency in cash has strengthened the status of Kazakhstan's national currency.

Another beneficial effect of the legalisation of black economy capital for the state treasury has been the increase in the taxable base and number of tax payers, and, consequently, an increase in budget receipts.

The Kazakhstan Way

Taking account of the positive results of conducting the first legalisation in Kazakhstan, we are currently working on legalising property as a logical continuation of financial legalisation. Its successful implementation will eradicate illegal property, put it on the legal register and introduce it to the economic relations system.

According to Ministry of Justice data, there are currently over 4.7 million real estate properties whose ownership deeds have not been registered with the appropriate authorities. In fact, 30 per cent of all real estate properties are unregistered. According to preliminary estimates, introducing these properties into legal circulation may attract around four billion tenge to the country's economy.

Why have we decided to conduct this campaign?

First, as I have already said, property legalisation is the logical follow-on from the amnesty on capital. The problems of the black economy and, consequently, 'grey money' and property, were caused by the inadequacy of the laws and instability of the economy situation over previous years. And now that these parameters have improved, we must try to introduce all these hidden assets into legal circulation. And here I should, I suppose, stress that, in accordance with the law, the legalisation measures do not extend to persons who obtained their money by criminal means.

There is no shortage of critics of this action, but we must not listen to them. As long as I can remember, there have always been people who have attempted to rouse social hysteria over nearly every one of our reforms. And what happened as a result? Where are they all now when we can really see the positive results of these reforms? When every citizen personally feels their effectiveness in his or her daily life?

Any criticism should be backed up by an alternative proposal. That's the principle I've always been guided by. Moreover, criticism should be positive and not of the kind we often confuse it with. It is a maxim I personally always follow. If I don't like something other people have done, I first of all ask myself what I could propose instead. However, nobody came up with any other ways of dealing with illegal property except those in common usage throughout the world. We are ready for a dialogue and veritably welcome all proposals. And I do mean proposals and not groundless expressions of discontent about everything under the sun. Criticism in our country often reminds me of the petty discussions in Soviet times on the never-ending subject of culpability. Should we really send all the owners of the 4.7 million properties to prison, even if the irregularities were the result of ignorance or negligence? I don't think so.

Conditions guaranteeing the confidentiality of the information provided were, however, not incorporated in the elaboration of the law. Work is now being carried out to eliminate this flaw. There is also a pressing need for broad-based explanatory work on the procedure involved in the state's recognition of property rights. Again, this is intended not as a means of tracking down people guilty of hiding property but to introduce this property into legal circulation where it will be officially registered and, correspondingly, the owners' rights properly guaranteed.

Only if a citizen's property is legally registered, can it be sold, resold or given away. And, most importantly, this property then becomes mortgageable, enabling its owner to receive bank credit to finance his business. We shall thus introduce more investments in the economy than we receive from foreign investors. And, finally, property legalisation gives ownership rights and peace of mind. That's what we need to explain to our people and make our officials understand.

Secondly, during the years of Soviet rule most of our people lost respect for property relations, and especially the idea of registering property in keeping with the law. Judge for yourselves: no Soviet law textbook or law contained the terms 'real estate' or 'law of estate'. Many people never even thought about the illegality of their actions which were not always a premeditated attempt to hide their incomes. For instance, the reasons for registering a property in someone else's name were quite frequently mundane. Take the period when internal USSR passports were replaced by new forms of identification. Citizens did not show much initiative, and the new documents took a long time to come into effect and sometimes got lost. If a good business deal was to come up at such a time, the entrepreneur had to conduct transactions in someone else's name so as not to miss out on it. This occurred because the person did not have a taxpayer's registration number, owing to various flaws in the republic's taxation system when it was first set up.

One way or another, I hope that legalising property will benefit our citizens and the country to the same extent as the first amnesty of capital did. The special feature of these measures is that people are once again being given a chance to legalise their money by paying the state a tax of 10 per cent of their capital. This applies also to funds located abroad. They do not have to be transferred to Kazakhstan. Moreover, we have warned citizens that this is the state's last action in respect of the amnesty.

Recalling the legalisation of capital, it is notable that it was conducted at a time of economic growth and high oil prices. The republic's oil revenues began growing sharply during this period. For instance, in 2000 alone, we produced over 35 million tonnes of crude oil. Exports that year totalled US$4.2 billion. For comparison's sake, in 1995, the figures were 23 million tonnes and US$0.7 billion respectively. However, what alarmed us was not the increase in oil sales revenues but the stable dynamic of their growth. With such growth tendencies we might have experienced the problem of an overheated economy and many other 'delights' of a market economy. To avoid problems of this kind we set about creating the National Oil Fund.

This initially meant making a study of other countries' know-how in this area and involving our ambassadors abroad in the work. Then we intended to set up our oil fund on the basis of this knowledge. The government was to have more dealings with the heads of transnational companies. With this in mind, in 1999, Kasymzhomart Tokayev, a diplomat of many years, who had acquired considerable experience as Minister of Foreign Affairs, was appointed Prime Minister. Unfortunately, there is not enough space in this book for me to describe the vast array of foreign policy actions he and I carried out together.

The Kazakhstan Fund for Future Generations
The idea of setting up this National Fund first came about in 1997, when the Kazakhstan to 2030 Strategy was being worked out. At the time many international consultants, Kazakhstani managers and economists regarded it as a folly. Not long after it had been publicly aired, there was a collapse in oil prices which subsequently brought about the crisis in Russia in 1998. As a result of all this, we only returned to the idea of setting up such a fund in 2000.

The National Financial System

The circumstances of the time demanded that we take measures to work out possible ways of stabilising the situation in the event of systemic risks such as a sharp fall in oil prices, the economy threatening to overheat and the 'Dutch disease' and oil resources running out.

The decision to set up the Fund caused a furore in society, first and foremost because most people could not understand the Fund's role in the state's development. Taking advantage of the public's misconceptions, critics of the Fund vigorously reinforced them by speaking of it in terms of being yet another excuse for local authorities to levy taxes.

Amid numerous interviews I was constantly asked to explain this issue and the reasons for setting up the Fund. In my responses to such questions, I spoke about how we were not thinking up anything new by setting up such a Fund. Many states earning revenues from raw materials created similar funds. After all, prices change in the world, and we should be setting aside the superlative revenues we are currently receiving from oil for the time when such a state of affairs ceases to be. I constantly emphasised that the state must secure its future by having internal reserves.

As a result of lengthy discussions and despite a barrage of criticism, the National Fund was eventually set up. Its aim was to safeguard the country's stable social and economic development by accumulating financial funds for future generations and reducing the economy's dependence on external factors.

During the decision-making process in respect of this Fund we made a study of all the oil funds in the world. Over the past 40 years such stabilisation saving funds have been set up in many different countries. Brazil was putting aside coffee revenues in one, Chile was doing the same with copper ore revenues and Venezuela, Saudi Arabia, Libya, Oman, Iran, Kuwait, the American State of Alaska, and the Canadian province of Alberta were following suit with oil and gas revenues.

During our study of these funds we always kept in mind whether the way the fund worked would fit Kazakhstan's specific features. Kuwait, for instance, set up its General Reserve Fund back in 1960, after the discovery of major deposits of hydrocarbons in the country in the 1950s and the regular increase of state revenues over spending. Over the next 15 years all state investments in Kuwait's economy originated from this fund, and by 1976 the country became so rich that it was able to set up another source in the form of a savings fund for future generations.

Alaska also has two funds: the Permanent Fund of Alaska has been functioning since 1976, and the State's Constitutional Budget Reserve Fund since 1990. The former is basically a reserve for future generations while the latter is used to cover the current budget deficit. The principles, rules and results of their work are regularly published and both funds are accountable not only to the executive authorities and legislature but also to Alaska's public.

Chile's Copper Stabilisation Fund was set up in 1985 to smooth out the fluctuations in the national currency's exchange rate and taxation revenues. The fund relies entirely on transfers from Chile's state copper company, and its resources are managed by the country's central bank.

In 1998, Venezuela's Macroeconomic Stabilisation Fund was founded on the basis of oil revenues. Its chief aim was to protect the budget and country's economy from the fluctuating prices of hydrocarbon raw materials.

Of all the available examples, that of the Norwegian Oil Fund, one of the world's largest funds, established in 1990, turned out to suit our needs best. It was set up as a result of public efforts in the wake of falling oil production. Hence it is both a savings and a stabilisation fund. First and foremost, it has to safeguard the stability of the budgetary sphere in the long term. In keeping with their legislation, the government is entitled to ask parliament's permission for the use of its funds both for short-term purposes (say, in the event of a fall in budget revenues) and in the long term, to even out budget revenues in the event of a decline, say, in oil production or an increase in public spending. The government or Ministry of Finance sets the main directions for investing these funds and also evaluates the expediency of using the 'stabilisation' funds. The country's central bank manages the fund's assets. At present, the Norwegian Stabilisation Fund's assets are state bonds, and the securities of companies not involved in the oil industry.

It was this model that best suited Kazakhstan's interests, as our countries shared many similar parameters in corresponding phases of social and economic development.

Running on ahead slightly, let me say that criticism has been voiced concerning the fund's management ever since it was first set up. I have always adhered to the principle that criticism should be constructive and can only then be of benefit. Sometimes, however, the comments made were such that you started having serious doubts about the common sense of the person voicing them. They ranged from the view that the fund simply was not needed as there was plenty of oil, all the way through to it being my own personal fund. I began simply turning a blind eye to all this unfounded criticism.

Some criticism was fair, however. For instance, opponents of the fund argued that depositing the fund's assets abroad would mean investing in other countries' economies when Kazakhstan's economy needed to be invested in.

Such comments were always taken into account when improving the working of the fund. However, at present the indices of social and economic development clearly show that if we were to leave the fund's assets inside the country, the level of inflation would be much higher than it is at present.

The accumulations in the fund are, on the one hand, significantly strengthening our economy's stability and, on the other, increasing other states' confidence in Kazakhstan. The periodic increase in the country's credit rating given by international companies may serve as an example of this.

However, comments of another kind have been voiced recently. Essentially, they are about transferring the fund's assets to one in which all Kazakhstan's citizens are to participate. Every citizen, including children, would be issued with a share. During the presidential election campaign our opposition handed out paper notes resembling one tenge banknotes with '17,000 tenge' stamped on them. This was the sum they were promising everyone if they won. They intended paying this money out of the oil fund. Can this really be compared to the considerable increases we made to all pensioners' pensions, the 30 per cent salary increases to budgetary organisations, the increase in benefits to families with a large number of children and to the disabled, and the increase in jobs? This is what showing real concern for people is all about.

But we should not again allow property to be redistributed on the 'share and share alike' principle. This has been tried out already. Take Saudi Arabia, for example, which distributed money to its public. They have stopped doing so now after realising the threat of encouraging parasitic attitudes in the nation. The Saudi King, custodian of two of Islam's sacred shrines, complained to me about the difficulties in getting Arabs to work again in industry and the service sphere.

In a market economy, it is up to the state to create the conditions for a person to fulfil his or her potential and receive fair remuneration for doing so. Maximum incentives should be given to productive labour. A failure to provide such conditions will result in the majority of the population simply waiting to receive dividends, and this is how parasitic attitudes are engendered. After all, the lesson of history is that applying the principle of taking and sharing everything equally among everyone is a sure recipe for disaster.

A summary of the National Fund's actual workings in this book will, I believe, lead to a better understanding of the expediency of setting it up and its significance for the economy and the country as a whole. Essentially, the National Fund is not a legal entity but an amalgamation of financial assets concentrated in the Government's accounts at the National Bank. The Fund has two functions – a savings fund (containing accumulations for future generations) and a stabilisation fund (to reduce the dependency of budgetary revenues on the state of world prices).

Any surplus from taxation and other compulsory payments from raw material sector organisations that have been confirmed in the republican and local budgets are transferred to the fund to ensure that it carries out its stabilisation functions. These transfers consist of corporate income tax, VAT payments, super profit tax, bonuses, royalties, and Kazakhstan's share in agreements on the division of production and funds arising from the transfer of state-owned greenfield land into private ownership. So that it can fulfil its savings functions, the fund also consists of transfers from republican and local budgets, at a rate of 10 per cent of the sum total of the aforementioned revenues.

Management issues are decided by the Council made up of the President of the Republic of Kazakhstan, the Presidents of the Senate and Majilis of Parliament, the Director of the President's Administration, the Prime Minister and his first deputy, the Chairman of the National Bank, the Minister of Finance, the

The National Financial System

Minister of the Economy and Budgetary Planning, and the Chairman of the Accounts Committee overseeing republican budget execution. Obviously, the executive and legislative branches of state power are represented in the Council, thereby virtually excluding a conflict of interests. All the Council's decisions are taken collectively. None of the Council members can individually dispose of the Fund's assets. The Fund is controlled by Parliament and is truly a public and national reserve.

The National Bank is directly in charge of managing the Fund's assets on the basis of an agreement with the Government on principal management and investment strategy. The latter defines the general order in which the Fund's investment operations are to be implemented, including the limits on the types and percentage of the cross-section of currencies, classes of instruments, external managers and custodians. It also set up the management of the risk involved in running the fund, the choice of a standard portfolio, and the periodicity and content of the National Bank's reports to the Government on their activity within the framework of the Fund's principal management.

On 1 November 2006, the assets of the National Fund of the Republic of Kazakhstan exceeded US$12 billion. The accumulated sum provided cover for a period of approximately two and a half years: in other words, in the event of a fall in oil prices, we would have enough money for one and half to two years to fully carry out the social obligations the state has taken upon itself. Moreover, this index will steadily rise in line with the planned large-scale development of Kazakhstan's sector of the Caspian Sea and expanding export of oil resources.

By 2010, overall output will have exceeded 100 million tonnes. In view of this and the planned large loading on the currency market, the National Fund's activity as a powerful instrument for sterilising the inflow of money will steadily increase.

However, more will probably need to be done. It is essential for the influx of money to be assimilated by the real sector of the economy. Only movement in this direction will enable the securities market to start working at full capacity and make banking structures focus their attention on the functions of transferring capital between the branches of the economy. You see, whereas there is a relative abundance of capital in the currency and finance sector and export-oriented industries, it is in short supply in the manufacturing industry, agriculture and other branches with potential competitive capacity that has still to be fully developed in the market.

This money can be used not only as a stabiliser but also as a kind of insurance in the event of a reduction in oil prices. If used properly, the super profit may become a source for the modernisation and development of all the other branches of our economy.

That's why we capitalised the state institutions of development with part of the funds that had been channelled to replenish the fund. In particular, 24.3 billion tenge were transferred to capitalise the Bank of Development within the framework of the Strategy of industrial and innovation development, 11.5 billion to the Innovation Fund, and 7.7 billion to the State Insurance Corporation specialising in export insurance. Provision was also made in the budget for 2005 to allot funds to the Bank of Development of Kazakhstan, the Centre of Engineering and Transfer Technology, the Centre of Marketing and Analytical Research, the Innovation Fund, the Agriculture Development Programme and the Mortgaged Housing Construction Programme. What's more, over 550.5 million tenge were allocated to develop information technology stock. This entire packet of measures was intended to help increase the economy's diversification.

I would like to note separately that as well as increasing the size of the Fund, it was also necessary to make both the National Bank and the Government more responsible for the efficiency of the Fund's management and transparency of this process as a whole. What I have in mind here is not only the search for new sources to replenish the Fund with, but also a higher level of efficiency in the management and investment of the quite considerable sum already available. Thus, in view of the size of the Fund, in the near future an optimum correlation between its stabilisation and savings sections is to be established, with due regard also for the long term. We must adhere to our long-term investment strategy in deed as well as in word. Short-term fluctuations in revenues ought not to have a cardinal impact on general investment strategy.

The size of the Fund is also of topical importance. This should depend on the total amount of revenue we transfer from raw material resources. In the next decade revenues from oil production alone, according to experts' estimates, may total around US$20 billion, so there is no sense in setting an upper limit to the Fund's size.

It also needs to be borne in mind that the Fund is in the initial phase of its development. Its success in many respects depends on how professionally managed it will be. The state must estimate exactly how much we must save and how much we must leave in the budget. It is important to envision the various possible dynamics for replenishing the Fund, depending on the scenarios of economic development and the situation on world markets.

It is also necessary to consider the closer coordination of money and credit policy, and the taxation and management of revenues from the raw materials sector with a view to increasing the competitiveness of the economy and avoiding the 'Dutch disease'. Certain steps have already been taken in this direction.

Thus, since 2005, the National Fund has functioned as an integral part of the budgetary system. This makes the picture clear both for the National Fund and the budget. What's more, a precise mechanism is being worked out for setting up a guaranteed transfer from the National Fund to the budget in the medium term and, possibly, the long term as well.

Generally speaking, the National Fund in particular and oil export revenues in general are two of the most popular topics both among our journalists and many others besides. Nowadays we gain our main revenues from the sale of non-ferrous metals, copper, the export of pig-iron, zinc, gold, aluminium, and ferro-alloys. We also export mineral fertilizers and grain. Kazakhstan is not only an oil, gas and coal producer. We need to realise this ourselves before trying to prove it to the rest of the world.

The Treasury and Ministry of Finance of Kazakhstan keep a close watch on this money. All of it, oil revenues included, goes into the budget. Regular oil revenue to the budget currently comprises only 26 per cent of the total. And these sums are just the start: much more is due in the future.

So, where is this money going? First, to the budget, which this year comprised US$14.5 billion – that is, 1.5 trillion. You see, we have passed the magic figure of a trillion! Secondly, to the National Fund for future generations (US$10 billion to their stabilisation fund).

Every cent is accounted for. We publish an annual report in the press, indicating all the facts and figures. So everything here is transparent and open. As for oil, if you consider the taxes paid by the foreign developers of our resources, public taxes and corporate taxes – I mean payment for the resources, for the ecology, for the labour – then it turns out that over 70 per cent of all these oil companies' revenues go to Kazakhstan's Treasury. When I say that we will achieve growth of 3.5 times our GDP, when I say that we want to increase GDP to US$5,800 per capita, and then to US$9,000, I am basing my calculations particularly on the development of these branches in the economy.

We are also currently transferring sums of money from privatisation to the fund. However, another segment is going to develop agriculture (1,150 million tenge), housing construction and the industrial programme. We have capitalised all our development institutions, and development bank, development fund and so on.

The oil money may get spent in such a way that the economy becomes overheated and 'Dutch disease' sets in, along with a host of other problems we are currently being scared with; but it is also possible, despite all these forecasts, to use them to strengthen the economy and support and develop areas of priority for the country. It may happen that this period of high oil prices gives Kazakhstan a chance to tighten its belt and gather strength before embarking on the fierce struggle for its place in the global economy and in the world as a whole. It is to our advantage for the time being, but we must not rely too heavily on oil dollars. Look upon this time as a starting point, a breather we've been given by history. What are we getting ready for? Our future; fierce competition; the challenges of the outside world. I believe that the Kazakhstan way has only just got going over the past 15 years. The hardest, as well as the most wonderful, part is yet to come.

We started with empty state coffers and now we are talking about our reserves. *Allaga shukir*! (Glory to the Almighty!)

I previously mentioned that we did not even have US$500 million dollars in our gold and currency reserves to introduce the tenge. Now we have currency reserves of around US$25 billion.

The National Financial System

Recognition is the Highest Praise

The fact that Kazakhstan has been awarded an attractive investment rating is a sure indication of the international community's high estimation of its economic development. It is the first CIS country to receive an investment-level rating from three world famous agencies – Moody's, Standard & Poor's and Fitch Rating Ltd. The recent rating forecast upgrade from 'stable' in 1995 to 'positive' in the ratings of the most authoritative agency, Standard & Poor's, is a considerable achievement. Let us summarise the history of rating conferment:

June 2006: ratings forecast upgraded from 'stable' to 'positive'.

May 2004: long-term ratings on obligations in national and foreign currency raised to 'BBB' and 'BBB-' respectively; short-term rating in respect of foreign currency debts raised to 'A-3'; forecast – 'stable'.

May 2003: long-term ratings in respect of national and foreign currency upgraded to 'BBB-' and 'BB+' respectively; short-term rating in respect of national currency debts upgraded to 'A-3'; forecast – 'stable'.

May 2001: long-term ratings in respect of national and foreign currency debts upgraded to 'BB+' and 'BB' respectively.

July 2000: long-term ratings in respect of national and foreign currency debts upgraded to 'BB' and 'BB-' respectively.

Sept 1998: long-term ratings in national and foreign currency debts downgraded to 'BB-' and 'B+' respectively.

Nov 1996: 'BB+/B' ratings conferred in respect of national currency debts and 'BB-/B' in respect of foreign currency debts; forecast – 'stable'.

Standard & Poor's: *Republic of Kazakhstan – credit rating,*
11 November, 2006.

The Kazakhstan Way

Among the numerous other plaudits for Kazakhstan's economy one can cite the one given in December 2002 by consultants of the IMF mission: 'In recent years Kazakhstan has achieved significant successes in stabilising the economy and has extremely favourable prospects in the medium and long term and has no need of IMF funding.'

> 'As was mentioned in December 2002, the IMF's permanent mission in Kazakhstan will be closing in August 2003. This decision has been taken in response to the impressive achievements in stabilising the economy, extremely favourable medium- and long-term prospects of Kazakhstan's economy and very faint likelihood of the country having a need to use the Fund's resources in the future.'
>
> From the IMF's final statement to RK on Consultation in accordance with Article IV, 10 March 2003

Recalling the distance we have come since setting up our financial system, I am yet again convinced that we acted correctly by following our very own Kazakhstan way of development. There is much to support this. For instance, the financial system now meets international standards, as its recognition by the world community confirms. Then there is the joint collaboration between world-famous, leading financial institutions and our banks and companies – and the recent expansion of Kazakhstan companies into CIS space. It is thanks to the state's partnership with the financial sector that we identified problems in time and helped resolve them as rapidly as possible.

Young Kazakhstani managers of a new calibre are currently making a name for themselves in the financial world. Many of these managers I know personally and many we have helped on their way and given 'a head start in life', so to speak. It has not simply been a case of setting up second-level banks. The old system went on working: commercial enterprises, both privately and state-owned, and local budgets kept on taking credit and, making use of loopholes in the laws, failed to repay banks. Sometimes this created serious problems for banks. For instance, occasionally I personally had to help Kazkommertsbank, the People's Bank and TuranAlemget get their money back. It was like that then. They needed my personal support.

The National Financial System

Developing the banking system to comply with international standards was partly facilitated by the fact that at the start of the 1990s they virtually all accompanied me on all my foreign visits. They then had a chance to meet the 'sharks' of global business, gain expertise from leading world banks and companies, and use leading Western know-how in their work, adopting the principles of financial practice. Nowadays Kazakhstan banks have the highest ratings in the territory of the CIS.

What matters most is that our present banking system is one of the most highly developed in the territory of the former Union.

The National Bank's independent monetary and credit policy took stock of the economic challenges of those years and succeeded in meeting them. One of this policy's most important achievements was to overcome hyperinflation and create the conditions for the gradual growth of the country's economy.

Thanks to the reforms and state support, our Kazakhstani businessmen and citizens are now able to use the entire spectrum of the banking and financial services directly from their places of work and homes.

Representatives of world-famous financial institutions are already working in Kazakhstan. I should mention that our domestic commercial banks have already practically assimilated the most valuable expertise from the global financial sector and are now competing on equal terms worldwide. What's more, domestic capital is going abroad and opening up associations and expanding into foreign markets. At the same time, it is essential for us to fill our market with new financial instruments, and, first and foremost, project bonds. Several investment projects of importance for the country will be selected for their issue, such as, for instance, infrastructure projects encompassing the construction of railways and roads, stations and sea ports. The joint launch of new investment projects and state development institutions onto the capital market will resolve the problem of financing newly re-established factories and give impetus to the implementation of the industrial and innovation development Strategy.

All this is allowing the transition to a structurally diversified economy with a view to increasing competitiveness, taking up a worthy position in the world division of labour, and further developing the integration processes in post-Soviet space.

The Kazakhstan Way

The measures we have taken in this direction are inevitably of interest to other nations. We have visitors from many different countries who are seriously interested in our methods. And during my visits abroad I am frequently asked about them. It is certainly worth mentioning that whenever I meet foreign business people and politicians, and students at the world's top colleges and universities, they always speak in glowing terms about our financial system's development. And you can often see from the look on their faces that they are wondering how a country that until only a short while ago had been on the world's sidelines could have achieved such success, and how Kazakhstani companies are now their strategic partners and closely collaborating with them.

I think that it is all down to the reforms we have carried through, including those in the financial sector, and I again would like to stress the importance of the human factor I mentioned previously. Of course, it is impossible in one chapter, as I have already said, to discuss all the features of our financial system's development and this is only a brief overview.

We are now harvesting the fruits of our endeavours. The institutional reforms aimed at building a market economy are now mostly complete in Kazakhstan. In recent years our country has been steadily maintaining high rates of economic growth. And in many respects the success of this economic development has been down to the country's developed financial system. Kazakhstan now has financial markets with developed infrastructures and a pension system I am proud of. But we must not stop here. I believe we still have very promising prospects ahead of us.

I have always defended and done all I could to support the banking sector. In the past we concentrated all our efforts on developing this segment with a view to giving Kazakhstan's economy a reliable source of finance. Radical reforms were carried out and essential laws efficiently enacted. We provided favourable conditions for its development, for instance, by introducing directly stimulating measures, especially in the area of favourable taxation. Now that the banking sector is firmly established, I think it will be fair to request similar help from it in the future to keep the development of the country's economy on track. What I have in mind here is the concept of 'social responsibility' in business. This means that an organisation must act in the interests of the society whose resources it is using.

To my mind, this principle should be inculcated in our companies' operations. The area of business responsibility is inevitably going to expand as this sector's influence does. Every businessman in our country is, first and foremost, its citizen, and must contribute to the economic prosperity of the country as a whole.

The process of setting up a financial centre in Almaty is currently under way. This important and complex project should attract the world's major banking institutions. Laws have been enacted and preferences provided for, and now it is up to our personnel in charge to see the project through. I hope they will do their best and make a success of it.

7

THE EVOLUTION OF THE LAND USE ISSUE

On 27 February 1994, all the republic's top agrarian officials, and collective farm chairmen from all over Kazakhstan, gathered in Akmola for a republican agrarian conference to mark the 40th anniversary of the assimilation of the virgin and fallow lands. The celebratory occasion turned into a serious discussion about the future of the republic's agriculture, which was on the brink of a catastrophe.

The third year of independence was drawing to an end. Society was gradually recovering from the symptoms of shock therapy and adapting to the new economic conditions. However, while urban citizens' individual initiative was acting as a catalyst for the rapid growth of small and medium business, the situation in rural areas was developing along quite different lines. Economic reforms were clearly stalling in the agrarian sector.

What concerned me most was the attitude of rural people who were used to waiting for decisions from above. Traditionally, agriculture has always been the focus of special attention in our country. There are numerous examples of this, from all-union campaigns to assimilate the virgin lands to Kazakhstan being hailed as the 'Soviet country's granary' and then all through the Soviet period receiving substantial state aid to develop and support its agriculture. However, the disintegration of the centralised planned economy stopped the influx of capital to the rural economy. And this, in turn, led to a fall in production and a decline in rural living standards, resulting in an increase in social tension in rural communities.

And yet in the 1990s, despite the grave crisis and deteriorating situation in the countryside, agricultural producers in the provinces still expected state aid to be reinstated and all their economic problems solved externally. Most interestingly, however, this expectation of special treatment has survived all through 15 years of independence and is still prevalent among our farmers today.

Take, for instance, the annual demands to the state for a reduction in fuel and lubricant prices during sowing and harvest-time – despite the fact that for a long time now fuel and lubricant producers have been private companies with similar costs and aims to gain profits.

This is why we had to precisely define state relations to agriculture. Even though I realised I would have to say a lot of unpleasant things, I still started by explaining the situation. What I said at the time can be summarised as follows.

After the disintegration of the Soviet Union, the political and economic situation changed in Kazakhstan. The state could no longer afford to subsidise agriculture at former levels. What's more, new market relations required the radical reform of the agro-industrial complex, first by setting up an economic mechanism that would, on the one hand, stimulate the effective operations of the state farm network and, on the other, eventually cause the old production relations to become redundant. I made it clear that the state would be reducing its presence in agriculture, and relying on rural people's personal initiative and the increasing development of farming enterprises, which would eventually result in collective and state farms being dismantled and private ownership introduced. When I told the conference delegates that the collective and state farms would soon cease to exist, 99 per cent of them, I recall, thought I was joking.

The special irony historically was that I was airing these ideas at a conference to mark the 40th anniversary of the assimilation of the virgin and fallow lands. We all know what a major role the virgin lands played in the development of Kazakhstan's agriculture and that of the Soviet Union as a whole. It would be simply stupid to dispute this fact, but it did not all go as wonderfully and smoothly as the Soviet leadership imagined.

'When attempting an analysis of the pros and cons of the virgin lands policy from a modern market perspective, the picture you come up with is not entirely rosy, and I cannot fail to mention this today. It is enough to recall that ten years of its forty-year history were racked by drought. Kazakhstan itself often had to buy in grain and forage. Some years over 2 million tonnes were bought in. Throughout these 40 years agricultural debts were paid off annually by the state. During the last five-year plans around 350 farms, that is, one fifth of the total number, invariably made a loss. Producing grain regardless of costs and quality was the only principle adhered to. In 1992 alone, the maximum average harvest was 14.8 centners per hectare. And over the 40-year period, this index exceeded 10 centners in only 13 years. Not a single country in the world has such a level of spending on its agriculture. It would have gone bankrupt long ago. . .

We are well aware that our agro-industrial complex is currently going through most difficult times. They are the result of both miscalculations in the strategy and tactics of virgin land policy and the actual development of reform processes in the economy. And, of course, we are going to be constantly searching for and finding ways out of the critical situation and doing our uttermost to help rural consumer goods producers – but only those with profit-making enterprises who can pay back their state loans. The state cannot afford to and, indeed, has no intention of having unprofitable enterprises constantly round its neck.'

From the speech at the commemorative meeting of members of the public and employees of the republic's agro-industrial complex, 1994

The years 1994-96 were the most critical years for agriculture, brought about mainly by the so-called disparity in prices. The state had 'released' (liberalised) the prices of energy supplies, industrial goods and other services, but kept the prices of agricultural produce fixed to prevent a sharp rise in the price of basic food products. In these conditions agricultural concerns had to purchase their circulating production assets at market prices while still providing their produce to the state at fixed prices. The barter system was flourishing everywhere. Only a few producers were in a position to sell their produce on the external market, and in most cases this meant using one or more middlemen.

Numerous meetings with proactive farmers who were trying, come what may, to work independently, according to market rules, convinced me that there was now a pressing need to conduct agrarian reform to meet the new economic conditions. The development of new relations in the economy's agrarian sector and increasing tendency to use land ineffectively, highlighted the need to define the status of land ownership and form new land relations. In other words, an effective market mechanism cannot be created without first defining the real owner – the one who is to become the main economic agent making decisions and taking responsibility. And first and foremost, this applied to land as the main means of production in the rural economy.

During the first years of reform, however, there was no consensus regarding the need to introduce the right to private land ownership. What's more, most of the population on principle rejected the rightfulness of putting state-owned land in private hands. Such a prevailing attitude among Kazakhstanis towards developing the institution of private land ownership in the republic was mainly due to the rural population's limited adaptation to the new market relations. People simply had not started to live and, more importantly, think along new lines.

History played no small part here as well. Communal (clan) land tenure had been prevalent in Kazakhstan's history, virtually excluding private land ownership. Each clan had roamed within the boundaries of its territory, and these boundaries could not be changed by anyone individually. Later on, the administrative reforms of 1867-1868 conducted by Tsarist Russia in Kazakhstan strengthened the status quo, according to which the land was state property. What's more, it was permitted to transfer it for the use of *aul* communities. Subsequently, the Tsarist government took charge of all the land in Kazakhstan, on the basis of these legislative acts. Thus, for instance, the Bukeyev 'horde' was given land in the area between the Volga and Ural rivers, and the Kazakh communities ended up with one of the best territories. In other words, as an actual concept, private land ownership had never existed in our country. Our land had always been the property of a clan or the state – Tsarist Russia, the Soviet Union and, finally, the Republic of Kazakhstan.

As well as such a historical background, land reform in Kazakhstan had a number of other special features. It is primarily because of the complexity of the issue of introducing private land ownership and public opinion being so divided over it that agricultural reform has dragged on through all the years until now. People were not ready for the land to be put in private hands, and so there could be no question of any simple, fundamental reform of all agriculture. That's why, unlike all the other areas of reform – where there was always a race against time, and it sometimes got ahead of us – we did not set reform in agriculture such challenging deadlines.

Even though we realised agriculture could not function without state support, and despite the privatisation programme and development of a market economy being officially on the agenda in those days, we still delayed resolving the issue of private landownership, making do with half-measures and transitional models. And yet all the problems facing us in industry, say, remained on the agenda in agriculture as well. The ubiquitous embezzlement and squandering of state property and, to make matters even worse, the sharp decline in the production of food products were leaving the agrarian and food-producing sector in a pitiful state throughout the country. The older generation still retained a memory of empty shop shelves, food shortages and so on.

But we still could not rush it. The success of agricultural reform mattered more than the length of time it took. For our republic, with its rural communities comprising over 40 per cent of the overall population, reform in the agrarian sector had a social as well as an economic profile. Behind all the harvest, milk yield and additional weight figures were not only collective and state farms but rural people who were totally unprepared for market reforms and, therefore, socially most vulnerable.

We were facing a dilemma: the countryside greatly needed state support but if it relied on state subsidies, our agriculture would never become competitive. With such an argument as a starting-point, it was essential to select a course of development that would take account of both these factors.

So, for the time being, rural communities were left on the market reforms' sidelines. And yet the need for radical market reforms in the countryside became increasingly obvious. Then there were the experiences of other countries down the years, showing that in many cases successful economic development began with the development of the agrarian sector and implementation of land reform. This is what had happened in the countries of Western Europe, North America and Australia. As for the model closer to us of the countries of Eastern Europe, most of the land in Hungary was transferred to private ownership from 1989 onwards. The right to private land ownership was legally sanctioned in Poland in the same year. In 1990, Romania adopted its agrarian reform programme, aimed at establishing a broad stratum of competent private landowners who were entitled to manage and use the land freely and choose the type of farming they went in for. The right to purchase and sell land was enshrined in the law. The Czech Republic likewise introduced the institution of private land ownership after 1989.

All these land reforms passed off successfully, spurring on the development of these countries' economies. To be fair, however, it should also be mentioned that a limited form of private land ownership had existed in all the Eastern European countries even during socialist rule. And the institution of private land ownership had existed there long before the formation of the Soviet Union. But in Kazakhstan, as one of the Union republics, not only was land exclusively state-owned, but our rural economy bore the quintessentially Soviet hallmarks of grandiose scale and lack of balance. In other words, these countries' model, despite our similar starting positions, did not suit us.

There were other reasons why Kazakhstan was not like Estonia or the Czech Republic, where so-called *khutor* or farms had developed over the years. Kazakhstan's natural and climatic conditions put it in an unstable and risky agricultural zone, prone to frequent droughts and spring hoar frosts that affected crop productivity. Many specialists and scientists consider that, for these reasons, only collective forms of labour and agriculture are in principle possible in Kazakhstan. And, consequently, private land ownership loses its original purpose of defining ownership.

I cannot say I fully disagree or agree with such a position. All I wish to say is that even collective forms of labour have to be based on an exact definition of the type of labour involved, and each member of the work force's specific role in it, as well as the ownership of everything involved. The main shortcoming of collective ownership, still affecting many former state and collective farms, is the lack of personal responsibility and notion that 'everyone is to blame but us'. Who should be taking the decisions? Who should be responsible? The owner of the land, because the land is the fundamental principle. And even when a proactive farmer comes along and tries to make a go of some concern and manages to organise everyone involved, people just cannot help piling all the cares and responsibilities onto him and then waiting to see what happens. It is time to realise that if you have been cheated, it means you yourself have let it happen.

But then what kind of agriculture did we need? One existing exclusively on state budget subsidies and fulfilling a purely social function? Or one functioning only in keeping with the stringent and at times harsh laws of a market economy, according to which only the most competitive survive?

Asking these questions, we came to the conclusion that neither option was well and truly right for our country. At that time what we needed was a kind of symbiosis of our very own, based on our time-hallowed experiences and those of other countries. The end-result of these combined options was to be a well-developed agriculture capable of competing in external markets, and also receiving state support to carry through economic reforms and enhance the social sphere of rural areas.

In other words, we were not declining state support for the countryside. But, it had to be focused on investment in the social sphere there: rural community education, healthcare, leisure facilities, supplying rural communities with better amenities and infrastructures. After all, you have to agree that not even the most successful farmer can deal with the problem of drinking water or new motorways and roads on his own. But the actual agricultural producers must be elevated to the status of independent economic agents who sort out their own problems, receive their own profit and so on. Agriculture is a branch of the economy just like industry, transport and energy. It has its own goods, its own special features and its own advantages, and so it is also capable of being competitive and successful. All the phases of reforming the economy's agrarian sector have been aimed at achieving this goal. With no experience of systemic economic reform, we undertook this process one step at a time, often through trial and error.

The First Phase of Land Reform, 1991-94
As I have always said in my numerous speeches, and will continue to say, private land ownership is one of the necessary conditions of

a functioning market economy. Property is of principal significance because it provides stability and confidence. A society where doubts exist over basic property rights cannot expect to develop successfully over a long period of time. What's more, private property nurtures a sense of proprietorship and serves as a guarantee for private business investments.

On the other hand, introducing private land ownership for agricultural purposes in 1991-94, when most of the rural population was not ready to manage their own land, could have had negative repercussions. You see, in order to manage your own property competently, you first have to appreciate its true worth and to know how to go about it.

We could not make the direct transition to the introduction of private land ownership. In the initial phase of land reform, economic relations in agriculture lacked stability, the profitability of agricultural production had declined sharply, and the land had yet to be properly valued. All this might have caused the rural population to make rash decisions over selling their plots of land which many would possibly have regretted later. As a result, such reform would have created an even greater crisis and, above all, in the social sphere.

During preparations for the reform, we naturally came to the conclusion that the Soviet Land Code was going to be unable to meet society's requirements in land relations. Enacted in June 1991, the Law *On land reform* was called on to create the legal and economic conditions for various types of farming to function effectively. This law did not, however, introduce the institution of private ownership. Rather, it created the conditions for overcoming the crisis in the agrarian sector. Everyone understood that it was transitional in character. Land relations in agriculture continued to be based on the lease of land from the state.

The principal directions of the law were the setting up of a special fund with a view to redistributing land for more effective use, the establishment of rural community boundaries, and the official registration and re-registration of land use entitlement documents.

While ownership in agricultural production passed from the state to the collective and then eventually into private hands, in other areas of the agro-industrial complex (service, processing, supplies and so on) this process also saw the setting up of large state joint-stock companies (SJSC) which subsequently passed into private hands. Thus, the changes in the forms of ownership were carried through step by step, travelling through the full spectrum from minimum to maximum efficiency.

The dynamic of land reform is proceeding along similar gradual lines. In the case of land for agricultural purposes, it started with rural people gaining entitlement to an agreed quota of land and ended with the introduction of private property, set out in the 2003 Land Code.

The fundamental legislative and other normative legal acts enacted in the early 1990s set in motion broad-based work in dismantling state ownership and privatising agriculture. A national programme was introduced for this purpose, parallel with the reform in the agro-industrial sector. During the first stage of privatisation, state-owned agricultural enterprises were turned into collectively-run concerns. A total of 472 state farms in the republic were privatised in this manner. The privatisation of state agricultural enterprise property was effected by distributing property shares in the form of certificates to the working collectives' members. It should be noted that, with a view to maintaining the integrity of well-established large-scale state farms, all their top managers with 20 years' employment service in managerial posts were alloted a 10 per cent property stakeholding in their enterprise. Another 10 per cent was given to them to manage for a period of five years. In the event of their agricultural concern achieving positive results, this part of the property stakeholding became their private property at the end of the five years.

However important it was to maintain the production base of the state agricultural enterprises, what still mattered most was the land. Who should acquire the land of the privatised collective and state farms, who would really concern themselves with preserving the quality of the land and keeping it fertile, and how should the transfer of the land be effected? This important issue gave me no peace and I kept returning to it. There was clearly a need to find genuine owners for the land: caring, conscientious people totally devoted to it. And so the choice fell to rural people.

The decision was taken to distribute agreed quotas of land to every member of the rural community. The average size of the plot was worked out by the collective of every farm in question and sanctioned by the regional executive body. The estimate of the land in question included all the farm's agricultural land, excluding the plots forming part of the populated areas and the regional executive authority' special land fund.

During the second phase of privatisation (1993-95) 1,490 state agricultural enterprises were privatised across the republic. The owners of the agreed quotas of land and property stakeholdings were entitled, if they so wished, to join together and form small enterprises, agricultural production cooperatives, peasant holdings and associations based on private property ownership with a legal entity's rights.

These measures created the conditions for the members of agricultural enterprises to select voluntarily and freely the type of farming they wanted to go in for. Work on establishing the size of the agreed quotas of land for the employees of all agricultural enterprises was carried out in 1993-94. The registration of land-plot entitlement certificates and their distribution to the employees of reformed and reorganised enterprises was carried out from 1995 onwards.

A paradoxical situation arose during this process. Privatising the property of agricultural enterprises logically also entailed changing the ownership of the land. However, the 1993 Constitution proceeded from the principle of the state's exclusive right to land ownership and made no provision for the transfer of these plots to the privatised enterprises' owners.

In other words, although we had started on rural reforms and achieved certain results in privatising state property, the subsequent effective use of this property and investment in its modernisation had been thrown into doubt on account of investors' concerns over the still unresolved land question. What was the point of acquiring tractors and sowing machinery if there was no land to plough and sow? Apart from everything else, these measures had failed to save our vast and once developed agriculture: it was disintegrating before our very eyes, and to this day has yet to recover fully.

To conclude, it should be mentioned that in 1992, at the request of the Commission of European Communities (CEC), the Food and Agriculture Organisation of the United Nations carried out research into the food situation in the countries of the former Soviet

Union. After analysing its results, the Commission noted the general shortcoming in the work of organisations responsible for making assessments of the food situation in these countries. This shortcoming consisted of there being no real food balance. Unlike the rest of the world, it was worked out on a calendar basis, from January to January rather than from one harvest to the next. Such inconsistency resulted in the fact that in Kazakhstan and the other republics of the former Soviet Union, no records were kept of the quantities and types of surplus food that could be sold on and the quantities that needed to be imported from abroad.

In its analysis of the food situation in the region, the Commission also noted that among the other countries of Central Asia, Kazakhstan was in the most stable position for providing its population with food products. The republic was the only one of the CIS countries that at the time of the assessment had surplus food, and, in particular, grain.

Despite all the negative factors that had cropped up, we still started feeling slowly but surely that we could keep going with the development and reform of our agricultural system. The transitional Law *On land reform* of 1991 allowed the problem of rural property relations to be temporarily resolved. State property privatisation set in motion the processes for setting up the first farmers' and peasants' holdings. These results did not, however, completely halt the disintegration in the agricultural sector and could not continue to guarantee long-term rural development. Time and the logic of events demanded further reforms.

Phase Two of Land Reform and the Period of Bankruptcy, 1994-2001

The start of the second phase of land reforms was marked by the signing in 1994 of two Presidential Decrees, having the force of law, on issues concerning the improvement of land relations (on 24 January 1994, and 5 April 1994) in accordance with which the right to use the land became the object of civil legal transactions. The said decrees were also transitional acts of a sort and preserved the right of the exclusive state ownership of land. The procedure in the sale and purchase of the right of ownership to a land plot, use and lease of land were confirmed in the execution of these decrees. There was still no question of alarming the public by introducing private land ownership and so the latter was replaced by property ownership rights. It was really then that the first signs of a land market and private land possession began to emerge. It became possible on a payment basis to acquire the rights to private land possession which, in practical terms, differed very little from the rights to private land ownership.

The proprietors of privatised enterprises started acquiring the rights to land and managing it as they saw fit, without any permission from the state. A new institution appeared for the first time in the history of land legislation among the CIS countries: that of land rights management. Not the actual land plots, but the right to lifelong, heritable possession, the right to use and the right to lease land were put in public circulation. Public opinion at the time reacted quite warily to all this new jurisdiction, and some held the view that it amounted to the sale and purchase of land and we were violating constitutional norms.

Looking back, we can see how important these legal acts were. This marked the turning point in land legislation towards a market economy. It was after their enactment that the first signs of a land market began to emerge and the market price of land began to develop.

I repeatedly noted that a definition of the status of land ownership presupposed not only economic effectiveness but also the preservation of the traditions and interests of the Kazakhstani people, people's destinies and a high degree of responsibility towards future generations. That's why the opinion and interests of society across the full spectrum had to be listened to before coming to a final decision.

Ideas on the introduction of private land ownership in Kazakhstan had been aired virtually from day one of independence. However, it had been impossible for a variety of reasons to enshrine private land ownership in the law.

As I have already mentioned, increasing the effectiveness of land use was the key aim in the choice of a new owner. With the transition to new market relations under way, the land owner had serious problems to contend with: the success of his independent business depended on his ability not only to own land but actually manage it. The new landowners had to be really competent managers, and capable of doing a first-class job organising the production process.

To introduce private land ownership, the state, for its part, had to create the appropriate institutions (landowners' registration service, land valuation and so on). In order to take the final decision to introduce private land ownership, there first had to be a thoroughly tried and tested method for transferring it into private hands, with due regard for the prevailing conditions, the specifics of privatisation and transfer of state agricultural enterprise property. The old saying about measuring your cloth seven times because you only cut it once was certainly applicable here.

Until 1995 the land was exclusively in state ownership. For the first time in our history, the country's Constitution, adopted by the all-nation referendum of that year, laid down that land in Kazakhstan could be in both state and private ownership:

> Part 1 'General Provisions', Article 6, clause 3:
> 'The land and underground resources, water, flora and fauna, other natural resources shall be owned by the state. The land may also be privately owned on terms, conditions and within the limits established by legislation.'
>
> Constitution of the Republic of Kazakhstan. Adopted by nationwide referendum, 30 August 1995

This provision allowed for the drawing up of legal acts establishing the right to the private ownership of land for agricultural purposes. The original bill on this issue that went before Parliament did not get through. It was discussed for a long time but no consensus was reached. It got to the point where they started working out which of the nationalities had fertile lands and which not. What they were really alluding to were the virgin lands, which were mainly worked by people from other republics. I did not start pressing the point home at the time but firmly said that I was in favour of private land ownership.

In December 1995, I published the Decree *On land* in which the new land relations were defined in law. It became legal to transfer to the private ownership of the republic's citizens and non-state legal entities land plots intended for the running of a subsidiary smallholding, horticulture and the construction of country cottages (dachas) and also for the construction of industrial and non-industrial buildings, including residential housing, buildings and structures, including the lands intended for their service. At the same time, according to this decree, the following were excluded from private ownership: agricultural land and also land used for defence purposes; woodland and water sources; specially protected areas; land plots with natural complexes and sites of special ecological, scientific, historic and cultural, recreational and therapeutic interest; of public use in populated areas.

The decree still bore the hallmarks of a compromise, as its provisions endorsed the restriction on introducing the right to private agricultural land ownership. In 1995, when agriculture was a highly unprofitable branch of the economy (there was a 17.9 per cent loss level from agricultural production sales, 2.9 per cent from plant production sales, and 30.7 per cent from livestock sales) and rural consumers' effective demand level remained low, introducing private ownership might have caused a problem with food supplies in the republic.

At a session of the Kazakhstani People's Assembly I noted that given the lack of funds of our citizens working in agriculture, launching a mass-scale process to buy and resell land would mean robbing these people and condemning them to working as hired labourers. Unaccustomed to a sense of proprietorship and unable to appreciate the value of ownership rights, people would simply be seduced by the instant profit and sell their plots or simply be unable to compete with the capital attracted from elsewhere. And then they would go and work as hired labourers for the purchasers of their land. Our society was not yet ready for the full introduction of private land ownership.

In all, 162 state agricultural enterprises were privatised across the republic during the third phase of privatisation (1996-97). The owners of property stakeholdings and agreed quotas of land were entitled to sell or lease them. However, in view of the sharp cuts in state subsidies, agriculture continued to function in the same way as it had in the days of a planned economy. Many employees of ex-collective and state farms who had received property shares and the right to an agreed quota of land were inadequately informed

251

and naturally conservative, and so failed to appreciate exactly what was happening and were unable to manage this property to maximum effect. Most of the production cooperatives, which were hastily set up by the ex-directors of collective and state farms (the so-called 'red directors') with local authority assistance, quickly frittered away their capital and working assets. They sold off their shares in processing and service organisations for next to nothing, putting paid to the idea of agricultural goods producers taking part in the management process. Nor did they always competently manage crop production. There were instances when the managers of such farms sold grain for the ludicrous price of US$20-30 per tonne.

What's more, given the disparity in prices, the flourishing 'wild barter', and shrinking agricultural production commodity market, there was a rapid increase in agricultural enterprises' debts. By the start of 1998, the industry's debts were in excess of 120 billion tenge. Agriculture became highly unattractive to investors.

At the end of the 1990s, investment in agricultural production as a share of the economy had dropped to 0.4 per cent. The situation was exacerbated by the breakdown in the organised produce sales and supplies system of agricultural commodity producers, which in turn resulted in the loss of major grain, meat, vegetable and other agricultural commodity markets.

The fact that there was no internal market protection system in place led to an influx of cheap imported products and the sidelining of domestic goods, which became an additional reason for the declining production. A set of urgent measures needed to be taken to resolve the situation that had arisen by giving post-privatisation support to the reformed enterprises, and setting up a system of state support to help develop agricultural entrepreneurs in market conditions.

However, the history of the land issue will be incomplete if we do not describe the state's competent handling of the bankruptcy proceedings which numerous agricultural enterprises went through in 1998. At the time it was the only right way forward. The whole point of the process undertaken was to free farms from the debts they had accrued. The bankruptcy proceedings enabled us to 'cleanse' agriculture of inveterate debtors, which in turn brought about a change of proprietors.

The Evolution of the Land Use Issue

With a view, in particular, to strengthening the agricultural industry's finances, from 1998 onwards a process began to get insolvent farms up and running again by instigating bankruptcy proceedings against them. A special republican inter-departmental working group was set up who, once every decade, was to provide the Government with information, in line with recommended guidelines, on agriculture's financial health and regeneration.

All the republics' farms were divided into three groups: profitable farms with steady economic and financial indicators; farms which could become financially self-sufficient if financial enhancement measures were applied; and, finally, farms which had to have bankruptcy proceedings instigated against them after pre-bankruptcy measures had first been applied.

Obviously, applying bankruptcy proceedings in the classic manner might have resulted in the farms losing all their assets and their employees being left with nothing. That's why so-called 'pre-bankruptcy' measures were carried out on the farms before bankruptcy proceedings were applied. Thus, within the framework of existing legislation, the main means of production used in the production and technological processes of insolvent farms were distributed among the members of the work collective as a way of cancelling salary arrears, and to the main creditors involved in the management of the farm's production. After receiving the main means of production, the members of the working collective would leave the insolvent farm with their agreed quotas of land and set up a new agricultural enterprise along with the above-mentioned main creditors, free of all debts, and continue working with a clean slate. And the insolvent farm went through bankruptcy proceedings with what was left of the mainly non-liquid assets.

When an insolvent farm was going through these bankruptcy proceedings, most of the creditors remained dissatisfied, and so the debts were automatically written off. During the reforms in the agrarian sector between 1998 and 2001, 2,284 farms were declared bankrupt, of which 1,981 (87 per cent) were wound up by the start of 2001, including 1,574 settled in court, and 407 out of court.

What did we get out of instigating bankruptcy proceedings against agricultural enterprises? First we freed the farms in question from the debts they had accrued during the crisis and time when there was a disparity in prices. Thus, many farms were given the chance to start working virtually all over again, debt-free, not to mention the new enterprises set up on the basis of the wound-up bankrupt ones. So, during that very period (1998-2001) 35,000 peasant farms were set up on the basis of the former privatised collective and state farms, most of which were located in the Southern Kazakhstan and Almaty districts.

The move towards market relations happened slowly in the agrarian sector. This was linked both to this industry's special features and the huge amount of problems it had accumulated. The lack of working capital in agriculture slowed its development down. Releasing the agricultural commodity producers from their burden of debt could not solve all the financial problems. The need for circulating funds and assets forced rural people to apply to commercial banks for credit. However, credit was often refused because of the non-regulation of the normative legal base of mortgage crediting on the security of land rights, and the non-liquidity of mortgaged property. Private land ownership would give the economy the mechanism it had needed for a long time in mortgage crediting: clearly defined right of ownership would possibly become an acceptable security for the receipt of essential funds.

Agriculture badly needed long-term investment at the time. However, the temporary use by individuals of land whose boundaries were not fixed or protected by law could not provide an influx of capital to the agricultural sector.

An important role in establishing lease terms and agreement conclusions, extensions and cancellations was played by officials at a local level. Such a situation caused an increase in the unauthorised trading of administrative resolutions on the allocation of land, its illegal use and concealment of received incomes. According to individual experts, an administrative resolution allowing the rental of one hectare of agricultural land cost between 6 per cent-10 per cent of the crop yield.

All these negative elements formed the basis of arguments in the speeches of opponents of land reform. They also cited the fact that land-use efficiency had not improved since the land had been put in private hands. But no one had pretended that introducing the right to private land was something that could increase the effectiveness of land use and labour productivity in next to no time, especially given the state of Kazakhstan's economic development.

Fears were also voiced about an increase in speculation. It was argued that the legal recognition of the right to private land ownership could help financial speculators gain access to a limited asset whose price had the potential to increase substantially within a very short period of time.

Nostalgic points of view were also articulated. Supporters of state land ownership contended that land relations supposed two economic outcomes: entrepreneurial income and rent. While entrepreneurial income could be appropriated by the land's proprietor with total validity, rent should be appropriated by society, as the land's proprietor had not actually earned the rental income himself.

There were also certain critics of private land ownership who excessively politicised this issue by contending that the introduction of private land ownership in Kazakhstan contravened the Kazakh people's historic foundations and traditions and might result in a social explosion. In their opinion, the redistribution of ownership was inevitable and might become the cause of land conflicts.

Looking back, I would like to note that there were also well-reasoned arguments put forward by opponents to the private land ownership, which it was impossible not to take on board. In particular, we agreed with those who pointed out the benefit for the state of retaining the right to land ownership and leasing it out. Leasing land instead of selling and purchasing it might ensure that the market mechanism had a limited effect on the countryside.

The market economy's subsequent development and the emergence of new nuances in land relations demanded the adoption of a new Law *On land*. This was to be better attuned to the current situation and better able to guarantee a fully functioning market economy. At a meeting with parliamentarians I again put forward my case regarding the introduction of the private ownership of agricultural land. It was well-founded, in so far as not just our experience but that of all other countries showed that the state of affairs in agriculture greatly depended on the extent to which the land factor had an effect on market relations. Meanwhile, the legislative acts in force were already providing an adequate legal base.

Subsequent events showed that the economy's agrarian sector and our people were not yet ready for such a momentous decision.

The Kazakhstan Way

The draft law *On land* that had been elaborated and given a reading in the republic's Parliament was revoked by the Government in July 1999, because of criticism of the provisions for regulating the introduction of private land ownership, agricultural lands included. The draft law's developers had made a series of serious misjudgments as no scientists or agrarian sector workers had been involved in the project and, most importantly, rural people's interests had not been fully considered.

After nearly two years of debates the new Law *On land* was enacted in January 2001, as a compromise solution to this issue. Although it could not be considered definitive, it did grant Kazakhstani citizens the right to privately own and lease land with the intention of capitalising economic relations in the countryside. I consider that this law gave considerable momentum to the formation of a class of land owners. As they successfully developed, these land owners were later to become the main lobby demanding the land reforms be carried through to their logical conclusion.

In accordance with the law enacted in January 2001, state and private land ownership in the republic was recognised and protected in equal measure. Agricultural lands could not be privately owned, with the exception of plots for private, domestic (subsidiary) horticulture, market gardening and the construction of country cottages (dachas). As far as the state ownership of agricultural lands was concerned, the essence of the law enacted in January 2001 remained the same as in preceding legislative acts. Land could not be privately owned by foreigners or persons without citizenship who were likewise not entitled to use land on a permanent basis. Agricultural land could be leased by individuals and legal entities of the republic for agricultural commodity production, woodland conservation projects, scientific research, experimental and educational institutions, subsidiary horticulture, market gardening and livestock farming.

The outcome of the second phase of land reform was that every villager was given the opportunity to manage his agreed quota of land as he saw fit. Rural people started getting used to their role as land owners committing them to make the best possible use of their new opportunities. And it was this change in rural people's attitudes that allowed us to take a more decisive step towards introducing

256

private land ownership by adopting the new Land Code of the Republic of Kazakhstan.

Development and Adoption of the Land Code, 2002-03

The issue of adopting the Land Code and introducing the private ownership of agricultural land was not resolved instantly by the country, but evolved during a lengthy process of land-legislation enhancements in the transitional period when market mechanisms in the economy were being developed.

The first and second phases of land reform were more like temporary measures in the transitional period to tackle the continuing crisis in agriculture. The main aim of the first phase of reform had been to define the status of the people working on the land and regulate their mutual relations with the state. The actual concept of private land ownership had been unacceptable in the prevailing conditions at the time. The first phase of land reform supposed a departure from socialist land legislation. Everyone working on the land needed to be given clarification regarding their land relations with the state, which at that time possessed the exclusive right to land ownership.

The main objective of the second phase of land reform was to widely engage the agrarian sector in market relations, in so far as the introduction of the institution of leasing and the right to private ownership of various categories of land made such participation possible. As is well-known, the draft law *On land* of 1999 – envisioning the introduction of private ownership – was revoked from Parliament by the government. It had been an unsuccessful attempt to convince parliamentarians of the need to introduce the institution of the private ownership of agricultural land. Debates between Parliament and the government resulted in the adoption of a compromise version of the Law *On land* in January 2001. However, this law did not envision the introduction of the right to the private ownership of agricultural land either.

Both the first and second phases of land reform, as well as addressing the issues on the agenda at the time, were, in a way, preliminary stages of the most important event in the country's land reform: the introduction of the private ownership of agricultural land. Over 150,000 peasant holdings were already operating in the republic by this time, using nearly 40 per cent of the agricultural land, and thus preventing the land from being concentrated in the hands of a narrow circle of people.

By 2003, the country's economy had not only fully recovered from the crisis of the 1990s, but was already showing high growth rates. Stable GDP had been observed for several consecutive years. Thus, in 2003 alone, the country's GDP growth was 109.3 per cent. The favourable situation in the republic's economy enabled substantial additional funds to be allocated for the implementation of incisive reforms and support of the agrarian sector. However, the support was to be selective rather than all-encompassing as it had been in the days of a centralised economy.

On my instructions, the State Agricultural Production Programme for 2003-05 was elaborated to set the strategic directions for the industry's development. It was also called upon to identify the industries where state support was most needed to make them as competitive as possible, and also the mechanisms and specific amounts of state support.

In my Address to the People for 2003, I identified rural regeneration as one of the main priorities in the government's work, and the period between 2003 and 2005 as the period within which this regeneration was to take place.

> 'We must remember that it is the rural population who genetically represent any nation most. It is they who strive most for stability and healthy evolutionary development. And it is they who most incisively and intuitively perceive the ideals of an independent and strong state in as much as, on a genetic information level, they preserve and reproduce our ancestors' hopes and aspirations.'
>
> From the *Address to the people of Kazakhstan for 2003*, April 2002

On the subject of the rural population, I always regard Iran's land reform as a warning to us. Kazakhstan chose a suitable time for radically reforming a sector as difficult as agriculture. The economy as a whole is currently undergoing a lengthy period of growth and its prospects look fairly encouraging. Iran under the Shah experienced something similar. When a world energy crisis loomed after yet another period of Arab-Israeli hostilities, the country's oil export revenues immediately increased several fold. The government in Tehran, it would appear, had nothing to worry about. But just then millions of peasants, who had been left landless and lost their traditional livelihoods as a result of the agricultural reforms, began flooding into the cities. And, particularly in Tehran, there was a rapidly increasing risk of conflict and protests erupting. How this ended is common knowledge. And yet, the end of the 1970s was practically the best time for the economy of Iran under the Shah. Nothing seemed to portend the lamentable outcome. Although everything in Kazakhstan itself seemed to be calm in those days, the disintegration of the Union and deterioration in living conditions had very seriously traumatised our people.

As we introduced our land reform, we were always concerned about not repeating what had happened in Iran.

Whereas grain had once been known as 'yellow gold' in a similar way to oil, Kazakhstani villagers were now hardly managing to make ends meet. They could not always understand the reasoning behind the cuts in state subsidies. In these conditions, the implementation of such socially sensitive changes as reforming the countryside and rural population's way of life was fraught with unforeseen consequences. As economic indexes improved and the urban population's standard of living went up, we increasingly realised that agriculture and its work force had suffered most from the Soviet economy's deficiencies and it was they who had personally borne the brunt of the transition to a market economy. At the same time, we made it perfectly clear that a return to the Soviet system of totally subsidising agriculture was out of the question.

'It has to be clearly explained to everyone that support for the *aul* should not and will not consist of general state subsidies and non-repayable funding of absolutely everything. We cannot and will not resurrect the one-time practice of free-for-alls and state paternalism.

From now on there needs to be a policy of purposefully creating the conditions for a person so that he can earn a living for himself and his family and supporting those who can and are able to work and show their industry. This is the state's responsibility to the people and its future.

All financial and economic state policy, social and agricultural included, must be selectively targeted only at areas with good prospects as far as people's vital activity and a functioning market are concerned.'

From the Address to the people of Kazakhstan for 2003, April 2002

Compared to the high growth rates of the other branches of the economy, the country's agrarian sector was still in an appalling state. For instance, agriculture's share of GNP for the period between 2000 and 2003 was, on average, only 8.2 per cent, whereas the rural population accounted for around 35-40 per cent (depending on the season) of the republic's total population. Rural workers' productivity was conspicuously low on account of the slow introduction of new technologies to agricultural production, shortage of financial resources, and the low level of managerial qualifications of the personnel in positions of leadership.

Of exceptional importance also was the fact that a strong agricultural sector in the country would help substantially elevate concomitant industries such as mineral fertilizer production, agricultural machinery construction, and the light and food industries, as well as others on the technology chain. The knock-on effect for the country's economy would therefore be enormous. Mention should also be made of the demographic, migratory and social factors that contributed to our special relationship with the *aul*.

Instructions were issued by me to elaborate a model for resettling rural people in different communities with promising futures. There was also a need to decide the fate of a number of rundown small towns. The country urgently needed state policy to stimulate internal migration from unpromising regions to developing regional centres and small towns. There were also the issues of planning and managing the migration flows and providing amenities, land, housing and retraining programmes for the migrants.

Previous attempts to resettle people in rural areas of Kazakhstan had proved unsuccessful, especially in the era of the Soviet command-administrative economy, from a market-economy perspective as well as in social and ecological terms. As a result, many rural regions had depressed economies.

260

'...the crisis in agricultural production caused a population drain and the collapse of the life-support structure of rural populated areas. This process continues to this day. Around 300 populated areas were abandoned in 2000-2002 alone. According to akimats' data, there are 136 registered rural populated areas that are now totally deserted.

Of the 7,660 rural populated areas officially represented by provincial akimats, over 500 are inhabited by fewer than 50 people, and there are numerous stations and halts (257), and villages within the territorial boundaries of towns (317) where the population is actually engaged in agricultural work. The 579,540 people living there consider themselves villagers and hope the state will focus its attention on rural problems....'

From the State Development Programme for Rural Areas of the Republic of Kazakhstan for 2004-2010

No truly incisive reforms of the agrarian sector can take place, however, without first resolving the crucial issue of land relations, and doing away with exclusive state land ownership. The main shortcoming of the prevailing form of state land ownership, past and present, has been people's lack of concern for the land, and its ineffective and even illegal use. For instance, research carried out by the Administration of the President of the Republic of Kazakhstan in 2001 revealed evidence of illegal crops in an area of 3,000 hectares.

The legislation envisioning only temporary land use has not helped develop stable land relations in agriculture or increase land users' confidence in the short term. It is this lack of private agricultural land ownership that has hampered the growth of investment in the agrarian sector. With a view to minimising risks, private capital has mainly gone for short-term investments in the best lands capable of giving a return in the very first year. By the start of the third phase of land reforms only 1.5 per cent of all investments were in agriculture.

Nor has current land legislation helped the development of mortgage relations. Inadequate information on soil quality and up-to-date valuation methods have made it impossible to fix and

261

differentiate land tax rates accurately. The lack of an economic mechanism to stimulate an improvement in soil fertility has also reduced farm holdings' responsibility for the use of lands. As a result, existing land rights have actually held back the development of market relations in the countryside.

Mindful of the situation that had arisen, in my Address to the people of Kazakhstan for 2003, recorded in April 2002, I instructed the Government to elaborate and put before Parliament a draft law *On private land ownership*. A year later, as a result of the debates on the draft law, there was a stand-off between the government and Parliament that eventually culminated in the Government's resignation.

A series of specific points led to this confrontation. The first of these, which the draft law's developers could not agree with, was the deputies' proposal to distribute land plots free of charge to the owners of agreed quotas of land, because it breached the constitutional rights of citizens who did not have such quotas. The situation was aggravated by the fact that land is a special means of production with a basic and cadastral value. The second point the Government was insisting upon was the sizes of plots to be sold to private owners. The original draft stipulated that they were to constitute no less than 10 per cent of the overall area of a region's agricultural lands, and the final decision, what's more, would rest with the local authorities. The Majilis (Parliament) was proposing the land plots fixed in the draft Land Code to be half this size. Experts, however, considered this would result in the segmentation of 60 per cent of all agricultural enterprises. In other words, some of the agricultural plots on major land owners' property would be state-owned and others in private hands. This might scare off investors and cause a chain reaction, dividing up existing agricultural concerns.

Parliament's next objection concerned the setting up of various terms for introducing private ownership for individuals and legal entities. The version proposed by the deputies envisaged transferring the ownership of agricultural lands to individuals immediately after the Land Code's enactment, and to legal entities after a period of three and a half years. This violated the principle of equality of the parties concerned, since peasants were immediately entitled to purchase plots of land and gain ownership of them on an individual basis, while production cooperatives and agricultural associations – as legal entities – were only entitled to do so after a period of three and a half years. And if you also consider that the lands of these legal entities were an amalgamation of the land quotas of their members – that is – individuals, and during these three and a half years the legal entities had to lease the land quotas of their own members, it meant that the working collective would be leasing land from itself. This caused astonishment.

Another divergence of views was caused by the sub-leases the Majilis deputies were proposing to extend until 2007. In the Government's view, this option would result, on the one hand, in extending lessors' terms of dependence and, on the other, in an unwarranted increase in the cost of agricultural production.

The last point was fundamentally important: funds from the sale of agricultural lands would accumulate in new institutions rather than the established National Fund, thereby causing additional budgetary spending. There were clearly fundamental conceptual differences of opinion. The government was basically arguing that were the Land Code to be adopted in its current form, it might ruin our agriculture.

Realising this law had a chance of being enacted and the government was evidently prepared to make several concessions, the deputies began a form of blackmail.

They let it be known that they would not vote in favour of the law in its entirety unless their changes were introduced to it. And so it went on, one concession after another, one article after another, and as a result, the members of the Cabinet came to the conclusion that an entirely different bill had been transferred from the Majilis to the Senate. It was virtually another legislative act and it was revoked in the Government's edition.

All the deputies' arguments were important because they expressed the electorate's views but not all were acceptable. Every argument and objection of both sides was considered, analysed, assessed and taken account of. And yet, despite the government changing the wording in a number of the draft law's articles, the deputies maintained a position totally at odds with the Government's on the issue.

The only legal way left was for Parliament to raise the issue of confidence in the government. If Parliament were to pass a motion of no-confidence by two thirds of the vote, the President would have to decide whether to dissolve Parliament or the government. If Parliament failed to win the vote of no-confidence, the government's draft law would be accepted. The result of the vote was as follows: 55 of the 77 Majilis deputies and three of the 37 deputies of the Parliament's Senate voted against the government. Since the support of two thirds of the Senate was required, the motion failed; but Imangali Tasmaganbetov decided that if 55 Majilis deputies (the majority) were against him, he could not remain in his post as Prime Minister, and so he stepped down. A role of no small importance was also played by the uneasy relations between him and the Majilis Speaker.

With the good economic growth rates, we got a chance to improve our citizens' social well-being by devoting considerable attention to culture, education and healthcare. This work suited a person with experience of working in the public sector. Such a person was Imangali Tasmaganbetov. My loyal comrade-in-arms of many years, he had worked as an Akim and had considerable experience working in government. Energetic by nature, he found the slow examination of laws put before parliament most frustrating. In this context, I would like to say by way of a lesson to the younger generation how important it is for a state's top leaders to control their emotions when the country's interests are at stake.

After the government's resignation, I met with the deputies of the Senate and Majilis. The version of the draft law proposed by the Government had to be repeatedly studied and defended. Resolving the land issue was a process reminiscent of a pine sapling that keeps growing steadily upwards, regardless of the drought conditions and periodic squally gusts of winds. However, obstacles in its way continually threaten to reduce this imposing and powerful tree to an ugly, gnarled stump. The question of whether or not to introduce private ownership was an obstacle in the way of agriculture's future development and growth and so by delaying its resolution we might always keep floundering in a quagmire of doubts.

I appealed to the Constitutional Council: if it were to consider that all the provisions of the Land Code complied with the Constitution, I would sign it and the draft law would come into effect. After discussing the differences of opinion with the deputies once more, we came to a common understanding. This is how dramatic the struggle was for this Code and how the last major step in the country's agricultural reform came about, allowing the new Land Code to work for the good of every rural person and formation of *auls* in Kazakhstan.

On 20 June 2003, my signature was put to the Land Code, which now included a most important, substantial amendment regarding the introduction of the institution of the private ownership of agricultural land.

Taking account of the republic's specific features and the previous code's provisions, three types of land use were envisioned: permanent use, temporary use (leasing) and private ownership. According to the code, state enterprises became permanent land users, foreign citizens and foreign companies acquired the right only to lease land with a maximum term of ten years, and the only transactions with land plots they were entitled to complete were for mortgaging purposes. State-owned agricultural land plots could now be acquired by individual and non-state legal entities of the Republic of Kazakhstan on private ownership terms. What's more, the right of ownership to the said land plots could now be acquired at cadastral (validated) value or at a privileged price, set by the government and constituting 75 per cent of the cadastral value. In both cases, the purchase of land by instalments over a ten-year term was envisaged. Along with the institution of private ownership, provision continues to be made for leases with terms of up to 49 years, but no transactions can be conducted with it, except for mortgaging purposes. In other words, land did not necessarily have to be bought from the state but could continue to be leased. The funds arising from the state's sale of agricultural land plots to private owners are deposited in the National Fund.

The land issue was certainly controversial and caused a great many divergences of opinion and contradictions in different circles of Kazakhstani society. An analysis of the criticisms revealed that many of the arguments advanced by the opponents of private ownership were insufficiently well-grounded, and did not comply with the Kazakhstani practice of land use.

For instance, a central misgiving was that the land would be bought by so-called 'latifundistas', who were actually investors working in agriculture by subleasing land. The land would therefore become inaccessible to peasants. In many countries of the world, including the USA and Russia, such companies are known as 'production integrators', and they own virtually no land. Certain measures were envisioned by the code as safeguards in these areas. With a view to preventing large amounts of land being concentrated in the same hands, limits were put on the size of land plots which could be privately owned by individuals and legal entities. With a view to securing an absolute primary right to the acquisition of agricultural lands, provision was made for citizens with agricultural training and experience of working in the agrarian sector, and resident in a given village, to be granted a preemption on a land plot to be used as a farm smallholding.

Supporters of the land market's total liberalisation suggested removing all restrictions on the purchase of land, including those imposed on foreign citizens. Their main argument was the need to attract foreign investments in agriculture. This argument was invalid because it failed to take account of agriculture's specific features, and the fact that in all countries of the world the agricultural sector is subsidised and only national capital functions in it.

After the Code's enactment, discussions on its key points went on for another month but then the annual harvest forced rural people to get on with their usual work with the new Code now in effect.

After the Adoption of the Land Code

Over two years had passed since the adoption of the Land Code and introduction of private land ownership when I started writing this chapter. I yet again stand by the correctness of the decision taken and policy chosen. Private ownership was, and still is, the foundation of political stability in society. Land reform was aimed precisely at developing and strengthening market institutions. The forecasts of the opponents to the introduction of the private ownership of agricultural land and their misgivings about land being purchased by 'latifundistas' have proved unfounded.

According to data of 20 August 2004, private ownership has been acquired of approximately 30,000 hectares (70,000 acres) of agricultural land. Experts estimate that a maximum of 10 to 15 per cent of the land will be purchased within the next ten years. Owing to the high price of land, the best option for farmers remains leasing land from the state. This has been corroborated by the experience of East Germany, which has also been through a transitional phase from a planned to a market economy: from 1993 to 2003, only 6 per cent of the lands in state ownership were purchased there. Regardless of this evidence, however, certain restrictions introduced by the deputies during the debates still found their way into the Land Code. To my mind the said restrictions, particularly the ban on the resale of a land plot within ten years of its purchase, are excessive and even ineffective. But that's not the main thing.

The land reform's success is going to depend on carrying through further long-term measures. The Land Code allowing the private ownership of agricultural land is merely one of the first steps on the way to improving land relations and the development of a land market in Kazakhstan. It should be noted that even this step has made a difference to the economy's agrarian sector. Private capital has confidence in the state's rural affairs policy and has already started investing substantial funds in the agro-industrial complex.

The *aul* support programme for 2002-05 has produced timely results. The state has spent US$1.5 billion on rural consumer subsidies. Exclusive tax benefits have been applied in the process. Families pay a land tax equivalent to only one fifth of the taxes paid in all other industries. The state subsidises tribal life, seed-growing, irrigation, and mineral fertilisers. A separate development programme for rural areas has got under way, targeting infrastructure, drinking water supplies, and the construction of schools and hospitals. After acquiring ownership of a production unit released for sale, state farm workers were able to lease modern equipment. Laws essential for the agrarian sector's systemic development were enacted. Credit is due to Agriculture Minister Akhmetzhan Yesimov, who is resolutely carrying out work to systemically resolve rural problems. An experienced specialist and manager dedicated to his work, he has been the best Agriculture Minister we have had since independence. He has already achieved a great deal in rural affairs and is continuing to do so.

Agriculture's overall gross output for the first half of 2006 across the whole republic was 77.5 billion tenge, which is over 3.8 per cent up on the same period in 2005.

However, I also realise that considerable work will be needed to conduct more incisive land reform in the future and get a civilised land market up and running in Kazakhstan. The state must constantly keep the rural population informed about the provisions of the latest land reform and the ways and means for carrying it through. There has to be a permanent consultation and legal support system for farmers and methods developed for encouraging rational land use and better soil fertilisation.

At present, land tax rates are calculated on the basis of soil quality ratings and not linked to cadastral (validated) land value. To prevent cases of ineffective land use, breaches of farming regulations and changes in land usage, the Land Code makes provision for punitive measures only such as the deprivation of ownership and land-use rights. But in a market economy these are inadequate for increasing incentives to maintain soil fertility levels and rational, effective land use. To put it more simply, we should not only be taking measures to prevent irrational land use but also encouraging solicitous land management. After all, it is much easier not to break regulations than take positive action to improve soil quality.

There is an urgent need to develop an agricultural crediting system. Agricultural commodity producers are still unable to get credit because of the underdeveloped mortgage base and high bank rates. As the land market develops, these problems will gradually disappear.

Measures must be taken simultaneously to keep reducing red tape. For instance, the 'one window principle' is now successfully up and running virtually all over the country. The number of different types of licenses is being reduced. The land rights registration procedure is gradually going to get simpler. The problem here has to do with the flawed duplicate system of registering real-estate rights carried out by various state bodies. As government in Kazakhstan becomes more computerized, an electronic registration system will be set up, making it easier for villagers to obtain land deeds.

At the same time, as the reforms are carried through, special attention has to be given to the industry as a whole, as agriculture is not just a branch of the economy but also a large block of social issues. And it will continue to play a special role in state life. However, while the state continues to subsidise agriculture, there has to be an understanding that with its support the state must not allow a parasitic mind-set to develop.

The state is going to create favourable conditions, but only in places with prospects for development. This support will take the shape of investments in the infrastructure and social sphere, and particularly in the creation of schools, hospitals, roads and water supply systems. Making agriculture work is going to depend primarily on the farms themselves, and people choosing to retrain and work in keeping with the new market principles. Take, for instance, the following statistics as examples of effective agriculture. The annual output per farmer in the USA is US$38,000, in Australia US$22,000, and in Canada US$17,000. In Kazakhstan an agricultural worker's current output is US$900.

That's why the state's main aim is to create favourable conditions as soon as possible for a highly productive and competitive, private agro-industry without any direct state intervention. And I am confident that civilised land relations are going to develop very soon in Kazkhstan's agriculture, making the industry economically more viable and more attractive to invest in.

What grounds are there, in my making such optimistic forecasts? First, there are the achievements in reforming land relations: introducing the right to private agricultural land ownership, abolishing the institution of subletting, codifying land legislation. Secondly, agrarian sector economists' indicators have pointed to steady growth over recent years, which is also evidence of the improving situation in the countryside. And, thirdly, the enactment of the Land Code has certainly not put an end to land relation reforms.

The evolutionary process goes on forever, and so together we must think about the future. For instance, the Law *On the inclusion of addenda to the Land Code of the Republic of Kazakhstan* has been adopted, in accordance with which addenda have been included in Articles 9 and 13 that envision granting land plots free of charge to scientific centres with international profiles, as well as extending the competence of the country's government to ratifying the regulations for granting land plots to individual housing construction projects.

The Kazakhstan Way

Now that private land ownership has been introduced, we are able to take more decisive measures to get the agricultural model we have chosen up and running. Increasing agricultural producers' competitiveness is a top priority here. This is a topic I speak about very often, and yet at times it seems to me that what I'm saying is still not getting through to villagers. They are anxious about us soon joining the World Trade Organisation (WTO) and the ensuing influx of imported goods. This, to my mind, is ridiculous. Judge for yourselves: our producers don't have to concern themselves with transporting and distributing their goods, and this reduces costs considerably. What's more, they know our consumers and market better. And, most importantly, consumers know them. For any Western companies these advantages would be more than enough. Cut costs, increase quality, work with consumers, and no European chicken or flour will ever take over your market. But you can forget about any special protective measures or harsh protectionist policy on the part of the state. We will never go back to this. We will support our agricultural producers by creating the conditions for them to develop their business without placing restrictions on anyone wanting to enter the Kazakshani market.

On top of everything else, we need to develop agricultural production's processing sector. Kazakhstan is a major grain exporter. However, once processing gets under way, we shall start exporting much more profitable finished products. Our agricultural produce must be brought up to international standards. Quite a lot has already been done to set up grain, milk, fruit and vegetable, and cotton processing plants. We shall be devoting considerable attention to developing agrarian science. Kazakhstan has special natural and climactic conditions, working both for and against us. One day, I hope, our agrarian scientists will devise crops that will make optimum use of the specific features of our land and climate.

Another direction envisaged in the design of a new Kazakhstani agricultural model is the development of our rural areas. Substantial rural regeneration is impossible without decisive improvements in the quality of peasants' living conditions and way of life. Hence it is essential to put significant effort into these areas. Most importantly, we need to create the conditions to enable peasants to improve their own work environment and locality.

The Evolution of the Land Use Issue

What's more, as part of the plan to develop Kazakhstan into one of the world's top 50 most developed countries, public enterprise corporations are going to be set up alongside the Kazyn Stable Development Fund and Samruk Holding, and KazAgro National Holding is to be established for the agricultural sector's development.

There is another extremely important achievement of land reform we simply cannot ignore. As the old adage goes: 'We don't inherit nature from our forebears, we have it on loan from our descendants'. Such an approach is essential for resolving land relation issues. I am sure of this because of my conviction that only a genuine owner will look after his land carefully in order to pass it on to his descendants in a suitable condition.

As for the emotions I experienced at the time, they can probably only be understood by someone who has himself taken such decisions at some point. I empathise with what many outstanding historic figures and heads of state have said about the loneliness of being a state's leader weighed down by public responsibilities. A head of state has exceptional responsibility for the entire country and electorate. He has to do everything to prevent his country from being caught off-guard, and sense how a situation is really developing.

It is virtually impossible to consider absolutely all the pros and cons, difficult to see into the future and impossible to change the past. In such situations you feel nothing but doubts and angst. Of course, you have advisers, some of whom are from abroad, and aides, and the government to advise you. But after listening to all the recommendations and opinions, poles apart and incompatible at times, you still have to take the most crucial and life-changing decisions yourself. This, too, is the tremendous responsibility and burden of being a state's top leader.

Members of the erstwhile managerial elite who had been used to working in the old country declined to, and indeed were unable to, work in the new conditions. Many voiced concerns that without collective and state farms there would be famine in Kazakhstan and the rural economy would collapse. But life has proved the opposite. I had to part with old friends I had worked with for years. I understood them, but could not leave them in their posts since they were slowing things down. Some of them realised this while others

271

went and joined the opposition – but I feel no hatred or resentment towards any of them. Let history be our judge.

Despite this, one has every reason to say that thanks to the effectiveness of the reforms, we have created the basis on which we can guarantee the country's stable development and future economic growth, and enhance public well-being.

Essentially, the institution of private land ownership has been introduced for the very first time in our country's history. And it has been an object-lesson for Kazakhstan. I have always held the view that ideas and projects should not be rejected merely because they have never been tried out by anyone else before. Everything happens for the first time at some time or other. So it was that in 1991, independent Kazakhstan's first astronaut was launched into space, heralding a new era of achievements.

8

KAZAKHSTAN'S WAY TO THE STARS

Zher kindigi – 'Earth's Umbilical Cord'

Recalling events of over a decade and a half ago, I was astonished by the symbolism of a historic coincidence. The establishment of Kazakhstan's sovereignty was first begun in space. In August 1991, just before the Soviet Union disintegrated, Baikonur Cosmodrome was declared republican property. That October the first Kazakh astronaut went into space, and in December we passed the Declaration on Kazakhstan's independence. In other words, it turns out we announced our intention to become a national state in space before doing so on earth! And now, many years later, this seems to me like a sign from above.

Like many others, I have always been enthralled by space. This great mystery enveloping the universe and extraterrestrial civilisations – a living link with our ancestors' spirits – has always fascinated and intrigued me.

Curiously, the Baikonur area's special cosmic future was predicted long ago by the philosopher Korkyt-ata. According to the legends and chronicles that have survived, Korkyt-ata spent his entire life on a quest for the sacred land and eternal life. And everywhere he went he was haunted by the terrifying spectre of death. Eventually, he heard a prophecy that if he were to find Earth's umbilical chord, death would pass him by. So, he travelled through many countries of the Orient, searching for a land where there would never be war, natural disasters or death. He truly believed a sacred place of this kind existed on Earth and always worked to disseminate the idea of it.

At long last, he returned to his home on the banks of the Syrdarya River and took up a stringed instrument called a *kobyz*, convinced that eternal life could only be found in art. Legend has it that whenever he spread a rug across the river and played his *kobyz*, the power of the *kiu* (melody) would keep him afloat and prevent him from drowning. It is also said that whenever Korkyt-ata played the *kobyz,* death would disappear and life was happy. But while the wise man was asleep one day, a small serpent slithered out of the water and bit him. Shortly afterwards he died and was buried in the steppe. Before his death he claimed to have found the sacred land after all, on the bank of the Syrdarya. He named the place of his death *zher kindigi*, 'earth's umbilical chord', because, he said, it was here he had sensed the wondrous link with heaven and the Creator.

Several centuries later, a team of Soviet scientists headed by Sergei Korolev chose what is now Baikonur as the site of the future rocket-launch facility, not far from Korkyt-ata's burial place. And they got it right. Of all the several dozen launch facilities in the world, Baikonur, which is quite close to the Equator, is considered to have the best location. According to the laws of physics, less fuel is consumed on take-off here. However, unlike other launch facilities directly on the Equator, there is hardly any rainfall here and the sun shines on 300 days of the year.

Baikonur did indeed become the cradle of world space science, a space centre and a launch pad. It was here, on Kazakh soil, that people became astronauts.

But where's our own Kazakh astronaut? This logical question loomed before me, as President of the Kazakh SSR, very clearly and distinctly in 1990. Its topicality was becoming especially evident because of the momentous changes the USSR was about to undergo. After preliminary talks with the heads of Russia's space and military departments, who supported the idea as a whole, the USSR Minister responsible for general machine-building, Oleg Shishkin, and I flew to Baikonur on a specially organised flight.

On 12 January 1991, we landed in Baikonur in bad weather. Walking down the aircraft's gangway at Leninsk's Krainiy Airport, I took in the dreary landscape set against the military chiefs' equally grey greatcoats. Then all of a sudden, braving the wintry slush and wind, little children carrying a bouquet of flowers came scampering out towards me like dancing dots of firelight. The little Kazakh boy, aged about five or six, held the bright red carnations out to me, and at that moment I intuitively knew that all our plans for Baikonur were going to work out. I gratefully shook hands with the little boy, who had suddenly come to symbolise Kazakhstan's future space programme for me, and I patted the little girl who was standing next to him and holding him by the hand.

We worked for two full days at Baikonur. Our very tight schedule included a detailed study of the facility's operations, a meeting in Leninsk with people living in the villages of Tore-Tam and Akai close to Baikonur, a visit to the Republican Space School and, most importantly, a political announcement I was intending to make on Kazakhstan's behalf concerning Baikonur. At the press conference attended by Central and Kazakh television journalists, I spoke of Kazakhstan's intention to take part in space exploration, stressing that only with the general support of the Soviet Union's republics would it be possible to keep the space complex up and running. The idea of the facility's new Kazakhstani status was still hanging in the air, and that's why there was obviously a mixed reaction among the people present. During this visit to Baikonur, my first as Kazakhstan's President, we saw the Progress transport spaceship being prepared. At the time, just as now, two manned launches took place in the spring and autumn every year. I raised the question of our having an astronaut in space, the most likely time for it being September-October 1991.

The Baikonur Cosmodrome became the universe's first mooring. A state commission was set up in 1954 to select a site on which to build the launch facility. Artillery Lieutenant General V.I. Voznyuk, head of the Kapustin Yar Polygon test site, was appointed the commission's chairman. After reconnoitring several of the country's regions, the commission put forward the proposal to locate the facility several hundred kilometres from the village of Baikonur [*Baikonyr* in Kazakh nomenclature] in a desert region of Kazakhstan, east of the Aral Sea. This place had a number of advantages over the others: low population not only in the facility's vicinity but also in the launched rockets' flightpath; flat, semi-desert terrain; the major central Asian Syrdarya River close by; a railway and vehicle thoroughfare in close proximity; over 300 days of sunshine annually, and, most importantly, its location fairly close to the Equator, meaning that the additional speed of the Earth's revolution could be used for launches.

Baikonur had been closed off to Kazakhstan for years and now the time had come for a Kazakh astronaut to fly into space. My

275

argument was simple and logical. Fortunately, many of the Union's top leaders realised this flight was a just reward for the republic whose land had been used for launching spaceships into space for the past thirty years. I was very conscious of the fact that this was Kazakhstan's much-needed first step into space, a step dictated by history itself.

Next began the complex process of looking for a potential astronaut. Military pilots were considered, and I asked the USSR Minister of Defence to look among Kazakh pilots serving in the armed forces. Two or three were selected but none proved suitable. Another possible candidate was Talgat Musabayev, a flying instructor and the small aircraft altitude record-holder. But time was needed to train him. The Soviet Space Agency was not very keen on having our astronaut as they had a list of candidates of their own. However, I wanted the issue tied up quickly, especially as an agreement had already been reached in difficult talks with Mikhail Gorbachev and the Ministry of Defence. One morning I read in a newspaper that our compatriot, military aircraft test pilot Tokhar Aubakirov, was holidaying on Mount Chimbulak. I immediately invited him to a meeting. There were a great many hurdles in the way, what with him being 45 years old and having health problems. But I persisted, and eventually he flew into space.

Within a few months, on my instructions, a group of the republic's leading scientists, led by President of the Kazakh SSR Academy of Sciences Umirzak Sultangazin and Viktor Drobzhev, began setting up Kazakhstan's first national space programme. It should be said that the scientific part of the programme had been developed long before and was just waiting to be put into action. Alterations were made to it so that it tied in with the first Kazakh astronaut's flight programme.

But while everything was fine with the preparations for the space programme, the astronaut's training was proving more difficult. The flight was a schedule add-on and there was little time for training, so Toktar Aubakirov, by then a Hero of the Soviet Union, and Honoured Test Pilot of the USSR, was made a member of the main crew and Talgat Musabayev became his back-up.

Owing to substantial changes in the plans of Russia's space agencies and astronaut training centre, numerous talks and consultations had to be held with managers, specialists and military personnel. As a result, I had to contact the USSR Minister of Defence Dmitry Yazov and even President Gorbachev for this important political decision to be finally reached.

In February 1991, at our invitation, a large group of scientists and space experts visited Almaty from Moscow. They included, among others, General Director of the Russian Space Agency Yuri Koptev, General Director of the Energia NPO Yuri Semenov, Head of the Astronaut Training Centre Vladimir Shatalov, and the director of the USSR Institute for Space Research. A meeting was held at the republic's Academy of Sciences at which Kazakhstan's first space programme was approved.

At the same time, parallel talks were taking place with the heads of the Union and Russian departments on organising the 30th anniversary celebrations of Yuri Gagarin's space flight at Baikonur. The decision was taken just before the first Kazakh astronaut's flight to hold the festivities at the launch facility under Kazakhstan's aegis. I gave instructions for the republic's Council of Ministers to take personal charge of the preparations and running of the festivities. A colossal amount of work was done in three months.

On 12 April 1991, Baikonur hosted a live broadcast to Moscow featuring a spectacular show in which I also took part. Thousands joined in a carnival procession through the streets of Leninsk, and demonstration flights of the unique Mriya transport aircraft with a Russian Energia-Buran rocket-carrier on board were shown at the central stadium. The programme also included horse races at an improvised racetrack near Baikonur and a sold-out gala concert of Soviet variety stars at the Gagarin launch pad.

In a word, the festival was cosmic both in scale and emotion. According to festival-goers, to this day Baikonur has never seen anything quite as spectacular as the Stars of Space, Sport and the Stage International Festival to celebrate the 30th anniversary of the Planet Earth's first man in space.

It was my second visit to Baikonur and a new political step for Kazakhstan towards space.

And so the historic day of 2 October 1991 arrived. It was now my third visit to Baikonur within a year. I flew into the cosmodrome at seven am, well in time for the Soviet-Austrian launch at 11:59am. During the next few hours several dozen aircraft landed at Yubileiniy Airport's landing ground No. 251, bringing Austrian Chancellor Franz Vranitsky, Chairman of the USSR Supreme Soviet Ivan Silayev, the leaders of nearly all the Union republics, numerous delegations from Russia, Kazakhstan, Ukraine and Austria, and representatives of foreign states' space agencies. The international team's launch attracted even more attention than usual, partly for political reasons. Over a month earlier, on 31 August 1991, the Baikonur Cosmodrome had been declared Kazakh property. And so my anxious thoughts were focused not only on the imminent launch but also on Baikonur's general future.

At ten am the astronauts – Russia's Alexander Volkov, Kazakhstan's Toktar Aubakirov and Austria's Franz Fibek – came out onto the square in front of the Soyuz launch complex's assembly and testing building. Weighed down by all their heavy equipment, they walked clumsily along, like children taking their first unsteady steps outdoors.

Colonel Volkov, the flight captain, reported loud and clear to State Commission Chairman General Vladimir Ivanov that the crew was ready for take-off. General Ivanov, fully aware of the gravity of the moment, looked at me and then turned the microphone towards Aubakirov, giving him the opportunity to say something.

Without a moment's hesitation, Toktar announced in Kazakh: 'Esteemed President! Astronaut Aubakirov is ready for his launch into space from Kazakhstan soil.' I nodded approvingly to him.

Everything went according to plan. The guests and I went to all the different areas in the launch preparation procedure, accompanying the astronauts all the way to the rocket. After wishing them success, and the same to NPO Energia's general director Yury Semenov and the head of the Baikonur Cosmodrome Lieutenant General Alexei Shumilin, who were remaining in the bunker to direct the launch, I drove over to Observation Point No 18.

The small observation platform was festooned with flags, and there were yurts spread out all around, with a young white camel – a living symbol of Kazakhstan's space programme – standing nearby, and folk music playing. The atmosphere was reminiscent of a small *aul* during a festival.

Only minutes were left before the launch. I had to give in to journalists' insistent requests and comment on events. In my interview I made a point of saying the following: 'I consider that in the future we should develop space with all the Union's republics taking part, because today the Cosmodrome is arguably the only advantage we have in the global economic competition.' And standing nearby on the platform, Chairman of the USSR Supreme Soviet Ivan Stepanovich Silayev added, 'I totally support you, Nursultan Abishevich. A new economic formation – I mean the CIS – has just been set up, and this has repercussions for the Cosmodrome's future and conquest of space. Now all the republics' leaders are here, and in the present situation it's very important for them to see Baikonur's resources, potential and grandeur for themselves.'

Just then one minute to countdown was announced over the intercom. I synchronised my watch, and as a gesture of support, said to a relative of Toktar's standing nearby, 'A safe journey to them!' An immense silence fell and all you could hear were the clipped orders: 'Key to start, ignition, lift off!'

Thousands of eyes were fixed on the launch pad and the Soyuz TM-13 spaceship in its metal casing. We had a perfect view of it all. The girder-like trusses slid smoothly apart and the majestic fireball carrying the spaceship rose up amidst clouds of white smoke. Passing through the Earth's gravity, the rocket headed in awesome splendour towards the skies. And only seconds later did we hear a powerful roar rumbling the earth.

It was a special feeling when everyone there sensed the real power of the universe and people's togetherness in the cosmos. All of us were now equal in the face of this elemental cosmic force, one big family of the Earth seeing our sons off on a long and dangerous voyage.

I had previously had occasion to watch spacecraft launches but this one was special, of course. Someone started clapping. 'Not yet, wait till they've got into orbit,' I admonished him.

The rocket was heading off into Baikonur's clear autumn sky. Everyone continued staring up, keeping it in their sights and following the trajectory of its flight. Like everyone else there, I, too, felt a buzz of excitement but tried to keep looking calm. Trying to catch sight of the rocket before it disappeared over the platform's roof, Ivan Stepanovich Silayev leaned over so far that he ended up almost lying on the rails. The live televised broadcast sent pictures of the launch all over the world.

For about ten minutes everyone stared intently up at the sky although the 'star' had already vanished, leaving a white vapour trail behind.

The stands emptied and everyone rushed onto the open square to get a better view.

Only Metropolitan Pitirim of Moscow stayed on there, gazing pensively into the distance. 'He must have seen with his own eyes how indivisible we people are before both God and space,' I thought to myself.

And then, at last, the radio announcer, changing his official tone, exclaimed, 'It's separated! The ship's in orbit!'

The silence was broken by thunderous applause. Everyone there started hugging and kissing. Many had tears in their eyes. Receiving the many congratulations, Chancellor Vranitsky and I were feeling equally happy: the way to the stars had been opened for both our countries!

In keeping with the traditions of Kazakh hospitality, and thanks to the efforts of the Kyzylorda district executive committee and local executive authority, the Gagarin Launch Complex was transformed that day into a colourful small settlement of yurts where there were sumptuous refreshments, artists in national costume, gifts, souvenirs and, most importantly, a general sense of triumph, which my Kazakh people well and truly deserved. This warm autumn day in Baikonur marked the start of Kazakhstani astronautics.

A short while later at the observation point, Chancellor Vranitsky and I gave a press conference in which I once again noted, 'Baikonur is not only the Soviet people's property and the entire country's treasured possession, it is also our trump card in the world.'

I then announced that by my decree an Agency for Space Research would shortly be set up in Kazakhstan and run by one of the republic's academicians. We would also be facing the challenge of making the space facility's potential comply with Kazakhstan's economic interests.

Everyone was well aware the country's budget could not finance the space departments, and the space projects would have to stop. And so, addressing the leaders of all the republics at the Cosmodrome, I said, 'Everything must be done to prevent work at Baikonur from stopping.'

I well remember the first radio link-up with the Soviet-Austrian crew in space. The Flight Control Centre employees setting up my conversation from Almaty with the Mir Space Station openly expressed their surprise that the country's President wanted to talk to the astronauts. My message to the international team was simple, friendly and even, I would say, fatherly.

Yes, for the first time a son of the Kazakh people had flown into space and I was manifestly proud of this. Toktar, whom we spoke to in our mother tongue, told me how beautiful our Earth was from space and what experiments he was conducting to study the territory of Kazakhstan. All in all, the crew was very friendly, good-humoured and witty, and as the head of the Flight Control Centre, Vladimir Soloviev, later remarked, the men worked in orbit without a single breakage, a sign not only of professionalism but also of the really tremendous camaraderie among the team.

Baikonur – a Difficult Creation

Baikonur is truly a creation of the Soviet Union. However, after the 'sovereignty parade' in which Kazakhstan went last, it became clear that space programmes were out of the question for our former Union republics. Realistically, the Cosmodrome could only be maintained by Russia, whose main space programmes were bound up with Baikonur, and Kazakhstan, which by dint of historical circumstances had become its owner.

The young sovereign state's new form of executive power, the institution of administration heads, also involved the city of Leninsk. In February 1992, by my decree, Vitaly Brynkin was appointed the first administration head of the city of Leninsk in Baikonur's history.

The city of Leninsk, the Cosmodrome's administrative centre, then acquired the status of a city of republican significance, and the nearby villages of Toretam and Akai were merged with it. Despite all the difficulties of the transitional period, it was then that the foundations were laid for setting up a municipal communal service, the state bodies of the Republic of Kazakhstan were formed and Kazakhstani communal services were actively developed at the Cosmodrome. Our republic's blue flag was confidently unfurled over Baikonur.

The Kazakhstan Way

On 25 February 1993, the Agency for Space Research of the Kazakh SSR was reformed as the National Air and Space Agency of the Republic of Kazakhstan, and the first Kazakh astronaut, Toktar Aubakirov, appointed as its Director General. The directorate of the Kazakhstan Air and Space Agency was immediately set up at Baikonur under the general heading of the 'Baikonur Cosmodrome'.

These two years of Kazakhstani administration at Baikonur enabled many of our compatriots to visit the Cosmodrome and the Kazakhstani press to be shown the closed-regime facility, since one of the ideological objectives of the time was to align the space facility's potential with Kazakhstan's economic interests. In the summer of 1993 a large delegation of Kazakhstani journalists visited the Cosmodrome for a meeting of Kazakhstan's Union of Journalists.

Baikonur needed protection and support as the media were attributing all the problems of the transitional period, and the economic and social slump right across the CIS, to the ineffective executive authorities in Kazakhstan's provinces. Russia's central television channels kept showing shocking pictures of Baikonur in decline, indirectly pointing the finger of blame at ambitious Kazakhstan.

Time and circumstances were dictating their own agenda. Urgent measures had to be taken to maintain the space facility, which had begun to fall into decay because the Russian side had cut off funding. Kazakhstan was totally in charge of all the running costs of the city of Leninsk but budget funds were inadequate for a city of Union-wide significance. And it was then the so-called 'human factor' crisis occurred which might have really destroyed Baikonur.

Excellent, irreplaceable space technology specialists, idealists and patriots of the universal space port started leaving Baikonur for the land of their forebears. The migration was not of a nationalist nature: people were simply looking for a better way of life and stability.

Meanwhile, the republic's National Air and Space Agency started actively searching all over the world for joint space project partners. The idea of setting up an international space company with Baikonur as its base became central to its work. However, time was passing by and once again Russia and Kazakhstan proved the only viable parties interested in running and developing Baikonur's space potential.

On 28 March 1994, President of the Russian Federation Boris Yeltsin and I took an unprecedented, crucial decision on Baikonur and signed an inter-state agreement *On the main principles and conditions for the use of the Baikonur Cosmodrome* in which the issue of leasing the Baikonur launch facility was raised for the first time in the two sovereign states' history.

When the Russian President and I announced the decision, exclamations of astonishment rippled across the Kremlin's St George's Hall. The Russians were pleased, as for them it was the only acceptable way of continuing work. The Kazakhstanis, on the other hand, were disappointed, because over several years they had got used to the idea of setting up an international space company.

What's more, many did not understand what a lease would actually entail. I heard specialists contending that the lease should only cover the Cosmodrome's facilities and technology but not its human resources. In actual fact, however, all the problems were yet again related to the same 'human factor'. It was impossible to separate the Cosmodrome from the city, and so we used the formula of the 'space facility', which included all the Cosmodrome's units and the city of Leninsk with all its population. Only on such conditions were the Russians prepared to continue running Baikonur in the future and our side accepted them. I realised the morale of my compatriots at Baikonur might be affected, but the urgent need to preserve the space facility's scientific, technological and intellectual potential was greater than even Kazakhstan's state interests. It was a challenge on a global scale – especially as we Kazakhstanis still had a lot to learn from the immensely experienced Russians in space project development.

The Kazakhstan-Russia treaty on the Baikonur facility has a specific character all of its own. Essentially, the signed new agreements encompass not only joint space projects as such but, chiefly, all aspects of the Baikonur facility's functions within the conditions of its lease by the Russian Federation. In this context, the 'Baikonur facility' has to be interpreted as the research, technological, scientific, production, technical, communal and maintenance units of the Baikonur Cosmodrome and the town of Baikonyr, which is home to both Russian and Kazakhstani citizens whose social rights also have to be regulated by appropriate bilateral agreements.

The next practical step in strengthening our relations with our principal Baikonur partner was an agreement between the Governments of the Republic of Kazakhstan and the Russian Federation that formed the basis for signing the Baikonur Space Facility Lease Treaty for a term of 20 years with a ten-year prolongation, on 10 December 1994. In this document's preamble the parties noted the historic significance of this step for Russia and Kazakhstan, emphasising their mutual intention to ensure the future development of space research in both states' interests.

The annual lease for the Cosmodrome's use was set at US$115 million. A Baikonur facility sub-commission of the Inter-Governmental Commission for Cooperation between the Republic of Kazakhstan and the Russian Federation was appointed as the parties' regulatory body.

I often thought about Baikonur's difficult destiny. With its sublime space projects on the one hand and earthly problems on the other, it was always at the centre of international interests and never let either party gain the upper hand. This creation of the great Union became the shared, troublesome but much loved charge of Russia and Kazakhstan, never letting on which of them it favoured more.

Only time could be the principal judge of it all. But the past 16 years since our first Kazakh astronaut's flight, and 13 years since the signing of the lease treaty, have proved the decision was correct. During this time Russia has maintained and modernised the main launch pad for carrying out its main space programmes.

Due to its close collaboration with the Russians, Kazakhstan has secured flights for two astronauts: Toktar Aubakirov, who carried out the first national scientific programme in space, and Talgat Musabayev, who completed three flights in space in the Republic of Kazakhstan's interests and became the record-holder for the longest stay in orbit.

Speaking of Kazakhstan's space achievements, I would like to specially mention Talgat Musabayev here. The story of how this Hero of Russia and People's Hero of Kazakhstan, and pilot-cosmonaut of both countries became an astronaut has remarkable resonance with the history of Baikonur. A Kazakh by birth – after his first space mission in 1994 – when he spent six months in orbit working as an aviation engineer – he and astronaut Yury Malenchenko were presented with Russia's highest award. The scientific experiments he had been conducting during the first flight needed to be continued, and he consulted me before starting preparations for his second mission. He wanted to fly as spacecraft commander, but in order to do so, in keeping with Russian Federation Law *On Space*, he first had to take Russian citizenship.

There were quite a few arguments in favour, but it was the ethical side of taking on citizenship that jarred. So I dispelled his doubts by saying, 'You were born a Kazakh and will always be one, but you should comply with these conditions if that's what it takes to carry out Kazakhstan's space programme.' Musabayev displayed courage and heroism on all three flights. I was not surprised to learn that he had virtually saved the Mir Space Station in an emergency situation during his second mission in 1998. In 2001, it was he who was entrusted with taking the world's first space tourist, American millionaire Dennis Tito, into orbit. As well as carrying out the two countries' space programmes, Talgat also devoted time and attention to Kazakhstan whenever possible. For instance, he sent a goodwill message to the *Azia dauysi* International Festival, broadcast one of our great poet Abai's songs from space, and took part in the inauguration ceremonies of Kazakhstan's new capital, Astana.

The capital's residents will most likely recall what an exciting moment it was to get a goodwill message in Kazakh from space. The first flag in orbit; the Muslims' sacred book, the Koran, consecrated with cosmic light; a handful of Kazakh earth that journeyed into space – we have Talgat to thank for all these.

During space flights and after his work in orbit, he always found the place where he was most needed. Now that he has completed his active aviation service he is running the Russia-Kazakhstan Baiterek joint enterprise, and is responsible for the major challenge of setting up a new rocket space centre. Musabayev's personal expertise of Russia-Kazakhstan relations played a key role in his appointment to this responsible post.

He has also spoken publicly about the need to think of future astronauts. In 1997, he sent me a report on the delays in organising the training of potential astronauts of the Republic of Kazakhstan.

A working group was then set up to deal with the selection process. Only four of the 800 candidates were passed by a medical commission. However, Mukhtar Aimakhanov and Aidyn Aimbetov, who had been sent to train in Russia's Zviozdniy Gorodok (Star City), were both passed by the chief medical commission in Moscow.

T. Musabayev completed his first space flight on board the Soyuz TM-19 spaceship on 1 July 1994, after working in orbit for 126 days as an aviation engineer with Y. Malenchenko and V. Polyakov. He completed two space walks logging 11 hours and 7 minutes.

Between 29 January and 25 August 1998, he made his second space flight, this time as space commander of the Soyuz TM-27 spaceship and as operations commander of Mir on programme EO-25 (NASA-7/'Pegasus') with N. Budarin and L. Eyharts (France, until 19 February 1998), and E. Thomas (USA, until 8 June 1998). During the flight he performed five space walks, logging 30 hours and 8 minutes. The duration of the flight was 207.5 days.

From 28 April to 6 May 2001, he completed his third space flight, this time as commander of the Soyuz-TM32 spaceship with Y. Baturin (aviation engineer) and the first space tourist, US citizen Dennis Tito.

But let us return to the time in the story where I left off, in 1995. The status of the city of Leninsk changed in keeping with the inter-state agreement. While remaining an administrative and territorial centre of the Republic of Kazakhstan, for the duration of the lease it acquired the equivalent status of a city of federal significance in the Russian Federation. This meant that it was under the jurisdiction of the Russian Federation and its funding sources were also Russian. The constitutional rights of the citizens of Kazakhstan residing in the city of Leninsk were protected by a special representative of the President of Kazakhstan at the Baikonur Cosmodrome. On my decision, the Baikunor veteran who had built the Cosmodrome, Yergaza Nurgaliev, was appointed to this new post.

Life in the city and Cosmodrome gradually settled down. In the autumn of 1995, I received an official request from the residents of Baikonur for the city of Leninsk to be renamed, and at the end of the year this decision was taken and the city acquired its original Kazakh name of Baikonyr.

Kazakhstan's Way to the Stars

Along with the Cosmodrome, on 5 May 1955, construction began on a settlement for the scientific personnel, who first named it Zarya but then renamed it several times, in keeping with the political situation: Tashkent-90, Tiura-Tam, Leninsky settlement, Zvezdigrad, Leninsk (21 June 1966) and, finally, on 20 December 1995, Baikonyr. Today the city is a modern cultural and administrative centre that can rightfully be called an oasis in the desert. The city's infrastructure is made up of 1,200 units; it has 367 multi-storey residential apartment blocks with an overall area of over one million square metres. The city has 13 schools, nine pre-schools, a branch of the Moscow Aviation Institute, an electronics and radio technology college, a medical institute, and a vocational training school. The city of Baikonyr has a population of approximately 80,000. The Baikonyr's residents celebrate 16 national holidays of Russia and Kazakhstan.

Nowadays Kazakstani state management bodies work alongside the Russian authorities in the city of Baikonyr, protecting the jurisdiction of the Republic of Kazakhstan and constitutional rights of Kazakhstani citizens, who make up over half of Baikonyr's population.

There are over 7,000 Kazakhstani citizens working in Russian enterprises and institutions of the town and Cosmodrome. Since 1994 the number of Kazakh-language schools in Baikonyr has risen from one to six – that is, half of all the city's schools.

One of the lease's conditions concerned the training of Kazakhstani personnel for work in the space industry, and this issue is now being given priority. According to Ministry of Education figures, within the past five years over 100 people have graduated from the Baikonyr branch of the Moscow Aviation Institute. Thanks to the Ministry's efforts, the number of students on full state grants has increased to 100. Over the past 40 years, hundreds of graduates of the Baikonyr electronics and radio technology college have been able to apply their skills at Baikonur/*Baikonyr*.

Today Baikonur Cosmodrome is a state-of-the-art scientific and technological facility. The cosmodrome's surface infrastructure consists of 11 assembly and testing facilities for the assembling and testing of spacecraft, launch vehicles and take-off blocks; nine launch pads (14 launch platforms); eight shaft launch units; four refuelling neutralizing stations for refuelling spacecraft, and take-off blocks with fuel components and compressed gases; two airfields; a measurement facility within the Computer Centre; and five measurement points.

Further, Baikonur's infrastructure includes 360 km of heating system lines, 470 km of railway lines, over 1,200 km of vehicle thoroughfares and 2,500 km of communication lines.

Baikonur has 13 rocket and space technology maintenance and testing centres up and running. Since the Cosmodrome's establishment approximately 2,500 rockets have been launched for space science and military purposes; over 3,000 spacecraft and satellites, and over 150 Russian and foreign astronauts, have flown into orbit.

Baikonur Cosmodrome currently has facilities for launching five types of rockets. There are nine launch systems with 15 light-class launch vehicles (Cyclon-2), medium-class (Proton-K) and super-weight (Energia) launch vehicles; and 34 technology preparation facilities for rockets and spacecraft.

The development of space exploration in Kazakhstan can be divided into several phases.

The first, between 1991-94, was of a distinctly national character: two Kazakh astronauts flew into space and Kazakhstan's first space programme was implemented.

The second, the setting-up phase over the following decade 1994-2004, was inseparably linked with the space facility's economic and political position. During this period over 30 international treaties and agreements regulating space, social and legal activity under the terms of the Baikonur facility's lease were concluded between the Republic of Kazakhstan and the Russian Federation.

And the third, begun in 2005, I look upon as the phase in which space activities in Kazakhstan will be actively developed in real terms. I would like to describe it in greater detail as it includes our prospects for the future in this area.

'Baiterek' – Kazakhstan's Cosmic Tree
During Russian President Vladimir Putin's official visit to Kazakhstan in January 2004, we signed an agreement in Astana on extending the Baikonur lease until 2050, thus envisaging the long-

term space programmes of both sides. And exactly a year later, on 25 January 2005, I passed a decree approving the state space development programme in the Republic of Kazakhstan for 2005-2007. Accordingly, work began on the Russia-Kazakhstan Baiterek joint venture to build a space rocket complex in compliance with the high demands of environmental safety and protection.

To date, draft work schedules have been drawn up for the development of the Baiterek joint venture's technical and launch facilities, buildings, technical systems and technological equipment.

Engineering prospecting works are now complete at Baikonur Cosmodrome's Site 200, where Baiterek is to be developed. There is also now a full list of the Control Centre No. 40 buildings designated to be leased and transferred to the joint venture. Proceedings are still under way to agree the contracts in compliance with the lists of specified amounts of work to be executed.

The Kazakhstan-Russia Baiterek joint venture has been set up to develop the ecologically safe, new Baiterek space launch complex based on the facilities of the Baikonur Cosmodrome's ground infrastructure. Baiterek is to be used to carry out commercial space programmes and projects as well as conducting the national space programmes of the Republic of Kazakhstan and Russian Federation.

The end result of the project will be to provide favourable conditions for the Republic of Kazakhstan to develop its own national aviation and space industry and space programme, use ecologically friendly rocket and space technology complying with all international standards, and also create new jobs.

The Baiterek complex is designed for the launch of spacecraft for various purposes, with a view to carrying out the space programmes of Russia and Kazakhstan, and also commercial programmes in low, medium and high circular and elliptical orbits (including solar synchronic, geostatic, polar, and half-day orbits). It will also offer take-off trajectories to the other planets of the solar system. The launch of space communication satellites to complete a variety of tasks is of the greatest interest to the national space programme of the Republic of Kazakhstan.

The national company KazCosmos, set up in March 2005, now has nine space projects on its books, including one to develop a specialised space technology design office jointly with Russian

Space Corporation Energia at the Cosmodrome.

The company is currently working on the development of the Sary-Shagan test facility; a national space system for the distant probing of the Earth; a spacecraft for scientific purposes; a multi-functional system; and personal satellite communications. Work is also under way to produce a draft project and feasibility study for the Ishym aviation and space launch facility.

Another project in the state space activity development programme in the Republic of Kazakhstan for 2005-2007 was commissioned at the start of 2006: Astana's Centre for Flight Information on rocket launches from Baikonur Cosmodrome.

The Astrophysics Research Centre is making headway in its space research, developing an international space radiation monitoring system and producing on behalf of the Republic of Kazakhstan a complex draft programme for conducting scientific research and experiments on board the International Space Station. These include the study of optical phenomena in the upper atmosphere.

Today we must focus our national potential for space activity on Baikonur as a prospective space industry centre. With this in mind, branches of KazCosmos and the Baiterek joint venture are now up and running in the city of Baikonyr, and departments of the Astrophysics Research Centre are moving there.

Space research in Kazakhstan goes back a long way. The V.G. Fesenkov Astrophysics Institute was established in 1950 to conduct astrophysical observations and theoretical research of galactic and outer galactic sites – stars and planets of the solar system. Since 1983, the ionosphere institute has been engaged in the study of solar-terrestrial communication mechanisms, and dynamic processes defining the interaction of various media (atmosphere-ionosphere-magnitosphere), as well as monitoring and forecasting weather in space over the Kazakhstan region.

On the initiative of Academician U. Sultangazin, the Institute of Space Research was established on 12 August 1991, with a view to developing space monitoring and ecological prognostication methods and technologies.

The launch of Kazakhstan's first satellite KazSat was the next real step on its way to joining the ranks of space powers.

On 18 June 2006, I arrived at Baikonur with President Vladmir

Putin to participate in this memorable event. The Proton-K rocket carrying Kazakhstan's first space satellite on board took off from Site 200 exactly on schedule, at 4:44 am on 18 June. It was the first time Vladimir Vladimirovich had watched a rocket launch at Baikonur, and how symbolic that it was the KazSat launch, made possible by joint cooperation.

Contrary to press expectations, we did not pass comment on the launch's success, as the satellite's principal work was due to start later, in orbit.

At eight pm the same day, the Akkola ground control complex received a signal from the satellite indicating that the aerials of the aviation retranslation complex were functioning and the spacecraft was ready for work. After two months of satellite in-orbit testing by Russian and Kazakhstani experts at Akkola's flight ground control complex, KazSat was put into operation by Kazakhstan.

KazSat has 12 active Ku-band transponders – four providing continuous telecommunication and eight for fixed communication in the BRTK Ku and BRTK 72 MHz frequency range. The transmission signal is to be provided by the ground control complex and communication monitoring system at Akkola, 100 km from Astana in Kazakhstan, and qualified personnel who have been trained in Russia.

In orbit the satellite will provide all Kazakhstan, Siberia and the Volga region with satellite communication and TV transmissions.

KazSat underwent flight design tests at an orbit of 92 degrees longitude and was moved to an orbit of 103 degrees east longitude, where it set to work. This orbital position is reserved for Russia and, by agreement, made over to Kazakhstan until 2021.

For the first time since the start of the Baikonur space facility's lease, Kazakstan is going to be taking part in the development of the city's and Cosmodrome's infrastructure. As a result of Prime Minister of Kazakhstan Danial Akhmetov's working visits to Baikonur, it was decided to build a national educational centre in the city of Baikonyr and reconstruct a building to house all the Kazakhstani space agencies, as well as several houses for Kazakhstani specialists.

I want to mention Danial Akhmetov's constructive work in carrying out Kazakhstan's industrialisation and residential housing programmes. Always proactive and determined to succeed, he has devoted considerable effort to carrying through the space activity development programme, the flight of our first communication satellite and the construction of the Baiterek facility.

Training personnel and increasing professional skills have been made a priority of Kazakhstan's state space programme. Within the President's Bolashak Programme, space-related study visits have so far been organised to foreign institutions of higher education in Russia, the USA, Britain, France, Germany, the Netherlands, Canada and China. Grants are currently being awarded to around 100 students engaged in space-related areas of study.

Two would-be Kazakhstani astronauts have completed a general course at the Y.A. Gagarin Astronaut Training Centre and are waiting for a flight programme to be decided upon. On the joint instructions of President Putin and myself, a joint group of Kazakhstani-Russian specialists have conducted a study of the use and application of global navigation satellite systems (GLONASS) and presented it to the Government of the Republic of Kazakhstan. In short, consistent, purposeful work is currently being carried out in the country to develop our space programme.

Vladimir Putin and I have visited Baikonur twice in the past two years. In 2005, we took part in the celebrations to mark the Baikonur space facility's 50th anniversary. In my speech to the people of the city of Baikonyr – people who have honourably served the space industries of Russia and Kazakhstan – I reminded them that at the start of 2004 we signed a document on extending the Baikonur lease until 2044, and decisions were reached on joint space programmes and training for Kazakhstani astronauts and space industry specialists. Then I made a point of saying: 'So, as far as the lives of our generation and joint work at the Baikonur Cosmodrome are concerned, Vladimir Vladimirovich and I have got them sorted. I, in fact, regard this facility as the principle and concrete evidence of our eternal friendship.'

My words were met with thunderous applause. I was grateful for this appreciation. Baikonyr people are special, and they were genuinely delighted that the Cosmodrome was in safe hands as far as the mutually favourable international cooperation between Kazakhstan and Russia was concerned, and their future was under the personal control of these countries' leaders.

Generally speaking, I was inspired by this visit to Baikonyr, the first after the facility was leased. After not visiting the Cosmodrome for 11 years, I could see it was as strong in spirit as ever. Figuratively speaking, this most complex, divinely gifted creation, Baikonyr, now resembled a strong, intelligent and educated young man full of ambitious plans for the future.

It may have had to endure the stiffest ordeals, but these have only given it more resolve, strength and faith. And Kazakhstan as one of its creators can rightfully take pride in it.

Over recent years substantial positive changes have taken place in the Republic of Kazakhstan as a whole and at the Baikonur facility in particular. Kazakhstan now has a developed market economy: within a tight time-frame we have succeeded in carrying through reforms securing the country's stable economic growth.

Kazakhstan today is one of the world's most dynamically developing states. A new economic management system is currently being set up, and an industrial and innovation strategy implemented with economic diversification as its goal. And one of the most progressive financial systems in post-Soviet space has been developed. Our sights are set on an economic model with priority industries which have competitive economic potential. Our agenda includes further modernisation and democratisation, and Kazakhstan's integration and placement among the world's fifty most competitive countries.

The challenge of developing our space programmes is being aligned with this strategic aim. The country's economic growth has paved the way for these programmes to be developed and carried through. The programme for 2005-2007 was launched successfully, and, on my instructions, a long-term programme covering further space activities, until 2020, is currently being developed.

The Republic of Kazakhstan is now a subject of international space law.

In 1995, Kazakhstan became a member of the UN Committee on the Peaceful Uses of Outer Space. In 1997, the Republic of Kazakhstan joined the five main international UN outer space treaties:

- The treaty outlining the principles of state activity in respect of outer space research and use;
- The agreement on the rescue of astronauts, the return of

astronauts and return of objects launched into outer
space, 22 April 1969;
- The convention on international responsibility for
damage caused by outer space objects, 29 March 1972;
- The convention on the registration of objects launched
into outer space, 14 January 1975;
- The agreement on state activity on the Moon and other
celestial bodies, 18 December 1979.

Our republic is now on course to take up its place among the
world's space powers. International proceedings are currently
under way for the Republic of Kazakhstan to join the Missile
Technology Control Regime, enabling the Republic of Kazakhstan
to become a fully fledged participant in international space activity.

In recent years the world space industry has undergone
substantial change, linked with the increasing scale of international
cooperation on the use and exploration of outer space, rapid
globalisation, and the commercialisation of space activity.

Many states, including Kazakhstan, have come to realise the
importance of geopolitical interests in outer space, as a consequence
of which these things have become a priority in national priority.

They are also playing an increasing role in our state's economic,
scientific, technological, and social development.

At the beginning of October 2006, the 15th anniversary of the
first Kazakh astronaut's flight in space was widely celebrated
throughout the republic. This event formed the basis of an
international forum on 'The results and prospects of the
development of space activity in the Republic of Kazakhstan' held
in Astana on the initiative of the Ministry of Education and Science.
The forum hosted delegations from Russia's Federal Space Agency,
Russia's astronaut training centre, Russia's space corporation
Energia, Russia's aircraft construction corporation MiG, Russia's
Zhukovsky Higher Military Engineering Academy, and the
Baikonur space facility, as well as guests from Austria, Kazakhstani
scientists, and representatives of the republic's space departments
and organisations – in short, everyone connected with setting up
and carrying through Kazakhstan's first national space programme.
The meeting became a grateful tribute to the memory of those who
forged Kazakhstan's way into outer space.

Kazakhstan's Way to the Stars

For all of us living on planet Earth, 12 April 1961 will always mark the day of humanity's breakthrough into outer space. No wonder, then, that it has been declared World Aviation and Astronautics Day. Like, undoubtedly, many other countries that have taken part in space flights, sovereign Kazakhstan does not have a day in its calendar specifically celebrating astronautics. However, the day the state first sent one of its citizens into space has become a historic date marking the official start of the country's space history.

In the years since 1991 the steps Kazakhstan has made in exploring space have been like an orbital circuit round the Earth. Soaring ahead of our country are new and distant vistas over the Earth where mighty Baiterek, the cosmic tree of Kazakhstan, stands rooted in the ground at its very centre, *zher kindigi*.

9

A NEW CAPITAL FOR A NEW ERA

I have to admit, poetry is not my strong point. But whenever I recall the process of transferring the capital from Almaty to Astana, a single line of Olzhas Suleimenov's verse always comes to mind: 'To elevate the steppe without abasing the mountains' – a line which took on an entirely new meaning for me, because it was precisely this extremely complex challenge we had set ourselves: to build a new capital in the steppes, and in so doing (and, to a great extent, for this very reason) preserve the beautiful city in the foothills of Alatau.

The idea of the transfer and construction of a new capital came to me a long time ago, back in 1992, but I did not breathe even a word about it then because Kazakhstan's economy was unable to carry the plan through.

And now here I am driving through Astana's streets, admiring it all. Like many other residents, I have gained a unique and wonderful feeling of being at home here: a sense of joy and peace. You feel as though even the street lights are winking at you and the trees stroking your head with their branches. But, you know, it always seems to me that all these buildings are not being built fast enough, even though building rates are amazingly quick. After all, only a short while ago there was nothing here but wide open steppes! A short while ago, the city was still Akmola.

I visited Akmola in 1992, a year after being elected President of Kazakhstan by an all-nation vote. I stood on the old bridge across the Ishym, watching the river.

A river gives special colour and significance to a town. Take, for instance, Atyrau on the Ural, Kyzylorda on the Syrdarya, Kostanai on the Tobol and Pavlodar on the Irtysh. And how many of the world's capital cities were founded on rivers: St Petersburg on the Neva, Moscow on the Moskva, Paris on the Seine and London on the Thames. Akmola, moreover, is in the centre of Kazakhstan and all Eurasia.

A New Capital for a New Era

Of course, just dreaming of building a new capital and actually making the dream come true are two different things. In fact, even in your wildest dreams you could never have imagined it actually happening.

There is a detailed account of how our young capital was built and developed in my book *The Heart of Eurasia*, and so here I intend to describe how we decided on the transfer in the context of the role the new capital was to play in the formation of independent Kazakhstan.

In this new phase of the country's development, the new capital was not only to become its main city, uniting the Kazakhstani nation, it was to guarantee buoyant economic activity and ultimately develop into one of Eurasia's economic mega-metropolises. With these factors as our starting point, we had to locate the capital in the centre of a transport network. There had to be industry nearby and suitably qualified personnel available. Akmola had all the above-mentioned qualities.

It was repeatedly argued that here, in the steppe, it would be virtually impossible to build a modern city and that the development of this area had only begun in the Soviet period with the assimilation of the virgin and long-fallow lands. But the area of modern Astana had, in fact, always been inhabited. A closer look at the research carried out long ago and in recent times clearly indicates that the Akmola steppes were home to different interacting ethnic groups and cultures from the earliest times. The so-called Steppe Way, mentioned by the Ancient Greek historian Herodotus, crossed these open steppes in the middle of the first millennium BC.

In 1998, archaeologists discovered the medieval urban settlement of Bozok five kilometres from Astana. In the 16th century a caravan route traversed this land, linking Siberia with Central Asia. Bozok was the capital of the Kipchak khanate.

The second era of development in Akmola's history is linked to the Soviet period. It was owing to the area's favourable geographical position that railways were then build in Akmola, enabling it to join the Union's railway system and become actively involved in the transport network. This, in turn, resulted in the widespread development of various branches of its industry, turning it into a major transport hub.

During the Great Patriotic War (the Second World War), Akmola was not only an economic centre of the Soiet Union but a military transport centre as well. One cavalry and three infantry divisions were assembled here. It was a place of evacuation for businesses and civilians from the country's front lines and thousands of injured people were cared for in its hospitals.

The 'virgin land epic' gave new impetus to the development of all the town's economic sectors. In 1950-60, businesses started being set up in the town in a great many different light and heavy industries including machine-building, construction material, energy, all forms of transport, communications and tele-communications. Agricultural, teaching, medical and construction engineering institutes and a number of vocational training schools and colleges were established.

Akmolinsk, as it was by then called, was renamed Tselinograd (*tselina* - virgin land, *grad* - town) in 1961, and became the centre of the virgin lands comprising several of the republic's largest districts. In those days the Union leadership under Nikita Khrushchev was already seriously discussing the option of transferring Kazakhstan's capital to Tselinograd.

After the Union's disintegration the republics acquired their own statehood and right to decide their own history. The transfer of Kazakhstan's capital to Tselinograd, now Astana, marked the start of a new era of development for Kazakhstan as an independent state. By becoming Astana, the city embarked on the third era of its history and in this chapter I shall be describing how this era began.

Taking the Decision to Transfer Kazakhstan's Capital

Before publicly announcing the idea of transferring the capital, I held talks with the Parliament and presented it with my draft speech. I frequently heard caustic remarks along the lines of: 'What's he got against Almaty? He'd do better paying wages and pensions on time.'

On 6 July 1994, in my speech at the plenary sitting of the session of the Supreme Soviet of the Republic of Kazakhstan, I put the idea of transferring the capital before the parliamentarians. My argument for the transfer was that Almaty no longer met the requirements of the independent state's capital in either economic or geopolitical terms. With its population approaching the one and a half million mark, its future prospects were quite bleak in terms of territorial scale and geographic location. There was an urgent need to increase the Almaty area, but on account of the high density of its buildings and shortage of open spaces the city was simply unable to expand.

Moreover, because of Almaty's high propensity for earthquakes, new construction in the city cost much more, comparatively speaking, than in Kazakhstan's other cities. And as a sovereign state, we now needed new types of administrative buildings there had previously been no need for, such as a building complex for the Parliament of the Republic of Kazakhstan, a Ministry of Foreign Affairs, a Ministry of Defence, banks and other institutions, such as the embassies of foreign states.

Almaty is, without doubt, the country's loveliest city. The Alatau mountains give it a particular beauty. I myself was born and grew up near Almaty and am very attached to it. However, the country's interests and objective factors mattered more than any personal inclinations. Almaty, as a capital, really did have specific, insurmountable disadvantages. For instance, the city's ecological situation worsened with every passing year. The former capital suffered from air pollution, particularly in winter, more than any other city in the country. Its streets and air had difficulty coping with the all-pervasive 150,000 or so vehicles of various kinds. The airport was located virtually within the city limits in a notoriously fogbound area and so frequently closed to flights.

The country's northern districts are much less densely populated than the southern ones. There were greater economic and social advantages in redirecting the migratory flows to other regions of Kazakhstan. The new capital was to be closer to the major industrial centres with promising futures and would not have many limitations.

A thorough survey of all the republic's territory was carried out on my instructions with a view to identifying the best location for the state's new capital. The capital had to meet 32 criteria, the most important of which were social and economic indicators, climate, landscape, seismic conditions, environment, engineering and transport infrastructures, communications and prospects for their development, suitable building conditions and human resources.

From the outset we were attracted to the idea of building the capital in the very centre of our country. And the very centre of Kazakhstan was Zhezkazgan and Ulytau where the khans had once resided and the mountains rose out of the middle of the steppe. In by-gone days Kazakh tribes from all over Kazakhstan, from the west and north, south and east, used to gather in Ulytau. It was here that the Kazakh nation became, as it were, cemented.

Nowadays, however, there is nothing in Ulytau: no water, no railways, no roads, and no airport. And vast amounts of money would have been needed to transfer the capital there. Building a new city in such a location would have been even more difficult.

I also considered Karaganda. I knew this city well. For those of us working in Temirtau, it had been the centre of civilisation. But it is a mining city and its land is constantly sinking and it also has water supply and ecological problems.

The third option for the capital was Aktiubinsk, but then we would be moving a long way from the country's eastern region. After all, we were leaving Almaty because we considered it to be a south-eastern dead-end; but Aktiubinsk in the north-west would also be cut off from the country's other regions.

One way or another, the survey showed that of all the options Akmola was the most viable. The state of the town and its location suited any architectural approach. Akmola was almost in Kazakhstan's geographical centre, close to important economic regions and at the crossroads of major transport networks. It had a population of about 200,000 at the time, and according to its general development plan, the population could feasibly be increased to 400,000. Over time, however, the city's population growth has, in fact, exceeded all our expectations. According even to official statistics, there are now over half a million people living in Astana, and the number is actually much greater.

Akmola was the centre of the virgin lands, which also indicated it might be suitable to have the status of capital city conferred on it. What's more, such a decision had, as I mentioned earlier, been seriously considered by the Soviet leadership under Nikita Khrushchev. That's why quite a few imposing administrative buildings had been built there back then, including an arts centre (palace of culture), young people's centre (palace of youth) and others that are still functioning today.

A New Capital for a New Era

The state of the town's essential services did not pose any serious issues either. Heating and gas supplies were well organised, and the construction of the short Irtysh-Karaganda canal sorted out any water supply problems. Apart from everything else, Akmola had a well-developed transport infrastructure, and its ecological situation was, and still is, normal.

The capital's transfer did not happen overnight, and was mostly completed, as planned, by the year 2000. After the necessary preliminary work had been carried out in Akmola, the first to move were the principal state bodies and a number of the most important ministries and departments.

Initial architectural surveys recommended building the administrative centre separately, on 300-400 hectares in the city's southern outskirts. Later on, however, after Japanese architect Kisho Kurokawa won the capital's master plan and design competition, the plan was changed and the city began to grow on the left bank of the River Ishym. As Kurokawa said at the time, 'The best hieroglyph is produced when it is drawn on a clean sheet of paper.' In terms of scale and picturesqueness, the Ishym's left bank was better suited as the site of the new capital's centre. The diplomatic corps was also moved to the left bank, inside the city limits.

To begin with, individual ministries and departments were moved, as planned, to towns in the vicinity of the new capital. It was supposed that the capital's relocation would help the intensive development in the northern regions of innovation and science-based enterprises, high-tech agricultural machine-building, and a broad network of processing plants for rural industry. In Akmola we wanted to acquire not only a new social and political centre but also, after Almaty, the next most important economic, business, scientific and cultural centre of Kazakhstan.

Many at the time spoke of the investments in the new capital bring irretrievable, at times openly calling them a complete waste of state funding. However, the only irretrievable expenditure on the capital's transfer was on the move itself. All the rest were capital investments, and investments in the future. Everything derived from it was to increase the state's national wealth.

In Almaty we would continue, just as before, to have a dominant business, financial, scientific and cultural centre seriously

301

influencing social and political life in the state. What's more, now that Almaty is setting its sights on becoming a financial centre on a Central Asian and CIS scale, we can exploit the southern capital's vast potential to give it international status. Improvements must be made, however, to its infrastructure, communications, transport and many other essential parameters.

I will say frankly that I heard quite a lot of harsh criticism regarding the idea of transferring the capital. To say that parliamentarians quite calmly accepted my idea about the transfer would be untrue. The votes were divided, with some deputies supporting me unreservedly while others dug their heels in, declaring that given the deteriorating social and economic situation, spending vast sums on the capital's transfer was simply absurd. The debates were stormy and the deputies mostly against me.

I remember setting the day of my speech on my birthday. But my cunning ploy did not come off and in the heat of the discussion it was not even remembered. To make up for it, later on, having decided that the new capital was not likely to happen for 20 or 30 years' time, the deputies ended up voting for the transfer. The motion was passed by a small majority. At a session of the Supreme Soviet of the Republic of Kazakhstan the resolution was passed *On the transfer of the capital of the Republic of Kazakhstan* confirming acceptance of my proposal on the state capital's transfer to the city of Akmola and giving instructions to the Cabinet of Ministers to produce, by the end of 1994, a feasibility study and the dates of the capital's transfer.

Later that year, on 2 September, I gave a more detailed account of the transfer plans in an interview for the newpaper *Kazakhstanskaya Pravda*. There were people who tried to score points over this as they had no other way of making their presence felt. Then I announced that the brouhaha over Akmola as the new capital was political intrigue, pure and simple. I asked people to take a closer look at my speech at the Supreme Soviet and the resolution adopted. The date of the transfer was not indicated in the resolution: it merely stated that the government was to produce all the documents required for it. It was perfectly clear this issue was not on the immediate agenda or even that of the near future, but sometime after that. Its completion was linked with the 21st century when it was to meet the vital interests of Kazakhs and all the Kazakhstani people.

A New Capital for a New Era

There is a very accurate definition of the difference between a political intriguer and responsible politician and statesman. The former is concerned about future elections, the latter about public well-being and the country's future. Those speculating on the capital's transfer did not want to understand the real issues involved. It is very easy to whip up hysteria over unpopular decisions and present yourself as a kind of 'voice of the people'. We have a lot of so-called politicians of that ilk. But it's much harder and more important to convince people of the need for the decisions being taken and their promising prospects, in the face of discontent and lack of understanding. After all, the plan to transfer the capital was to be implemented on non-budgetary funds whose sources were being looked for.

And, anyway, would all that much expenditure be required, I asked? Premises for nearly all the different authorities were already available there so people could move straight into them and start working. True, buildings still had to be built for the Ministry of Defence, Ministry of Foreign Affairs and Parliament, but buildings suitable for these particular bodies would have had to be built in Almaty anyway. According to experts' surveys, per square metre, the construction costs of residential housing and office buildings were less in Akmola than Almaty.

Here are some simple estimates by way of an illustration. Let's suppose we were going to spend, say, ten billion tenge on transferring the capital and eight of them would be returned to the state in taxes from the industrial enterprises and construction organisations carrying out the various commissions. Then, as a result, new enterprises would presumably be opened where a lot of people could find employment. And it was also important not to forget that every new building was the property and treasured possession of the state.

September 15 1995 saw the issue of my Decree *On the capital of the Republic of Kazakhstan* having the force of law, in which instructions were given to form a State Commission to organise the relocation of the highest and central authorities to the city of Akmola. With a view to accumulating non-budgetary funds for the city of Akmola's development, the Government of the Republic of Kazakhstan was charged with the duty of setting up the New Capital Non-Budgetary Fund. The government was to prepare and

303

submit for my consideration proposals for offering preferential fiscal, duty and other terms to investors participating in Akmola's construction and the development of its infrastructure.

Building a state is not easy, but building a new capital is even harder. Our people had never built a capital of their own before. Virtually nothing was left of the khanate headquarters at Ulytau except for the earth ramparts encircling the camp. The form of transport in this capital had been camels and horses.

No capital was set up after Russia's conquest of the territory of Kazakhstan either, the provincial centres being located first in Omsk and then Orenburg. It was the Soviet Government that took the decision to transfer the capital from Orenburg to Ak-mechet (Kyzylorda), and then in 1929, during the construction of Turksib (the Turkestan-Siberia Railway), it was moved again to Alma-Ata. For exactly 70 years Alma-Ata worthily carried out its functions as the republic's principal city. It was here that the signing took place of the Declaration of State Independence and the adoption of the first sovereign Constitution. After acquiring independence the capital was renamed Almaty ('Father of Apples'). It was one of the most beautiful capitals of the Union republics, renowned for its unforgettable setting (and its apples).

Aged 19, I had moved from the Alma-Ata district to Temirtau, where I was to spend the rest of my youth. By then Akmola was already considered a young and promising city (Palaces of Youth were not built anywhere else in those days). It was specially being got ready to be renamed Khrushchevograd and turned into the capital. At that time it was the centre of the virgin lands. However, it should be noted that after Khrushchev, with the exception of the town centre, most of the buildings consisted of old log cabins.

I thought long and hard before taking the decision to move the capital, considering all the steps, consulting various expert historians, political and cultural scientists, and studying the history of the transfer of capitals in other states. So, let me summarise the main reasons.

First, the transfer was demanded by the need to strengthen Kazakhstan in geopolitical terms. That's why particular attention was paid to the location of the principal city. Astana is at the centre of the Eurasian continent, and a synthesis of European and Asian traditions. It has equal access to the South, East, North and West.

Secondly, not a small role was played in this decision by security considerations. Ideally, an independent state's capital should be some distance away from external borders and located in the middle of the country.

Thirdly, Kazakhstan's economy needed improving. The transfer has had a positive knock-on effect in that respect. For instance, district centres have started developing, and there have been upturns in branches of the economy such as the building material, road surfacing, energy and machine-building industries. Housing construction is developing at an unprecedented rate.

Fourthly, by transferring the capital to a region with a multi-ethnic population we have yet again confirmed our intention to set up a stable multi-ethnic state, maintaining and enhancing friendly relations between the peoples living in Kazakhstan.

Of course, after beautiful Almaty it was difficult deciding to move the capital to Akmola. Not many wholeheartedly embraced my idea of the transfer. Not even everyone in my family was in favour of it. Everything had to be started virtually from zero.

The New Capital: 'To be or not to be.'

Conversations and gossip about my reasons for being so determined to carry through my plans to move the capital began in 1994, and went on for four years until the actual preparations got under way.

The idea of transferring the capital was branded as 'virtual politics'. In other words, instead of tackling the country's real social and economic problems, the authorities were attempting to cover up their real inadequacies by taking symbolic decisions. The idea was regarded as inherently counterproductive: instead of performing their duties to its people, the authorities were inventing extraordinary functions for themselves, derogating from their responsibility to the people in favour of their 'responsibility to history'.

The reasons for transferring the capital fell into two groups: official (evident and implicit), and concealed (not officially voiced but discussed in the press).

Foremost among the officially announced reasons was the lack

305

of prospects for developing Almaty, as the city was located in a valley surrounded by foothills. Mention was then made of the old capital's increasing ecological problems, the area's dangerous propensity for seismic activity, its proximity to the Chinese border and geographically inauspicious location, making communication with the republic's other regions difficult. Further reasons included the need to develop Kazakhstan's northern region and desire to eradicate distressing memories of the unrest which brought students out onto the city's main square in 1986.

It should be noted that more often than not the arguments put forward in favour of Akmola were of a geographical and geopolitical character, mentioning the fact that it was in the centre of Eurasia and Kazakhstan and at the crossroads of transport networks.

Internal political and economic reasons were often voiced, such as the plan to send the stream of rural migrants northwards from the southern regions of the republic where there was an excess of manpower, and thus both increasing the percentage of Kazakhs in the population of the northern districts and solving the unemployment problem.

Other reasons discussed at some length were the ideas behind the language policy approved by me. Rumour had it that a list had been made of positions in the public services that could only be filled by people who had passed a Kazakh language qualifying examination, and this was causing concern among people who did not know Kazakh. The conclusion drawn from this was that most of the country's top posts were soon going to be held only by ethnic Kazakhs, regardless of their professional qualification levels. As you can see, this prognosis has not been justified, as the following facts indicate. People of 64 nationalities work in the public services: about 20 per cent of the general number of public service employees are of Russian nationality, and nearly 10 per cent of the general number belong to other nationalities. This corresponds more or less to Kazakhstan's ethnic composition.

Some argued that there was no rational explanation for transferring the capital, and no need for investing tens of billions of dollars in its construction. They put this down to Nazarbayev's ambition and his desire to be immortalised. What could be longer-lasting and more monumental than a capital, they asked?

A New Capital for a New Era

Opinion polls were conducted in Almaty, and 62 per cent of residents at the time were completely against any move to Akmola. Nor was the idea enthusiastically greeted by state employees in Almaty. It made some draw the conclusion that the professional management qualification level of government bodies in Akmola was bound to be lower than that in Almaty. It was pointed out that Akmola was also bound to lose in the intellectual stakes between the old and new capitals, and this would badly affect the state apparatus, as it would be unable to meet the rising challenges.

It was predicted that for all but the most senior officials the capital's transfer would mean a substantial reduction in their chances to find alternative employment and greater dependency on their jobs. Inevitably, this would result in a decline in the public services' prestige and a substantial decline in the number of independent-minded people. This, in turn, was bound to lead to the process of state decision-making becoming inordinately simplified, as the state apparatus would be merely an executor rather than a co-author. It was argued that the state apparatus would inevitably lapse into the role of executor of the leader's will and would not even be able to have a say in his plans, let alone come to any independent decisions. Against the backdrop of all these arguments there were also predictions on the positive factors for weakening bureaucracy that would come out of all this.

Despite a broad-based public information and awareness campaign, for many people the reasons for transferring the capital still remained a mystery. In many publications the official reasons were described as inadequate. Around this time an article appeared in the newspaper *Kommersant* under the headline 'President Nazarbayev's personal capital', which claimed that:

> 'Only in conditions where there is no democracy can epoch-making projects emerge that nobody understands. No strategic considerations can justify the diversion of vast funds from the payment of wages and pensions and solution of other of the country's social problems.'
>
> Salopov, D. 'President Nazarbayev's personal capital'. *Kommersant*, 28 October 1997

The Kazakhstan Way

This total lack of understanding of the state authority's actions generated suspicion regarding its sincerity. The idea inevitably arose that there were some secret motives concealing disagreeable aims. All this confusion over the secret and open reasons for the capital's transfer eventually ended up fusing into the single hypothesis that by the end of November 1997, the 'old capital' was going to be struck by a horrendous earthquake. Only this, according to virtually all observers, seemed like the most logical reason for my determination to leave comfortable and warm Almaty as quickly as possible. In the light of this, all other attempts to explain this initiative failed to be taken seriously. Later on, we, too, became reconciled to the fact that people refused to accept our official and totally logical and well-founded reasons, and ended up inventing the explanations that suited them best.

The official reasons for the transfer hung in the air and gained no support at all in the arguments about the new capital. Akmola's possible positive features were not regarded in public consciousness as signs of its 'capital city potential', nor did Almaty's problems diminish its status as a capital.

Ordinary people argued that in any case it was a risky business moving the capital to Akmola, a city with complex weather and climactic conditions, extremely windy in summer and prone to snow blizzards and infamous *buran* (severe snowstorms) in winter, standing on marshland and with no good quality drinking water supplies. Ecologists also issued warnings about the construction of canals depleting the already low levels of water in the Ishym, and construction on a massive scale on its lower, flood-prone left bank destroying the entire region's fragile natural balance. It was predicted that this move would herald the beginning of the end of the present political regime if it turned out to be an enormous bluff to confuse Kazakh migrants from *auls*, 'distract' them from Almaty and send a massive stream of poor people northwards from the south.

Some, for instance, could see no point whatsoever in moving out to the bare steppes where there were no engineering communications or roads, and spending exorbitant sums of money on strengthening weak terrain, building canals and constructing an entirely new city when the old one still had whole districts of adobe buildings that urgently needed demolishing.

Others countered that by arguing that Mr Nazarbayev was cashing in on prospective oil dollar revenues and making a capital investment ahead of time in what he was calling 'the capital's urgent transfer to the country's geographical centre'. Others still considered that the move from Almaty to Akmola was my individual decision, their argument based on the fact that as there had been no all-nation referendum, the decision was unlawful. In so saying, they disregarded the session of the Supreme Soviet and resolution adopted there.

All this, of course, reached members of my family, and they started trying to dissuade me from going ahead with the move. They expressed their doubts to me at a traditional Sunday family lunch party, but I turned the matter into a joke by saying to my wife, 'Sara, we're moving to your family home. Akmola's on the River Nura.' Somehow or other a new version of this quip got into the public domain, according to which I was obeying my wife and moving the capital to the area her family came from. My family – my wife, Sara, and daughters, Dariga, Dinara and Aliya – have always been there for me, supporting me in every possible way. But that's a separate issue. I'm eternally grateful to them for this.

It was in these complex conditions, ignoring conversations that were distorting the true reasons for the transfer, that the idea of developing Akmola as the capital had to be translated into reality. There were quite a few advisers on both sides, but it was up to me to make the decision and take responsibility for it.

Every politician dreams of changing something or other, and does his uttermost to see the challenge through, staking his authority and future on it. Without such dream of accomplishing something major, he might as well not be in politics. And if he does make a success of it, all criticism gets swept aside. If he doesn't, then he has to go. That's how it was then.

The Capital's Transfer as an Accomplished Fact
On 7 October 1997, in my speech at a conference of senior ministerial and departmental officials and construction workers, I once again focused attention on the fact that there were to be no hitches in supplying Akmola with electricity and water and so on.

Nobody believed we could get Akmola ready for the state authorities' move on such a tight schedule, but we did.

October 20 1997 saw the issue of my Decree *On declaring the city of Akmola the capital of the Republic of Kazakhstan*: as of 10 December 1997, the city of Akmola was to become the capital of Kazakhstan, and the capital's official inauguration was to take place on 10 June 1998.

Speaking before Parliament at the time, I noted that all the construction work had been completed in record time. Judge for yourselves: the decision to reconstruct Akmola was taken in October 1996, works got under way in February, and by October 1997 only the communications and electricity were left to install.

I do not think our descendants will have cause to criticise us for taking the wrong decision. Almaty will remain the country's major city, just as before. Having two powerful centres will, however, only increase the republic's economic potential. There are numerous examples of countries with dual capitals: Ankara and Istanbul, Moscow and St Petersburg, Karachi and Islamabad, Rio de Janeiro and Brasilia, Melbourne and Canberra, Ottawa and Toronto, Washington and New York. And, in my opinion, we are not the first and will not be the last to follow this course.

On 8 November 1997, Akmola received the standards of Kazakhstan's state symbols, and acquired an exceptional status as the custodian of the state flag, coat of arms, and Presidential Standard. I remember how particularly emotional I found this event. Because, after all, if you abstract yourself from the purely economic and geopolitical facts and figures, there is something sacred and familiar about the city that everyone senses.

Our descendants will sense it, too. And perhaps because they will not be weighed down by old images and memories, they will take to our new capital much more deeply not just as a symbol of renewal, or as a Rubicon marking the start of a new period.

Astana is a symbolic city representing a dream come true. For many decades the idea of freedom and independence had been roaming our steppes, gathering strength in people who were devoted to their land. And now it had come about. Kazakhstan's boundless steppes, hundreds and thousands of years old, were going to witness decision-making at state level! We had built the capital from zero. We had agonised over all the problems connected with its transfer. Once a dream and now this marvellous city, Kazakhstan's pride and joy.

Once the new capital had been inaugurated, we merely paused rather than stopping completely, because we expected the capital's transfer not only to make life more animated in the regions but also to give impetus to market reforms, help develop the country's infrastructure, and create new jobs. At this tense time of change we began sowing the field that was to produce harvests for both present and future generations.

Acquiring its new capital city status, Akmola had new golden threads embroidered into its biographical tapestry. As I said at the start, Akmola had repeatedly been at the epicentre of highly important public events during critical years for the republic. Take, for instance, the assimilation of the virgin lands, a period of time which brought deserved fame and prestige to the Akmola area, when it became home to thousands upon thousands of people. Here, too, the most enriching managerial expertise was accumulated.

It was not fortuitous that at this challenging time for the state our attention was once again focused on Akmola. The country needed a surge of patriotism, a feat similar to the assimilation of the virgin lands. Only this time it was connected with the new realities – strengthening independence, state-building and expanding the social, economic and political changes. And we were convinced that transferring the capital to Akmola would in many ways help achieve these aims.

Imagining how the city would grow and develop, I often used to lose track of time. Recalling the first months of construction works, I think about the people who were to become kindred spirits – a vast number of people. I want to express my tremendous gratitude to everyone who was by my side in those days, supporting me in my decision, and who, like me, held the new capital dear: Kisho Kurokawa, Vladimir Ni, Amanzhol Bulekpayev, Adilbek Dzhaksybekov, Nikolai Makievsky, Akhmetzhan Yesimov, Farid Galimov, Zhanabek Karibzhanov and many others.

I particularly want to mention the services of the first chairman of the State Commission responsible for the capital's transfer, Nikolai Makievsky, and project manager Vladimir Ni. They arrived in the city when water supplies were provided on an hourly basis, the temperature indoors never got above 10 degrees Celsius and there was nowhere to eat. The city was dark at night because there was no street lighting. The moment they arrived, they worked out a plan of action. Not once did I hear a note of doubt in their voices. They trusted me rather than what they saw in front of them. I am grateful to them. I also have great respect for the work of the new capital's first Akim, Adilbek Zhaksybekov, who was in this post during the stormiest first six years. He was born and grew up in Akmola, loved the city and knew it well. But he has grown even fonder of Almaty, where he has recently moved to. He contributed greatly to the way Astana looks today, and showed initiative. I liked his work and his confidence. He was my staunch supporter.

Turning a still Soviet-style provincial town into a modern capital was not the easiest of tasks. It was impossible to get rid of the old, post-Soviet legacy overnight: the shoddy, inconveniently planned houses, underdeveloped infrastructure, obsolescent industry and so on. The construction of the new city had to be well-planned, logical, founded on international know-how, and fully take account of national traditions.

Meanwhile, the human resources issue – personnel training and retraining – had to be sorted out before new ideas and innovative technology could be introduced. A special sense of responsibility needed to be nurtured in the people of Akmola as the country's showcase and, as it were, calling card. While gratitude was owing to them for their formidable work, in both volume and speed, in getting things ready for the state management authorities' move, they also had to be not only hospitable and convivial but also exceptionally enterprising, high-powered and creative. From the very start, the bodies of all the branches of power had to set themselves a rigorous work regime meeting high state targets.

Henceforth decisions of momentous national significance are to be taken in the vast country's centre. It is where the heart of our Fatherland is now beating, and where Kazakhstan will determine its historic destiny at the turn of the third millennium. Another decisive factor in the choice of capital is that Astana is one day destined to become an influential powerhouse on the Eurasian continent. The economic, technological and information advances in developing Eurasian space in the 21st century are also bound to filter through our new capital.

A New Capital for a New Era

This is the first time that we have taken an independent decision on the capital of our state. Gone forever are the days when decisions were taken for us, determining where and how we were to live and who were to be our friends and enemies. Arguably, for the first time in our national history we have inhaled the breath of freedom without fearing for our children's future. And at the turn of the 21st century we have announced our very own choice of a new capital under the sacred skies of the ancient steppes. Not only does the county's present leadership stand by this choice – so, too, do far-sighted Khan Tauke and great Khan Abylai, the sagacious legendary *biis* (tribal leaders and judges) and fearless young people who in December 1986 showed the whole planet what national pride was all about. And it is also the will of the millions of our fellow tribesmen who paid with their lives for the right to be rulers of their own destiny.

Opinions may have divided over the actual move, but one thing everyone agreed over later on was the need to rename Akmola. There were various ideas such as Karaotkel, Yesil, Ishym, Sary-Arka. There was even a suggestion to call it Kazakhstan after the country, or, among others, Nursultan. But then one night the perfect name for the capital came to me – Astana! It is distinct and easy to pronounce and understand in all languages.

In broader terms, with the capital's move we began large-scale work to overcome the lop-sided distribution of production forces, and eradicate the concealed unemployment in the south of the country caused by overpopulation. In due course this region will see the development of innovative, science-based, high-tech industries and the further expansion of agricultural machine building and, what is particularly important, networks of processing plants for rural industries. And this, in turn, will mean new jobs, the effective use of human resources and increased economic activity for the entire country.

However, apart from these perfectly obvious arguments, one also has to keep in mind factors of a strategic order.

In view of the fact that Central Asia stretches from Afghanistan to the northern reaches of Western Siberia, and from the Caspian to Mongolia, the new capital lies at the very centre of a promising region with the potential to attract vast investment. On the crossroads of communication lines extending from the shores of the Pacific Ocean to Europe, it may one day take on the role of a major transit crossing and powerhouse of the coming century.

All the previous transfers of the republic's capital had been prompted by considerations of 'revolution' or 'class', without addressing Kazakhstan's actual interests in the least. And the fact that for the first time in our history we had taken the decision to move and build a capital, acting on our national interests, had great political and moral import.

The implementation of the master plan for the capital's development began with the construction of a new centre. The Baiterek monument erected in Astana's new centre consists of a central column representing a tree trunk and a large sphere on top symbolising the sky. In general conceptual terms, Astana and Baiterek both embody three principal philosophical parts: the earth, life and the sky. For Kazakhstan and its capital, Baiterek is just as meaningful as, say, Red Square for Moscow or the Statue of Liberty for New York. It has taken on a philosophical, political and historic significance.

According to an ancient poetic myth, Baiterek, the tree of life, grows on the summit of Koktiuba, on the vast ocean's shore. Every year the sacred bird, Samruk, lays a golden egg – the sun – in Baiterek's crown, and every year the sun is eaten by a dragon-like snake; but it still reappears the following year. These symbols represented the changeover between night and day, summer and winter, and the struggle between good and evil, light and darkness. According to legend, Yer-Tostik kills the snake, saves Samruk's egg and, in return, is helped to escape from the underground kingdom by the grateful bird. The legend of the sacred tree perfectly reflects the ideals of regenerated Kazakhstan aspiring to live in peace and harmony.

In the final stage of the First Congress of leaders of world and traditional religions, a ceremony was held on the Baiterek monument's observation platform, 97 metres above the ground, during which the religious leaders and senior representatives of the major faiths signed a wooden plaque inscribed with the words 'Blessed be Kazakhstan – Land of peace and harmony' in Kazakh, Russian and English. The leaders of the world's religions blessed Kazakhstan's new capital as the capital of a state bearing the ideals of peace, goodness and concord to all the peoples of the Earth.

A New Capital for a New Era

A second Congress was held in September 2006. And with all the wars, catastrophes and disasters going on, it is very important that Astana's Palace of Peace and Concord has become a place for religious dialogue. In terms of religious architectural monuments, Astana's Palace of Peace and Concord is quite unique. Of course, there are other places housing various religious faiths under one roof but, unlike them, the Kazakhstani monument is one big space for constructive dialogue. And it is quite logical for the Museum of Culture, a library and concert hall also to be housed in the building where representatives of various world and traditional religions come together. Our pyramid is the architectural embodiment of Kazakhstan's religious tolerance and good will.

The new capital harmoniously combines the rich heritage of the past with the best achievements of the present. Many of its buildings have already gained recognition throughout the country and abroad. With its spectacular dancing fountains, Pyramid of Peace and Concord, and oceanarium, Astana and its wonders are causing a stir even among the most experienced and well-travelled art lovers and tourists. Our capital reflects the spirit of the whole country: it can be found in every one of its streets, nooks and crannies. The large models of 19th-century Kazakh jewellery, the jug with its cascade of different-aged coins, the sundial tower combining high-tech design with the ancient Turkish method of telling the time are all individual displays of Kazakhstani cultural originality. It is my hope that before too long the young capital will be hailed as the most beautiful city on Earth.

Recalling the initial phase of the city's construction, I always think warmly of the River Ishym, just as though it were a person, a close colleague, who has supported me and done a lot for Astana. During Soviet times, the Ishym was an average small river that only mattered in terms of providing sufficient water supplies. Its right and left banks were built up with country cottages (dachas). And practically nothing had been done to tidy up the river banks inside the city limits bordering the centre, while the river in the city centre was overgrown with rushes.

Everything changed with the city's transfer here: the riverbed and banks were reconstructed and the embankments became a favourite local local haunt. Looking at the Ishym's embankment these days, it is impossible to imagine the colossal work people had to do to fill

315

in the dwindling river's banks, conceal the city's entire life-support system below the surface, and prevent natural disasters. Nowadays the Ishym's water level is artificially maintained quite high. Were it not for the supporting dam, the river would possibly be shallow enough to wade across. The Ishym is now one and a half metres deep, like an *aryk* (irrigation ditch), and linked to the Irtysh canal and River Nura. There would be a sufficient supply of water here, if such a need arose.

There are two other rivers in Astana: the Akbulak and Sarybulak. The Akbulak is somewhat smaller than the Ishym but no less famous because of its rowing canal, flower clock, bridges and embankment overlooked by the main building of the Eurasian National University and a spacious new beach. The River Sarybulak flows behind the railway station, quite close to the busy main roads. The capital's waters will play their part in its overall architectural integrity.

A lot can certainly be said about Astana's architecture, and even more about what is still planned. Our capital is, and will always be, unique in every way, depending on how far our flights of fantasy, daring designs and creative expertise can take us.

Some preliminary results in carrying out this grandiose project may already be summed up. During this period, investments in Astana's development from all the various sources totalled over US$5 billion. That the builders' profit margin averaged 10 per cent of costs; the remaining funds went on the production of building materials, the payment of wages and taxes to the budget. Hundreds of construction and assembly firms, and dozens of factories in the construction industry from all over the country were employed here. Tens of thousands of our citizens were provided with jobs.

Astana has already received recognition in the world. In July 1999, the city was awarded a UNESCO City For Peace prize, and in 2003, Moody's Investors Service raised the city's credit rating by two levels at once from Ba3 (stable) to Ba (positive).

I am particularly grateful to the governments of friendly countries, and heads of foreign and domestic companies, who at my personal request allocated grants to the new capital's fund. I succeeded in attracting nearly US$400 million of such funds. We are grateful for this invaluable help to the Agip company (Italy), the Kingdom of Saudi Arabia, the Kuwait Fund, the Abu Dhabi

Fund, the Sultanate of Oman, the TengizShevrOil and Kaz-MunaiGaz companies, the Eurasian Group, the SSS, IspatKarmet, KazakhMys, KazTsink companies, and many others as well.

It will be impossible for me to describe all the details of creating our new capital in one chapter, especially since, as I have already mentioned, my book on Astana *In the Heart of Eurasia* came out last year. I believe that one day another book will be written about the new capital of independent Kazakhstan – but it will not be by me or even our contemporaries. And it will tell in detail about the dramatic years and heroism of Astana's builders, and all those who came here from all over our vast country. Here, though, I have only given a brief sketch of this remarkable period and its importance for every Kazakhstani.

City of the Future

Every year Astana celebrates its birthday on 6 July, the day Parliament passed my proposal on transferring the capital. The city Maslikhat passed a similar resolution. The city hosts a variety of festive events to celebrate Capital Day. After a short while Kazakhstanis' attitudes changed towards the administrative centre's transfer. Many of the migrants now feel well and truly part of Astana and genuinely regard Astana as their home city. It is not for nothing we Kazakhs have a saying about nomadic people constantly on the move acquiring new values.

Creating the new capital and new symbol of Kazakhstan was colossal work. I would like to express my immense gratitude to the builders, including the foreign companies and middle-ranking state officials who bore all the responsibility for organising the work of the President's Administration, the Government and ministries, and all those who were involved in this. Tremendous work was done: we did a great job. Back then I said that the following year we would already start building the city here in Akmola.

The main purpose of the capital's transfer is to maximise the state's potential for development. Of no small importance is the fact that Astana is historically a centre linking Europe and Asia, at the crossroads of major transport networks and republican railways and flight routes.

In the future the new capital will be a synthesis of Eastern and European cultures, like the idea of Eurasia itself, this ideal is turning out to be very controversial. This is no obstacle, however. Astana has inherited pragmatism from Western culture and spiritual refinement from the East.

The capital's transfer became a pivotal moment in the emergence of a state ideology. Just as Moscow was once the ideal for every Soviet person, so, too, Astana is becoming a symbol of the country's development as a state. And, possibly, the concepts of patriotism and statehood are taking on their full meaning through this city's construction. Thousands of young men and women are flocking to the new capital in search of a better future. And the young city is maturing with them.

I was once asked whether a true leader definitely had to have people's support, and how to win it when every decision taken benefited some while infringing the interests of others. I would like to say that the most important decisions in our state's history have been the most difficult and not the most pleasant. But a true leader definitely needs to have people's support. Every leader has to have lofty heights to conquer and a dream to achieve. If you don't have a dream, there is no reason for you to go into politics and take up the reins of a country's leadership. And you need to give everything of yourself and stake your authority and future in order to achieve this goal. So it was with the idea of constructing a new independent state and its new capital.

Today I can confidently say that this goal has been achieved. As for people's support, I have satisfied myself on more than one occasion that most of our people are perceptive and astute, and if your goal is to create or improve something, people will always take your side. Over the past few years, since the capital's transfer to Astana, the most substantial social, economic and political reforms have been carried through in the country. They have changed the way people think. The parasitic and paternalistic tendencies that used to prevail in society before and after the collapse of the USSR have gradually begun to die away. People have started believing in themselves and in their strengths, and realise they can and must build their future – and that of their children – with their own hands.

In the near future Astana will become a beautiful modern city and major political, scientific, cultural and business centre of the Republic of Kazakhstan. Looking at all these plans, I always imagine the people behind them. After all, none of them mean anything without people ready to put them into action. We have founded the new capital but it will be up to our progeny, young Kazakhstanis, to make the dream city come completely true. It is their city – a city which broadens Kipling's refutation of the adage that East and West shall never meet: here is a city where the East has indeed met the West. . .

A city of the steppes eternally dreaming of freedom. . .

A city it took us fifteen years to make our way to. . .

A city today pointing the way to the future. Our way, the Kazakhstan way.

AFTERWORD

My book is based on the most difficult and demanding events in Kazakhstan's recent history and my activity as the country's President. It may, I believe, become a reference book for the younger generation. Each of its nine chapters covers periods in Kazakhstan's development which were and, most probably, still are most important for us. It describes how we worked out strategies when the country needed clear pointers of development; the adoption of the country's Constitution, which gave us a legal foundation; the initial development of our oil and gas resources – the country's main source of wealth; the introduction of the national currency and development of banks and Kazakhstan's fully-fledged economic system; the implementation of privatisation and land reform which made the economic reforms irreversible; the construction of Astana to represent our young state. It also tells of a Kazakhstani's first flight into space and many other of Kazakhstan's experiences since gaining independence.

This book does not touch upon some of the important issues we dealt with as we were developing the state from its very foundations, such as the establishment of our national army, border control service, customs and a special operations force. A vast amount of foreign policy activity is required to give Kazakhstan an identity in the world. I could not describe all my colleagues who have helped me in this work. My meetings with heads of state and interesting people all over the world is a subject in its own right and a future project. This book, you see, is not a memoir, since it is mainly about the economy our self-sufficiency rests upon. The process has got under way in recent years to list our companies' shares on the London Stock Exchange Fund Market (IPO). This is an entirely new development and we are becoming part of the global economy. We are becoming transparent. This is encouraging confidence and will bring new technologies to the country. Kazakhmys, Kazmunaigaz are IPO pioneers, and other companies are getting ready to follow – but this is again a subject on its own.

An account of conducting energetic economic reforms in the country would, however, be incomplete without a brief overview of the education system. Now that we have entered a new phase of development, economic growth is requiring not only financial investments but also a national stock of human capital. An education gives a person not only knowledge but also the skills to seek new ways of using it. This is why I consider that a high level of education is also reflected in the beneficiary's high level of skills.

Obviously, a competitive education system plays a decisive role in a country's development and so I have decided to describe certain key landmarks. What matters most is that a state should always fulfil its most important duty of providing every citizen with equal access to an all-round, high-quality education that meets the present and future needs of the individual, society and the state.

When the Strategy Kazakhstan to 2030 was being adopted, we set ourselves the goal of joining the ranks of the world's developed countries by 2030. This presented us with new important challenges, especially in view of growing globalisation. And tackling these challenges is to be a top state priority.

This is precisely why in my Address to the country's people on 'The strategy for joining the 50 most competitive countries', I focused mainly on the education system, and ensuring its competitiveness by – among other things – integrating science and education.

Two equally important challenges may be singled out. First, it is the role of education to help nurture patriots capable of making conscious choices and taking independent decisions for the good of their county. Secondly, it is the role of education to help nurture competitive individuals, motivated towards continued self-improvement and able to look after themselves and their family, easily adapting to any conditions and taking on new ideas. What's more, in this age of globalisation there is also the challenge of preserving national identity.

Education, the State and Society

The Kazakhstani system gives young people equal access to a full education irrespective of their family's financial circumstances, place of abode, national origin and state of health. It is able to use its resources for the social protection of children and juveniles not in their parents' care. School plays a substantial role in the growth of children's intellectual skills: it acts as a powerful regulator both in terms of education, encouragement, and moral upbringing. The state also singles out and supports the most gifted and talented children and young people. The state will assist in the payment of their school fees, including those at top Western educational establishments.

In 2008, Kazakhstani schools will have transferred to a 12-year education programme. Taking account of the country's traditions in education and international practice, the new primary and secondary education system is to be structured on the principle of 5+5+2. First, primary school (Years 1-5) where Year 1 entry will be at six years of age. Secondly, the main secondary school (Years 6-10). It is important to emphasise that after completing Year 10, the student will have a wider choice of options for continuing education in smaller specialised classes, vocational schools, lyceums and colleges, and higher technical schools. Thirdly, Years 11 and 12 are to consist of specialised classes for this older student group. The transfer to specialised subject schooling will enable students to make a well-considered and informed choice of their future professional activities, and personal self-determination.

Here I would like to pause and discuss the issue of social partnership. Now that we can clearly see the results of the country's economic growth, it is essential for business, which is constantly experiencing a shortage of personnel, to understand its social responsibility in the field of education. First, there has to be a reduction in the numbers of unemployed young people in the countryside. It has become a fashionable trend among businessmen over recent years to erect mosques and madrasas (Islamic schools) in their home villages. The problem is that once a mosque is built, it is often not clear who should be teaching our young people there or what syllabus they should be following. Moreover, for one reason or other there is no tradition in our country encouraging businessmen to help the schools where they and their parents were educated. We have around 8,000 schools in the country, and one in every four of them requires major refurbishment. This has acquired particular urgency now that we are planning to transfer to a 12-year education system, set up vocational schools and resource centres, and expand the network of professional schools and lyceums.

Why can't businesses take one or two schools under their patronage? Why couldn't they repair a library or a design and technology room or buy sports equipment? In the West a patron who has donated the funds for a new building has auditoriums and halls named after him, and sometimes even the building itself. Why shouldn't we introduce the same practice here? Then again, throughout the world this patronage of educational establishments also extends to institutions of higher education.

During this process one should also not forget that very shortly our institutions of higher education should be offering degree courses which will be recognised worldwide. I want to believe that in 10-15 years' time a Kazakhstani university graduate will be rated just as highly as his peers from the world's top universities. Yes, at present such an objective is still a dream. However, as the popular saying goes, when the going gets tough, the tough get going. So, in order to achieve our goal, we must start right now setting up a network of world-standard, elite universities.

The education system must ensure that all the country's resources – human, information, material, and financial – are used effectively. And the state must guarantee education is accessible to all strata of society, and make supporting education a priority.

Education and the Individual

As we strive to create a rule-of-law, democratic society and effective market economy, we are encountering certain problems. These are caused by a change in people's attitude to vital values, and the economic and political difficulties they have encountered – and mostly likely will encounter again during the process of this transition. In these conditions, along with the top-priority social demands being made of the education system, there are also new spiritual and moral demands.

At the present stage of civil and economic development, Kazakh-stanis have to be equipped with versatile skills enabling them to adapt quickly to the changes taking place in society and the economy; solid basic knowledge and skills helping them to continue their studies; the ability to analyse information and, on the basis of this analysis, make choices and take decisions; know how to respect generally accepted norms of civil conduct, and also adequately grasp other people's views.

Our younger generation has to learn to be independent and able to deal with problems for themselves; to receive new information and knowledge; to think critically and creatively, and to show initiative and ingenuity. It is essential to remember that only those countries whose people make the most productive use of the information, skills and technologies they have learned will enjoy a promising future.

School is where personality is formed. It provides not only basic knowledge and skills, making further study possible, but also an initial experience of life. It is here the foundations are laid for the relations between the individual and society, respect for elders and peers, and respect for law and order. The student learns to understand the significance of the state and realise that through social institutions it helps realise his personal plans.

School gives the first lessons of life. While teaching how to live in society and obey its rules, school should not, however, stifle a child's individuality. A student who does not have an opinion of his own is unable to defend his position, think and generate new ideas in a well-reasoned manner. Such an individual is unable to make the right decisions and act innovatively. Such a school-leaver will be inclined to rely on other people's judgements instead of independently apprehending the truth. To avoid this, the teacher's paternalistic attitude to the pupil has to change. There is this wonderful aphorism: 'A teacher does not give the answers, he asks the questions. A teacher doesn't lead you by hand on the road to Knowledge, he simply points the way.'

Education and a Competitive Economy

People's living standards and Kazakhstan's steady economic growth are also going to have an impact on how our country uses its intellectual potential.

Afterword

In this era of the information society, the concepts of competence and skills have changed, and there are now new methods and instruments of transferring, receiving, assimilating and storing information. Given these conditions, a 20th-century education system is unacceptable and will be unable to function effectively and meet our society's needs.

Kazakhstan today is on the threshold of a new surge, a new period of its development. And a new time for us means, first and foremost, a time of new people and new challenges of the kind that will allow Kazakhstan to keep up the momentum of its development. In order for Kazakhstan to retain its leadership in the Eurasian region, it has to have the courage to set itself ambitious challenges and do much more than anyone else. Just such a challenge is Kazakhstan's ambition to join the world's 50 most competitive countries.

In the first chapter I discussed the nation's competitiveness. But what does being competitive mean for an individual? Individual competitiveness is a concentration of acquired vital skills, including readiness for the dynamically changing present and uncertain future. It is a capacity for using the challenges of an uncertain future to one's advantage. In other words, nowadays young Kazakhstanis have to acquire habits and skills that will not only help them lead worthy lives in the global world but also actively influence the real world, changing it for the better. People are needed who are not programmed, but able to improvise freely.

Time is speeding by, dictating new rules and waiting for no one. Kazakhstan simply does not have the right to lag behind the leading countries. Kazakhstan needs educational establishments of a new type right now. These should be elite universities – powerful, educational, scientific, research and production complexes closely linked with industry. The Kazakhstan Institute of Management and Economic Law (KIMEL), the Gumilev Eurasian University and the Kazakhstan-British Technical University have been founded with my personal participation. These universities are our first attempt to elevate the Kazakhstani system to a world level.

Education knows no bounds. That's why our universities need to really feel the pulse of global competition. A gifted school leaver who, for instance, wins an International Olympiad, gains access to the world's most prestigious universities. Our young physicists, mathematicians and chemists are attending Massachusetts Institute of Technology, Harvard, and Oxford free of charge. Universities are vying with each other to attract promising scientists with stipends and grants.

To this end, back in 1993, in the first years of Kazakhstan's independence – the most difficult of times, when there were no funds to pay the wages of employees in the budgetary sphere – the state formulated a purposeful personnel training policy and the international Bolashak grant was set up. Such grants were usable in Japan, Singapore and South Korea – countries which had succeeded in setting up their own competitive higher education system.

A prestigious university of international standard urgently needs to be built in Astana to create a similar Kazakhstani model of higher education and develop a unique academic environment. The master plan has already been approved for developing such a university. It will have new institutes and centres meeting the latest global requirements. Education at the university is to be harmoniously combined with innovation, research and enterprise.

The university is to create the conditions for developing Kazakhstan's intellectual, scientific and technical elite and developing and transferring skills, designs and technologies oriented towards the needs of the cluster sectors of the economy. A special corporate spirit and cult of knowledge is to become an inseparable part of this university, where students will adhere to the principle of 'education for the sake of knowledge and not grades'.

However, I also want to focus your attention on the fact that, along with all the other measures being taken by us, there is to be a substantial increase in the requirements of competence and training standards of the teachers themselves. The quality of education depends in many ways on the teacher, and his skills and erudition. The teacher is the one directly responsible for nurturing and developing specialists of the new generation we are focusing on.

Education and National Identity

When speaking of the nation's competitiveness, it should not be forgotten that competitiveness is, first and foremost, about making the most of one's advantages. However, before we can identify them, we must first understand who we are.

We are the descendants of people who have lived for centuries at the crossroads of world civilisations. The Great Steppe was always a crossing point for various cultures, languages, armies, goods and ideas. Throughout history the steppe has given life to peoples. And in the 21st century it is to give life to individuals of a particular calibre, and generate new ideas. The skills of the steppe mentality we have inherited in our genes perfectly reflect the global trends of mobility and systemic organisation. Nomads were always mobile, and all their actions, seemingly incomprehensible at first glance, always conformed to the set cycles of the weather and principles of social mutual relations.

How can these skills help us in the present situation? Let's take, for instance, mobile communications or wireless internet: these technologies give a person freedom of movement and do not tie him to any particular place. Transnational corporations depend in many directions on mobile groups of 10 to 100 people based on different continents and mobilised in the event of a specific task. The concept of 'lifelong learning' that places emphasis on continual education and the regular refreshment of personal skills is embedded in the field of education worldwide.

A competitive individual born in a distinctive environment must, first and foremost, get to know the culture and language of his people. Preserving the cultural sources of their mother tongue and spiritual traditions imbibed through the education system should help the younger generation acquire immunity to the all-absorbing, unifying and assimilating processes of globalisation. However, national baggage should not hamper the integration of the Kazakhstani younger generation in the field of general education worldwide, or reduce their competitiveness.

Every Kazakhstani should have a sense of his own worth and take responsibility for his actions and life. Learning to assess a situation in an analytical and critical manner and taking key decisions, being able to work creatively with information, including the latest IT – that's what really counts.

An urgent need is currently rising up the agenda to form a new Kazakhstani social awareness attuned to the core values of the reforms being conducted in the country. It should undoubtedly contain elements of universal human culture, the most up-to-date skills, and national traditions. Consequently, despite the changing world and new social requirements of the field of education, the education system's challenge remains unchanged – nurturing a fully-fledged, competitive citizen, and revealing the role of skills not only from the perspective of achieving economic gain, but also from that of bringing up future generations as reasoning citizens with a sense of responsibility to society and loyalty to the country. These elements should be fostered in each and every individual in the family, school and university.

The shortage of creative people sure of their potential and abilities to take worthwhile risks may be the greatest obstacle in Kazakhstan's way to developing a science-based economy. The Industrial Innovation Development Strategy adopted in 2003 is going to enable us to solve this problem. As the strategy is carried through, improvements will take place in the institutes of education, as they are the key factor in determining the economy's personnel and technological excellence. Another practical outcome of the strategy will be the funding and prodigious development of scientific research, aligned with the promising tendencies of scientific-technical progress. This is precisely why we are attaching such importance to skills.

I am confident that by opting for a knowledge-based society, we are developing in the right direction, as countries' comparative advantages are being determined less and less by plentiful natural resources or cheap manpower but increasingly by technical innovations and the practical application of these intellectual skills.

And, in conclusion, I once again wish to stress that the country needs a new generation of young people who can take on responsibility. It must learn to cope with solving major problems and adapt to the changed economic and technical circumstances, as well as taking advantage of these conditions with an intuitive sense of the global trends just around the corner.

My parting message to the young people of Kazakhstan is that you absolutely must get an education of good quality such as will serve as a reliable foundation. Otherwise, you will not be able to build your future, and that of your children and the country as a whole. You need to keep working, primarily, on your own account. You can always keep on learning and improving. 'Unlike a man's life, knowledge is eternal,' as the wise Chinese saying goes. You can't argue with that. And we also have our own Kazakh sayings about the power and great benefits of learning. For instance: 'Try to master seven languages and know seven sciences.'

And as the great Abai said, 'If you want to be rich, learn a trade.' His words, in my opinion, perfectly sum up modern education strategy.

In order to become a powerful and prosperous state and achieve steady growth, we need to focus on the intellectual elite, high technologies, and the country's scientific potential. Only through its intellectual potential will the country be able to take up a worthy place in the world. And so you, young Kazakhstanis, have a tremendous responsibility ahead.

Life is full of unexpected twists of fate and tests of endurance. It is not for nothing that people pray for the Creator's protection against evil and misfortune.

A person is forever being presented with a fundamental choice between good and evil, light and darkness, love and hatred, knowledge and ignorance.

All the problems and hardships in a person's way are, it would seem, put there solely for him to succeed in mastering them and finding the best way to achieve his goals.

True happiness is when a person makes the right choice every moment of his life, and thus attains inner harmony.

Young people will be successful if they opt for humanitarianism, knowledge, responsibility, justice and altruism.

Every evening I try and answer this important question about the day: 'Did it all go right?' And for me, as President, this means: 'Am I doing everything to make life better for my fellow countrymen?' This is the essence of my credo.

May you love your Homeland and take care of it. Look after our country, help one another, keep together, and then any ordeal and obstacle will be surpassed and overcome with dignity.

INDEX

Index

Index